The
Unmasking
of
Drama

The
Unmasking
of
Drama

CONTESTED
REPRESENTATION
IN
SHAKESPEARE'S
TRAGEDIES

Jonathan Baldo

WAYNE STATE UNIVERSITY PRESS   DETROIT

Copyright © 1996 by Wayne State University Press,
Detroit, Michigan 48201. All rights are reserved.
No part of this book may be reproduced without formal permission.
Manufactured in the United States of America.
99 98 97 96   5 4 3 2 1

Library of Congress-in-Publication Data

Baldo, Jonathan.
The unmasking of drama : contested representation
in Shakespeare's tragedies / Jonathan Baldo.
p.   cm.
Includes bibliographical references and index.
ISBN 0–8143-2598-X (alk. paper)
1. Shakespeare, William, 1564–1616—Tragedies.   2. Representation
(Literature)   3. Renaissance—England.   4. Tragedy.   I. Title.
PR2983.B26   1996
822.3'3—dc20   95-51670

Designer: Joanne E. Kinney

TO MY
PARENTS

CONTENTS

ACKNOWLEDGMENTS

The list of colleagues, friends, and teachers to whom I owe a debt must begin with Carol Jacobs, who early on set a daunting and even impossible example of what criticism might be capable of doing. Richard Fly, Aimée Israel-Pelletier, and especially Gretchen Wheelock generously provided detailed comments on the manuscript in its early stages. Others whose stimulating conversations have helped to improve the outcome of this work include Reid Barbour, Mary Cappello, Ralph Locke, Patrick Macey, John Michael, Marjorie Woods, and all of my colleagues, past and present, in the Humanities Department of the Eastman School of Music, the University of Rochester: Doug Dempster, Tom Donnan, Ruth Gross, Aimée Israel-Pelletier, Hans Kellner, John McGowan, Ernestine McHugh, Jean Pedersen, David Roberts, Lisa Roetzel, and Tim Scheie.

A portion of chapter 3 of this volume, titled "Generally Speaking," was delivered at a session of the 1992 meeting of the Shakespeare Association of America in Kansas City, Missouri. Earlier versions of chapters 2 and 4 have appeared in *Criticism,* and I am grateful for the permission to reprint. To the editors over the years of that journal, particularly Arthur Marotti and Leonard Tennenhouse, I owe an ever-compounding debt. The Eastman School of Music of the University of Rochester generously granted me a one-semester leave that enabled me to begin this project.

The helpful staff of the Office Automation Center, including Barbara Koeng, Steve French, Dawn Chock, and Ken Owens, saved me thousands of hours, first by coaching me in basic word processing and subsequently by their heroic rescues of files in peril.

Nathaniel, age seven, and David, three, regularly administered large doses of laughter. (One day, at the mention of "Shakespeare," David observed, "You like that beer, don't you, Daddy?" Watch for "Shakesbeer," an authentic publike brew forthcoming from an exciting new microbrewery.) The expert editorial advice and loving support of my wife, Roberta, made all the difference. She not only made this book possible but also made it seem worth doing. From initial conception, this is in every respect her child, too. Thanks to the staff of Wayne State University Press and its director, Arthur Evans, for a quick, painless delivery. I would especially like to thank editors Lynn Trease and Kathryn Wildfong for their careful and professional handling of the manuscript.

The continuing interest and encouragement of my sister Elizabeth and brother Christopher—a little more than kin and more than kind, to misquote Hamlet—were a constant help all along the way. Finally, to my parents, who have not only borne me but borne with me as I embarked on the strange, mad career of literary critic, I lovingly dedicate this book.

Fast Foreword:
Will and Representation

❁

"Belike this show imports the argument of the play."
—Ophelia, 3.2.136[1]

"that hint of parliament which is the dignity of the theatre"
—William Empson

I n a recent newspaper story on local Shakespearean productions, a
theater director tried to explain the famous longevity of the plays:
"The plays are not about others, they're about ourselves." Phrased in this
way, the commonplace assertion of the plays' universality seemed not
only banal but morally dubious as well. Like many of my colleagues, I
had been teaching for years that literature is largely a pursuit of elusive
"others," that it is not simply a corridor of mirrors in which to regard
(and perhaps adjust) our own reflections.

The widespread assumption of the plays' almost limitless capacity to represent, to speak on behalf of subsequent generations and
other cultures, has recently begun to be challenged. We are in the
midst of an explosion of books and articles seeking to discriminate
various Shakespeares. Such examinations represent decidedly different
constituencies: studies, for instance, on America's Shakespeare, on
the Shakespeares of particular nations, cultures, and races, and on
Shakespearean representations of gender, all driven by the knowledge
that a universalist Shakespeare, like other forms of universalism, has
been a powerful tool in the erasure of gender, class, and race and
in the underrepresentation and therefore the silencing of particular
constituencies.

One of the ironies of a universalist Shakespeare whose works are,
in Ben Jonson's prophetic words, "not of an age, but for all time," is that
Shakespeare produced a body of work that in large measure challenges
its own era's dominant ideas about representation: for instance, the

11

assumption that a single body, a monarch, can represent an entire people. Paradoxically, Shakespeare has been taken as fulfilling the very function that none of his monarchs can. From an interpretive point of view, one of the limitations of that corporate monolith, Shakespeare, Unlimited (not Shakespeare but a certain view and use of him), is its tendency to obliterate the ways in which representation is a subject of the plays themselves: a matter of considerable controversy, struggle, competition—drama, if you will. Recent literary and historiographical studies have explored the very different ways in which Queen Elizabeth and King James represented themselves and were represented to their people, as well as the ways in which their styles of representation were reflected and challenged by Shakespearean representations.[2] In the six studies that follow I will look at some of the major tragedies in which modes of representation—of the whole body politic by a universalized and universalizing protagonist; of various specific constituencies by a general type or by a generalizing rhetoric; of the visual by the verbal, and vice versa, and of power by its visible manifestations; of wholes by parts—meet resistance, either from within or from emergent, alternative modes of representation. In the process I hope to suggest ways in which the differences between Elizabethan and Jacobean styles of representation, both political and literary, may themselves participate in a larger historical shift in the concept of representation.

The theater would seem to invite a discussion of representation in the broadest range of senses, including the political sense. In the theater, literature's capacity for representation seems extended; the degree of "standing for" seems heightened. William Empson writes in connection with Dryden, "Even the aristocratic fool of the Restoration stage . . . is like the national hero who becomes a symbol of his nation; he 'stands for' the group satirised."[3] The theater is the closest thing in the literary realm to a representative institution, as Empson suggests in referring to "that hint of parliament which is the dignity of the theatre."[4] The premises behind dramatic practices of representation remain no more constant than the procedures of parliamentary representation. In many of Shakespeare's Jacobean plays, particularly *Coriolanus,* may be read the demise of an older, corporeal concept of representation tied to the body and visibility and even tentative steps toward a new concept of representation in the modern sense of "standing for," one that will be tied to the rise of parliamentary government.[5]

The shifting structures of Shakespearean representation belong to a larger history of the concept and practice of representation in the seventeenth century, a history closely tied to the English Civil War and the aspirations of those social classes who hoped to profit politically from that event.[6] Might Shakespeare's middle and later tragedies put their own representational practices into question so vigorously as to foretell—if only in whispered voices issuing from the margins of the folio or from the tiring houses—the cataclysmic midcentury dislocations to the concept and practices of political representation? The tragedies stretching from *Hamlet* to *Coriolanus* and *Timon of Athens* constitute English Renaissance tragedy's most strenuous attempts to unmask its representational practices and to penetrate its own ordering principles.[7] All the chapters that follow support the conclusion that in Shakespearean tragedy at the top of its form, Shakespeare is working as much against as with many of the basic ordering principles of the genre to which his plays belong.

Part I will suggest the twin reliances of absolutism and the English Renaissance theater on synecdoche, the trope that allows for substitutions of parts for wholes and wholes for parts. Part II explores the parallel proclivities for generalizing shared by Shakespeare's characters and his tragedies, where generalizing is an essential feature of representations of sovereignty. Part III is devoted to the ways in which Shakespearean tragedy is supported by, and also at its height begins to challenge, a cooperative relation between the seen and the heard, words and things, as well as the Elizabethan association of power with a "privileged visibility."[8] In each section my predominant interest lies in the ways Shakespearean tragedy renegotiated its contracts with the ordering structures to which it owed its very existence. Though I will consider a broad range of Shakespearean tragedy, including the apparently anomalous *Coriolanus* and *Timon of Athens,* the ghost of *Hamlet* will keep reappearing in each section because I believe it to be such a pivotal play—one that inaugurates many of the critical practices of Shakespearean tragedy in its middle and later phases.

In their assumptions about how a life may be represented, Shakespearean drama and the biographical novel exhibit vastly different dependencies on the trope of synecdoche. Drama, which presumes that the meaning of a life, a reign, or a historical period may be distilled into a single adventure from it, may be the most synecdochic of the literary genres and as dependent on the efficacy of the trope as was any version of English absolutism. The biographical novel, by contrast, is predicated on the inefficacy of part-whole substitutions or, alternately, may be said to actively block such substitutions. It presupposes that a life must be retold from beginning to end in order to represent it adequately. All novels, whether or not they take their shape from that of the individual life, imply that no single episode from a life or a history can match the typifying or summarizing force of the episode in a Renaissance tragedy. In my first two chapters, I explore certain complications in the operations of various kinds of synecdoche—the fundamental trope of representation, according to Kenneth Burke— in *Coriolanus* and *Hamlet,* two tragedies that seem particularly keen in exploring the interstices between political and theatrical forms of representation. The theater's economical means of representation, I will argue, echo assumptions about political representation. A dilatory play like *Hamlet,* which challenges the theater's economy, similarly challenges the economy of political representation, as does the increasingly less sympathetic nature of Shakespeare's tragic heroes in late plays like *Coriolanus* and *Timon of Athens.* Conversely, the quarrel over political representation in *Coriolanus* impinges upon premises governing representation in Shakespeare's theaters.

The two middle chapters are devoted to the generalizing tropes of Renaissance drama and the ways in which Shakespearean tragedy begins to reflect critically on those tropes. In the course of a discussion of *Gorboduc,* Franco Moretti writes of sovereignty in Renaissance tragedy that it "is a universal power, reaching and defining every part of the body politic, whose destiny is therefore enveloped within it. . . . Universal, the decision of the king will gradually affect his person, his family, the nobility, the people, and all society: in event after event, the royal act resonates over the entire political body."[9] Or as King James wrote in a more somber vein in *The Trew Law of Free Monarchies,* "The King is ouer-Lord of the whole land: so is he Master ouer euery person that inhabiteth the same, hauing power ouer the life and death of euery one of them."[10] In Shakespearean tragedy, too, ideal sovereignty entails universality in these specialized senses. A generalizing rhetoric is ordinarily instrumental in the representation of such sovereignty or in the pursuit of sovereignty in the case of a disenfranchised prince like Hamlet, just as certain generalizing tropes are an important foundation of Shakespearean tragedy; both the genre of tragedy and the conception of the sovereign in the Renaissance rest their claims to legitimacy and authority to some degree on the authority of generalizing rhetoric.

The authority of generalizing becomes foregrounded as a problem in the tragedies beginning with *Hamlet,* largely through protagonists who are habitual and sometimes self-critical generalizers. *Timon* in particular plays off the form of a generalizing allied with sovereignty against an intrusive form of generalizing, which Timon often labels "confounding." Though this second form of generalizing might seem subversive rather than supportive of sovereignty, it was familiar enough as an element in conservative discourses, playing a supporting role in carefully staged claims for the necessity of monarchy. For an Elizabethan audience all the forms of confounding in the play would have seemed appropriate to their setting because in ancient Athens, in Sir Thomas Elyot's words, "equalite was of astate amonge the people, . . . which moughte well be called a monstre with many heedes."[11] As *Timon* is itself is in so many ways abstract in form and characterization, it shares responsibility for and stakes in the various kinds of generalizing undertaken by its characters, from the Poet to Timon, Apemantus, and the general Alcibiades. Elyot's educational treatise *The Book Named The Governour* (1531) similarly opposes two orders of generality, reviving the specter of a fantasized levelling—a generalizing that confounds and disperses power—only to reinstate the sovereign as a figure of universality through a generalizing that concentrates power and supports hierarchy. But in Shakespeare's later plays, the outcome of this confrontation between two orders of generality is more uncertain, less contrived—in a word, more dramatic—than it is in Elyot's *Boke*.

A translatability between visual and verbal signs was crucial both to a theater in which so much of a "scene" had to be evoked through words, and to a culture in which the monarch's body, presumed to embody or mystically represent the entirety of the body politic and the complex array of signs of power surrounding it, could be "read" by the illiterate masses. The monarch's body, like a Renaissance play, functioned as both spectacle and text. To doubt the translatability between the visual and verbal, as I believe Shakespeare's middle and later tragedies began to do, was to disturb one of the fundamental premises of both English Renaissance theatrical practice and political representation, in particular the Renaissance association of power with what Stephen Greenblatt has called a "privileged visibility."[12] In the middle and later tragedies, I will try to show in my fifth and sixth chapters, the experiences of both characters and auditors foretell what Foucault in *The Order of Things* characterizes as the dissociation of words and things, the mutual estrangement of the faculties of eye and ear, and the general dominance of vision in all disciplines during the period roughly from 1650 to 1800.[13] Adjudication between verbal and visual evidence is more necessary in the middle and later tragedies. Those plays fascinate with their moments of disjunction or discord between word and image, as in the incongruity between dumb show and play in the middle of *Hamlet,* or the difficulties of the messenger in reporting the movement of Birnam Wood to Dunsinane, or the countless bloody sights that, unlike the severed limbs in the early *Titus Andronicus,* increasingly betray expectations that they will "speak," spilling rhetoric as freely as blood. The earlier tragedies tell a different story: of the relative amicability of eye and ear, of the facility of translating the evidence of one into that of the other.

To study Shakespeare's tragedies as instances of the unmasking of certain formal and ideological assumptions of Renaissance drama is implicitly to maintain that Shakespeare needs to be studied more in relation to his successors, both within and without the limited sphere of theater history, than has been the custom in Shakespeare scholarship.[14] That this is seldom done is owing partly to the assumption that a yawning gulf opened up around 1642 in English theatrical history. Another obstacle to prospective readings of Shakespeare is that—if I may use a metaphor that I hope will appeal to the groundlings among or within us—critics seem to have insisted, out of reverence, that his number and jersey be retired. Or, to use a more refined metaphor for readers seated in the upper gallery, we tend to suppose that whatever kingdom William conquered and ruled has long since vanished, like Camelot. He was a sovereign, we tacitly assume, who could have no successor.

The removal of Shakespeare from a history that would look more than a few years beyond him, our stubborn insistence on seeing him as a culmination (which he undoubtedly is) but not a transitional figure, has not helped to enrich Shakespeare criticism. Instead it has caused us to underplay many of the self-subversive elements in his so-called "mature" tragedies. That word "mature," so often applied to the tragedies of about 1600 and after, is a developmental metaphor embedded in questionable assumptions about the *telos* of Shakespeare's career. It implies that those tragedies so designated are Tragedy's tragedies, the Final Cause of tragedy, or what tragedy ultimately aspired to be, rather than the beginning of tragedy's undoing. I am aware that I am reversing customary practice, which is to regard earlier works like *Titus Andronicus, Richard III,* and *Romeo and Juliet* as the productions of an immense talent that hasn't yet fully mastered his craft. But viewing the earlier tragedies as something more than apprentice pieces has the advantage of putting into higher relief the vigorously interrogative character of the later ones. At some level it makes sense to say that Shakespeare is on his way to becoming less of a tragic playwright rather than more, even before *Coriolanus* and *Timon of Athens.* Moreover, my argument implies the need for a reassessment of these two late tragedies, too often still considered as evidence of the weakening powers of a tragic playwright in decline. Certain qualities of *Coriolanus* (its spareness) and *Timon of Athens* (its allegorical nature) may fit the canon better if we regard them as extreme developments of a process very much in evidence in the great quartet of tragedies: interrogating the ideology of dramatic forms.

16

Part I

❧

Representing

1
IMPOLITIC BODIES

D uring the span of Shakespeare's career, both the concept and practice of political representation underwent slow but significant
changes. Not until the end of the seventeenth century would Parliament
conceive of itself as a national body representing the sum of all the
interests and estates of the kingdom. It was not yet a representative
institution in the modern sense, a body willing to assert its legislative
independence and lay claim to a sovereign authority that rivaled that of
the monarch. But it was equally far from what it had been in the later
Middle Ages, the king's high court. The beginning of the transition may
be dated from earlier in the Tudor era, during the 1530s and 1540s,
when according to G. R. Elton, "the notion of the king's high court
whose decisions overrode everything else precisely because it was the
king's high ultimate seat of judgment, gave way before the developed
idea of a representative institution whose decisions bound everyone
because everyone was present in it either in person or by proxy. At the
same time statute came to be seen as an expression of free legislative
authority, and the limitations surrounding it came to be removed."[1]

During Elizabeth's reign, the House of Commons pressed for the
right of initiative in legislation.[2] In an "unresolved conflict, which
Elizabeth bequeathed to her successors," there emerged in the lower
house a sense that members were free to speak their own minds and
set their own agenda, "free from royal or conciliar restriction."[3] Shortly
after convening in 1604, the House drew up a bill for the restraint of
purveyance of supplies for the royal household, resulting in a vehement
warning by James in which he compared his parliamentary critics
to Roman tribunes and the subsequent drafting by the Commons

of an *Apology of the House of Commons, made to the King, touching their privileges* (1604). In this document the House insisted on the importance of the people's consent to legislation that affected them and "asseverated its powers as a representative body: 'Neither yet durst we impose it by law upon the people, without first acquainting them, and having their consents to it.' "[4] James's disputes with Parliament over electoral procedures are also reflected in *Coriolanus*. As historian Mark Kishlansky has shown, the play actually anticipates future electoral change by having one citizen suggest that what is needed to elect Coriolanus consul is not general acclamation (similar to contemporary English practice) but a majority vote,[5] and by another's "hint that the individual voice is as important as the collective one. . . . The clash of values at which Shakespeare dimly hinted would, over the course of the seventeenth century, emerge as one of the defining characteristics of the selection process."[6]

As late as the beginning of Elizabeth's reign, Parliament saw itself mainly as a corrective to bad government, a body that in ideal circumstances would meet infrequently. Under Elizabeth, Parliament, particularly the Commons, did grow substantially in the way of legislative independence. The open clash between Queen and Commons in 1601 over the power to grant monopolies, a decisive event in the history of the Commons' attempts to direct royal policy, was preceded by decades in which Parliament had an increasing role as keeper of the national purse strings and a somewhat independent voice, not simply the voice through which royal authority spoke. Under James, the unity of king-in-parliament, that sovereign power that, according to Sir Thomas Smith, might do "all that ever the people of Rome might do," "which representeth and hath the power of the whole realm, both the head and the body," and in which "every Englishman is intended to be there present, either in person or by procuration and attorneys . . . from the prince . . . to the lowest person in England," was breaking apart.[7] Relations between James and his parliaments became increasingly strained, largely over financial issues when the impoverished king tried unilaterally to raise the customs on various commodities.[8]

During Elizabeth's and James's reigns, representation in Parliament increased as well.[9] With their increase in number and political maturity during the late sixteenth and early seventeenth centuries, "MPs also became more organized and increasingly obsessed with defending their parliamentary privileges."[10] Those new members, however, for the most part did not regard themselves as "representatives" in the modern sense of the term, even though a few of the more outspoken parliamentary men were becoming "strongly conscious of their responsibility in Commons as representative of a broadly based, influential, and increasingly vocal squirearchy."[11] Though James complained of the extent to which parliaments concerned themselves with local and particular interests, "irrevocable decreits against particulare parties, being given therein under colour of generall Lawes,"[12] officially it was Parliament as a whole that was regarded as representing or embodying the nation as a whole. As Hanna Fenichel Pitkin relates, the noun "representative" doesn't make its first appearance in English until the 1640s, when it still usually refers to Parliament as a whole or bodies like it, not to individual members. The sense of the relation of an individual member of the Commons to his particular constituency isn't conveyed by the word "representative" until after the Civil War. In the course of the century, the meaning of "representative" as an adjective also shifts "from the earlier 'standing for' by way of substitution and substituted presence, to something like 'acting for.'"[13]

I will contend that *Coriolanus,* the Shakespearean play most explicitly concerned with representation in its political senses, reflects shifts not only in the practice but also in the very concept of representation. Struggles over representation take many forms in the play, including clashes between a patrician notion of representation, recognizable by an English audience in 1608 as parallel to the new claims of Jacobean absolutism, and a rival concept implicit in the demand for popular representation by tribunes. Representation of the body politic of Rome by Coriolanus—a representation that is never consummated because an impolitic Coriolanus refuses to show his wounds, let his body speak, and convert his natural body into a legible public and political body— is opposed to a newer order of representation that is independent of natural bodies and that construes the "representative" not in the older sense of making present through an embodying but in the modern senses of "the typical" and "an agent who acts on behalf of another." Bodies in *Coriolanus* are either grossly dilated, like Volumnia's, or privatized, willfully held from the public sphere of representation, like Coriolanus's: in either case, impolitic or incapacitated for a political role. The image of the body politic in Menenius's speech shows the idea of representation through the body, coincident with the great age of English theater and the system of absolute monarchy, to be a largely discredited fiction.

According to the logic of absolutism as set forth by Thomas Hobbes, "A Multitude of men, are made *One* Person, when they are by one man, or One Person, Represented. . . . For it is the *Unity* of the Representer, not the *Unity* of the Represented, that maketh the Person *One*."[14] An unorganized multiplicity before representation by a sovereign, a people

21

becomes a political body only through the unity of the sovereign's person. Hobbes's belated defense of sovereignty has connections with England's older conception of itself as a dynastic realm. As England came to view itself increasingly as a modern nation-state, its unity would depend less on bodily re-presentation by a monarch and more on distinct borders and uniform culture. Historian John Guy notes, "In the reigns of Henry VII and Henry VIII politicians had spoken only of 'country,' 'people,' 'kingdom,' and 'realm,' but by the 1590s they began to conceptualize the 'state.' "[15] Besides identifying England as "a defined territory," the concept of the "state" was supported by "three underlying beliefs: (1) that humanity was divided into races or nations; (2) that the purity of the English nation would be sullied by foreign admixtures; and (3) that English language, law, and customs (including dress) were the badges of nationality."[16]

As England gradually reconceived itself as nation-state rather than dynastic realm, its unity would increasingly seem to inhere in the nation itself, prior to representation by a monarch. National unity would depend less on representation by the single and unified figure of the monarch. The conceptual shift from dynastic realm to state may very well have helped pave the way for the possibilities of England's two revolutions later in the century. Coriolanus's denial of a public, political use for his body represents a critical moment in that shift. It augurs a phase of England's political history in which the monarch's body will no longer have the function of granting unity to a people who possessed none prior to and independent of monarchial representation.

Parallel to the revision of ideas of political representation in the play, Shakespeare revises his methods of dramatic representation. Coriolanus is an unrepresentative hero, if we understand "representation" in its older senses, just as *Coriolanus* strikes most critics as an anomalous play. That both hero and play seem so unrepresentative, however, may be precisely the point of this landmark in the revision of notions of representation, both literary and political.

Rymer and Shakespearean Representation

When the theaters were relit following the Restoration of the Stuart monarchy, a new concept of representation began to govern and direct the action of English stages. Whereas the Shakespearean tragic hero had been representative in the sense of being comprehensive, a summation, a microcosm, Restoration characters were representative in the sense of being types or typical. The Shakespearean hero was representative in much the same sense that the Renaissance monarch was understood to be the symbolic embodiment or re-presentation of the realm, a means of making present and visible to the people in symbolic form the whole of the body politic. The dramatic hero best embodied, in his or her little world, the totality of the larger world to which s/he belonged.

The representative quality of a Prince Hal, a Rosalind, or a Hamlet derives from their embodying characteristics (and imitating the discourses of) the whole of the body politic as it is represented in the play. Hamlet is a composite portrait of all the fragmentary characters in the play, including the courtier Laertes, the soldier Fortinbras, the scholar Horatio, the Gravedigger, Claudius, Ophelia, and even Osric, all of whom reflect "a piece of him" (Horatio, 1.1.22). Hal actually goes through an education in political representation in the sense of learning better to embody or symbolize the whole realm when his father mistakenly thinks he has taken a detour from politics by playing the political truant. In his apprenticeship in the taverns of the realm as in the soldiers' camp on the eve of the battle of Agincourt, Hal is learning and internalizing the discourses of those on the margins, thereby making him more fully a master of all the discourses and therefore the people of the realm, a more truly "representative" king than his father. Hal becomes a more potent "figure" than his father in two senses of that word, including the rhetorical one, for he is a far more potent synecdoche than Henry IV. A great deal of that potency derives from his mastering the discourses of the "other."

Even the closest thing in the Renaissance to Restoration characters, the "humour" characters of Ben Jonson, share with Shakespeare's tragic heroes the notion of an assumed whole condition that in abnormal characters becomes fractured and fragmented, and therefore stunted.[17] It is the assumption of a whole condition that I believe distinguishes the Renaissance understanding of representation—whether in the political or the literary sphere—from the Restoration's and also largely from our own. As Raymond Williams succinctly describes Renaissance representation, in a gloss of Charles I's surprising description of the Houses of Parliament as "the Representative Body of the Kingdome" (1643), "an assumed whole state or condition was *represented* by a particular institution; the *representative* quality came from the whole state outwards, rather than from scattered and diverse opinions brought together and, in a more modern sense, *represented*."[18] Just as political representation in the Renaissance assumes "a whole state or condition" represented by the monarch or by Parliament, so does the representation of the protagonist's life in a Renaissance tragedy appear to assume a whole state or condition that is legitimately represented by a single

23

adventure. And as the representative quality of Parliament following the Renaissance would cease to come "from the whole state outwards" and derive instead from "scattered and diverse opinions brought together and, in a more modern sense, represented," so does the eighteenth-century novel attempt to represent the protagonist's life in a part-by-part manner, building a sense of the whole from scattered and diverse adventures, none of which has the summarizing or representative force of the episode from a Renaissance tragedy. Novelistic representation, like political representation after the Renaissance, would increasingly work from the ground up, as opposed to the top-down procedure favored by Renaissance plays and monarchs. The eighteenth-century novel is predicated on the inefficacy of part-whole substitutions or, alternately, may be said to actively block such substitutions. In their assumptions about how a life may be represented, the Renaissance play and the novel exhibit vastly different dependencies on the trope of synecdoche. Drama, particularly in its Renaissance forms, may be the most synecdochic of the literary genres, and as dependent on the efficacy of the trope as was any version of English absolutism; the novel, perhaps the least synecdochic, belonged to an era in which the process of political representation was a good deal more complex and more cognizant of social divisions. A later age would despair of the prospect of representing the nation theatrically. In 1879 Matthew Arnold wrote, "Our vast nation is not homogeneous enough, not sufficiently united, even any large portion of it, in a common view of life, a common ideal, capable of serving as a basis for modern English drama."[19]

The words "represent" and "representative" have a significant history in the seventeenth century, one that is of considerable importance for understanding shifts in theatrical practices. From an early sense implying a substituted presence, the king and Parliament embodying or symbolizing the whole realm, a sense still informing to a large extent Hobbes's characterization of the king as Representative of the people,[20] the more extended political senses of standing for and acting for began to emerge in the seventeenth century.[21] The word "representative" gradually came to mean "standing for the opinions of those who elected them."[22] From the king and Parliament as substituted presence, the word "representative" came to suggest an agent standing for and acting for a particular constituency. It was only in the 1640s, Hanna Fenichel Pitkin notes, that the word "representative" was first applied to individual members of Parliament rather than to Parliament as a whole.[23] Concurrently, the sense of the "representative" as the "typical" began to emerge when applied to characters and situations.[24] It is a use of the word independent of the sense of a whole condition existing *prior to acts of representation* being made present to the mind through its symbolic representative.[25] As the family of words related to "representing" gradually loses its older sense of making present "an assumed whole state or condition" and acquires the meaning of typifying, Shakespearean tragedy will become vulnerable to charges built on this new understanding of representation.

After the Restoration, Thomas Rymer complained in what is perhaps the most notorious criticism of Shakespeare ever penned that Shakespeare's characters are not believable because not sufficiently typical or representative. Iago is an improbable character for Rymer because he doesn't have the traits of the typical soldier: simplicity and honesty. Neither the Venetians in *Othello* nor the Romans in *Julius Caesar* are representative in Rymer's sense.[26] Of course, the political meanings of "representative" and "represent" shifted in the politically convulsive era between the end of Shakespeare's career and the treatises of Rymer, and the bombast of Rymer's assault on Shakespeare, I believe, may be attributed in part to this very shift. Rymer's accusation that Shakespeare's characters are botched because insufficiently representative rests on a different concept of representation than the one implicit in Shakespearean tragedy. The newer concept owes something to a political context concerned more than the Elizabethan or Jacobean ones with the part-by-part representation of the people through Parliament, a context in which the "representative" came closer to one of its modern senses of "typical person."[27]

Coriolanus repeatedly stages the clash of two opposed concepts of representation: perhaps the deepest level at which faction operates in this extraordinarily factious play. One involves symbolic re-presentation of an entire political body by a single individual (like Coriolanus or King James) or institution (the Roman consuls or English Parliament). The other form is closer to our modern senses of the word. The tribunes who are chosen to represent the people—historically there were five, whom Shakespeare represents with two, Sicinius Velutus and Junius Brutus—are representative both in the modern sense of "typical" (a meaning that becomes especially prevalent in the eighteenth century) and in the senses of "standing for" and "acting on behalf of," meanings that over the course of the seventeenth century separated and diverged from what was soon to become an archaic sense of "symbolizing" or "making present."[28] It is such a divergence that seems to inform the people's demand for representation by the tribunes, a request that is far less subversive in its immediate political consequences—the granting of a more direct political voice to the Roman people—than in its implicit challenge to the rhetoric of bodied representation and to the assumption behind that rhetoric of a preexisting whole state or condition that only needs to be made present by the body of a single ruler or a political body (the consulate or Parliament). The questions of Coriolanus's election to the consulship and the people's representation by tribunes, his refusal to show his wounds in public, Menenius's mishandling of the fable of the belly, Coriolanus's famous ejaculation "There is a world elsewhere!" (3.3.135), the apparent reversibility of Coriolanus's names, and his disinterest in being "general" in both senses of that word: together these constitute a series of variations on the theme of re-presentation being confronted and challenged by a new order of representation.

One of the most striking aspects of the political rhetoric of the play is that, although the order of re-presentation is unequivocally aligned with the interests of the patrician class by Menenius's fable of the belly, challenges to the order of re-presentation come primarily from within the patrician class rather than from without. Coriolanus's own rhetoric goes far toward denaturing the rhetoric of the public or political body, which is already in deep trouble in Menenius's fable in the opening scene. It is implicitly a challenge to the organicist rhetoric of re-presentation and incorporation that Coriolanus, who should be a preeminent spokesman for re-presentation, issues when he refuses to show his battle wounds to the Roman people.[29]

Bodies, Wounds, and Voices

The figure of the wound as gaping mouth is commonplace in Shakespeare.[30] Usually the wound is credited with being able to speak, metonymically, of the soldier's heroic deeds that led to the wounds. In the early tragedy *Titus Andronicus*, Lucius avows, "My scars can witness, dumb although they are, / That my report is just and full of truth" (5.3.113–14). In reply to the King's accusation that Mortimer is a traitor, Hotspur says of his single combat with the Welshman Glendower in *1 Henry IV*,

> He never did fall off, my sovereign liege,
> But by the chance of war. To prove that true
> Needs no more but one tongue for all those wounds,
> Those mouthèd wounds, which valiantly he took. . . .
>
> (1.3.94–97)

Similar associations of tongues and wounds are made in *Richard III* (1.2.55–56) and *Julius Caesar*, where Antony in soliloquy refers to dead

Caesar's wounds as "dumb mouths" that "do ope their ruby lips, / To beg the voice and utterance of my tongue" (3.1.260–61). And later, toward the end of his rousing eulogy before the plebeians, he maintains that it is not he who, properly considered, is speaking, but Caesar's wounds: "I tell you that which you yourselves do know, / Show you sweet Caesar's wounds, poor poor dumb mouths, / And bid them speak for me" (3.2.226–28). Unlike these earlier wounds, Coriolanus's will not become tongues testifying to his deeds before the people he despises. Neither will he allow those wounds and the deeds that produced them to be mouthed by others, whose praises would aggravate rather than assuage his wounds: "I have some wounds upon me, and they smart / To hear themselves remember'd" (1.9.28–29).

In a substitute image, Coriolanus's wounds become graves in a speech by a Menenius desperate for Coriolanus to achieve the consulship: "think / Upon the wounds his body bears, which show / Like graves i'th'holy churchyard" (3.3.49–51),[31] an image designed to suggest both the size and quantity of the wounds, as well as the wound as "memorial to the enemy who inflicted it."[32] The image of wound-as-grave would seem in large measure consonant with the image wound-as-mouth. Both depict the wound as memorial to high deeds. Where it diverges in meaning from the more commonplace image is in its implication of silence. Of course, in transmuting wounds from tongues to graves, Menenius is surreptitiously justifying Coriolanus's stubborn refusal to show his wounds and thereby allow his body to "speak." Because graves, unlike tongues, are silent, it is appropriate that Coriolanus's wounds remain close and private. Menenius's figure also tacitly sanctifies Coriolanus's body, making it more properly an object of thought and meditation ("think" of those wounds, Menenius says) than of seeing and speaking. Menenius removes Coriolanus's wounds from the public realm of spectacle and rhetoric, placing them in the zone of private meditation. In addition, "holy" is etymologically connected to a family of words designating wholeness or integrity, including "whole," "wholesome,"[33] and "healthy," reinforcing an association in the play between patricians and a condition of wholeness or integrity, as opposed to the fragmentary and fractious plebs.[34] "Holy" serves to give the impression that the scars on Coriolanus are not fissures; far from being signs of fracture and division, Coriolanus's wounds paradoxically (like Christ's wounds) support his claim to be whole and integral.

Coriolanus's refusal to show his wounds challenges the very political rhetoric on which his own class has depended to keep the people's rebelliousness in check. The greatest threat to patrician rule in *Coriolanus* therefore comes from within rather than without the patrician class. This is apparent from the very beginning of the play, in Menenius's retelling of the fable of the belly, at once the most playful and the most serious extended treatment in all of Shakespeare of the organicist metaphor of the body politic. Menenius's treatment is serious and playful for precisely the same reason: the notion of a body politic in Menenius's hands degenerates into a self-conscious fiction, thereby laying bare the controlling and oppressive aspects of the metaphor and making it potentially a site of political contestation. The likable patrician Menenius finds himself confronted with a skeptical citizen, who seems to guess rightly that the metaphor is a rhetorical ploy to keep the people in line and deny them their due. Though it is a famous exchange, it deserves a further performance:[35]

> Men. There was a time, when all the body's members
> Rebell'd against the belly; thus accus'd it:
> That only like a gulf it did remain
> I'th'midst o'th'body, idle and unactive,
> Still cupboarding the viand, never bearing
> Like labour with the rest, where th'other instruments
> Did see, and hear, devise, instruct, walk, feel,
> And, mutually participate, did minister
> Unto the appetite and affection common
> Of the whole body. The belly answer'd—
>
> (1.1.95–104)

After interrupting, the First Citizen takes the initiative to dilate and review the figure of the political body:

> Your belly's answer—what?
> The kingly crown'd head, the vigilant eye,
> The counsellor heart, the arm our soldier,
> Our steed the leg, the tongue our trumpeter
> With our muniments and petty helps
> In this our fabric, if that they—
> Men.   What then?
> 'Fore me, this fellow speaks! What then? What then?
>
> (1.1.113–19)

On the one foot, "the great toe" of that body, a plebeian, usurps the privilege of elaborating the mainly patrician fiction through his constant interruption of Menenius; on the other, he begins to elaborate it in a much more conventional way than does the patrician to whom he is speaking. Rather than focusing our attention almost fetishistically on the secretive and private belly, the First Citizen begins to catalog the parts of the body politic in the proper order, beginning with "the kingly crown'd head." The First Citizen's brief rehearsal of the figure of the body politic, unlike the treatment it receives by Menenius, does not subvert the public nature of the ruling body that is presumed to be re-presentative of the whole political body.

There follows the rhetorical climax of this exchange: the belly (representing the patrician class) assures "my incorporate friends," the mutinous members of the political body, that the belly does indeed receive all the "general food," but only as a "store-house" and "shop of the whole body," distributing it thence "through the rivers of the blood / Even to the court, the heart, to th'seat o'th'brain": the court and throne of bodies natural and political. Such distribution of the "general food" to the whole public body, like Coriolanus's wounds, remains invisible, Menenius explains:

> 'Though all at once cannot
> See what I do deliver out to each,
> Yet I can make my audit up, that all
> From me do back receive the flour of all,
> And leave me but the bran.'
> (1.1.141–45)

After Menenius makes explicit to the First Citizen that the belly represents the senators of Rome, and the people its mutinous members, the image of the body degenerates into references to the First Citizen as "the great toe of the assembly" (1.1.154).

There are several aspects of this treatment of the body politic that make it, far from a useful instrument for controlling the people, a self-consuming figure. In general, the speech, though it sinks the rulers of Rome deep inside the interior of the body politic, brings the political purpose of the figure—to control mutinous members and silence their legitimate complaints—closer to the surface than any other instance of the figure in Shakespeare. Menenius's handling of the figure exposes a good deal of skepticism about its legitimacy, making it at times appear a monstrous and distended fiction, the rhetorical equivalent of his own belly or Volumnia's body: "For look you, I may make the belly smile, / As well as speak" (1.1.108–9), presumably pointing to folds in his stomach as he speaks these lines, thereby making the dilated fiction unexpectedly concrete. The identification of the nobility with the belly, rather than with a nobler part of the body like the head, conflicts with the more standard uses of the figure, as the First Citizen seems to understand

29

when he calls the belly "cormorant" and "the sink o'th'body" (1.1.120–21). In addition, the nobility are identified with one of the most private and secretive parts of the body, whose workings are invisible: " 'Though all at once cannot / See what I do deliver out to each." Though as a whole the speech maintains the Elizabethan fiction of the public body of the rulers re-presenting the entirety of the body politic,[36] the speech contributes to the general movement of privatizing the body in the play, for which Coriolanus is most responsible by refusing to show his wounds in public, thereby preventing the translation of his private body into public discourse; and for which King James might have been held responsible as well, given his reticence, compared with his predecessor Elizabeth, to theatricalize his presence by appearing in public spectacles.[37]

A pattern of conventional treatment of the body politic figure by the plebeians and subversive treatment of that figure by patricians holds true for the entire play.[38] For instance, Coriolanus, while standing for the consulship, mocks the people whose votes he must garner by repeatedly referring to them as "voices." By doing so, he suggests what he believes to be their partial or fragmentary nature, which he sometimes does far more explicitly as in his early remark, "Go get you home, you fragments!" (1.1.221).[39] Upon the entrance of three more citizens, he says,

> Here come moe voices.
> Your voices! For your voices I have fought,
> Watch'd for your voices; for your voices, bear
> Of wounds two dozen odd; battles thrice six
> I have seen and heard of; for your voices have
> Done many things, some less, some more: your voices!
>   (2.3.124–29)

As he publicly and politically disembodies himself by refusing to show his gaping wounds to the people, Coriolanus also symbolically disembodies the people of Rome by referring to them repeatedly as "voices" seemingly disconnected from any other part of a political or natural body. Of course, that is Coriolanus's point: these fragments are not an organic part of the body that is Rome. But by referring to the people as "voices," Coriolanus expresses something more far-reaching and ultimately destructive to himself and to his class: he shows himself to be a nonbeliever in the figure of the body politic, as in a less thoroughgoing way did Menenius in his retelling of the fable of the belly. By disembodying himself and the citizens that he is, according to the political rhetoric of Shakespeare's day, supposed to re-present in the sense of embody, Coriolanus further undermines what in the first scene still seems an operative fiction for controlling the multitudes.

By contrast with Coriolanus's refrain of "voices" to refer to the people of Rome, the people—both the citizens and their tribunes—refer to their voices in such a way as to maintain them "incorporate" with the rest of the political body. The First Citizen vows that Coriolanus "shall well know / The noble tribunes are the people's mouths / And we their hands" (3.1.268–70). Regretting the people's spineless confrontation with Coriolanus as he stood in the marketplace for the consulship, an exasperated Junius Brutus asks the citizens, "Why, had your bodies / No heart among you? Or had your tongues to cry / Against the rectorship of judgement?" (2.3.201–3). The rhetoric of the third citizen suggests that the plebeians' tongues are far from the disembodied instruments they are to become in Coriolanus's speeches: "For, if he show us his wounds and tell us his deeds, we are to put our tongues into those wounds and speak for them" (2.3.5–8). For one thing, he refers not to voices but to tongues, for unlike Coriolanus he habitually makes their political voices or votes bodied in the instrument that produces them. For another, those tongues inserted into Coriolanus's wounds (as if simultaneously repeating the violence done to Coriolanus's flesh and making love to his wounds) become figuratively interlocked with the body of Coriolanus.

Such references keep the people's "voices," which are of vital importance to the election or denial of Coriolanus and therefore to the health or sickness of the body politic, explicitly connected to the rest of the political body, whereas Coriolanus focuses almost fetishistically on the mouths of the people in such a way that they seem to become dissociated from all other body parts.[40] Punning on the reduction of the commons to voices, the "herd" reduced to the "heard," he snarls to the two tribunes,

> Are these your herd?
> Must these have voices, that can yield them now
> And straight disclaim their tongues? What are your offices?
> You being their mouths, why rule you not their teeth?
>   (3.1.32–35)

"Voices" are yoked in Coriolanus's truncated rhetoric of the body politic only to "tongues," "teeth," and "mouths." He both denigrates them by way of suggesting their fragmentary nature, and denies them a connection to the body politic that would repair or overrule their fragmentariness. In denying the plebeians a body, Coriolanus does more

31

to undermine the patricians' most potent instrument for controlling the plebeians, the organicist rhetoric of the body politic, than anyone else in the play. In disembodying the plebs as well as himself, holding onto his natural body as a private property rather than a public re-presentation of the body politic, the always impolitic Coriolanus votes himself out of office.

Coriolanus, Inc.

Ancient Roman culture placed great stress on membership in a family, a clan or gens, and a nation. In the context of the organicist political rhetoric of the play, the analogy between the state and the human body that was the lifeblood of Renaissance political rhetoric, those ever-enlarging and concentric spheres of membership in family, gens or clan, and nation are a means of incorporation, of positioning the individual within the whole of the body politic. In *Coriolanus,* however, the nominal form of incorporation is as problematic as the incorporative figure of the body politic.

There were four divisions of the Roman name: the praenomen applied only to the individual; the nomen, to his gens or clan; the cognomen, to family members within the gens; and the agnomen, an "addition" commemorating some special achievement. Caius Martius acquires an agnomen through his feats at Corioli, thereby becoming Caius Martius Coriolanus. As Philip Brockbank has noted in his New Arden edition of the play, "Fully described, Caius Martius Coriolanus has *praenomen, nomen,* and *agnomen,* but no true *cognomen.*"[41] The most distinctive thing about Coriolanus's name, however, is the odd tendency of the praenomen (applicable to the individual alone) and the nomen (applicable to all members of his gens) to reverse their customary order (at 1.9.64, 1.9.66, 2.1.163, 2.2.46, and in Volumnia's comments upon his name at 2.1.171–73).[42] Rather than ascribing confusion or memory lapse to Shakespeare, it would seem fruitful to see such reversals as belonging to a family (or clan) of failed acts of incorporation in the play. The assurance that should derive from the Roman name, the individual's progressive "incorporation" into a larger social and political body, are curtailed by the unsatisfactorily explained tendency of Coriolanus's names to fall out of place.[43]

The first miscarriage of Coriolanus's names happens, appropriately, at the moment he acquires his addition or agnomen, Coriolanus, for his feats at Corioles. He is hailed first by Cominius, then by the people, as Martius Caius Coriolanus (1.9.64,66). Some editors assume this is a mistake and emend the lines to "Caius Martius Coriolanus." Often the discrepancy in names here and elsewhere is ascribed to a difference in compositors or to editorial interference, theories that Brockbank rejects.[44] The discrepancy within Coriolanus's names, I submit, is perfectly consistent with his most salient characteristics. At the moment of greatest fame and celebrity, a disorder within Coriolanus's names suggests all sorts of questions about the inverted order of particular and general, or private and public interests that inform Coriolanus's outlook, as well as questions about the fitness of Coriolanus to stand for the consulship, to represent the Roman body politic. The reversal of Coriolanus's praenomen or individual name Caius and nomen or clan name Martius is a species of synecdoche, the trope that involves a substitution of whole for part and part for whole, general for particular or particular for general. Coriolanus's whole outlook, including changes in outlook in the course of the play, might be described by means of a particular version of this trope: one that substitutes parts for wholes without integrating them; one that would surgically remove unwanted parts or parties from the body politic and divide particular from general, private from public.

Coriolanus vacillates in his allegiance to the public and private spheres, but at any particular moment of the play, he polarizes private or "particular" and public or "general" interests and values.[45] Toward the beginning of the play, he seems to hold to an ideal of suppressing the private for the good of the state, an outlook conducive to effective warfare against the Volscians: only the soldier who holds "his country's dearer than himself" (1.6.72) may follow him. Even here, however, we have a whiff of a Coriolanus who will be equally fanatical in his allegiance to the realm of the private and "particular," for he implies that he is recruiting the singular and particular soldier, not the many: "Let him alone, or so many so minded, / Wave thus to express his disposition, / And follow Martius" (1.6.73–75). Only the highly particular soldier, paradoxically, will be able to ignore his own particular or private interests. After peace has been established, Coriolanus comes to stand for a synecdochic inversion of public and private interests that is mirrored in the inversion of his individual name and clan name. Coriolanus often goes against the dominant outlook of the Renaissance by placing the private before the public,[46] as I shall detail momentarily. Then at the end of the play, while among the Volscians, Coriolanus represents the fanatical suppression of both private affections and public interests. His sometime Volscian enemy Tullus Aufidius attests that he has "stopp'd [his] ears against / The general suit of Rome: never admitted / A private whisper, no, not with such friends / That thought them sure of you" (5.3.5–8).

Coriolanus echoes Aufidius's distinction between public (or "general") and private with his vow not to hear further suits from Rome, whether public or private: "Fresh embassies and suits, / Nor from the state nor private friends, hereafter / Will I lend ear to" (5.3.17–19). At each stage of the play, Coriolanus either polarizes the spheres of the private and the public in ways that suggest one is encroaching upon the other or else dismisses both. Either way he displays his political ineptitude, his inadequacy for mediating public and private interests.

Throughout most of the play, however, Coriolanus stakes out his allegiance to the private and against those terms that are synonymous in *Coriolanus* and throughout Shakespeare, the public and the "general." As an adjective, "general" can mean "public" as contrasted with "private" (as, for instance, at 5.3.6, Aufidius's line "The general suit of Rome"); as noun or adjective, it often refers in Shakespeare to the commons, the plebeians (as in Volumnia's jeering reference to "our general louts"). Coriolanus's contempt for the "general" in the latter sense is all too apparent. Less obvious is his hostility to the "general" in the former sense: his commitment to the private sphere to such a degree that it represents almost a treason against the "general." In spite of his considerable rhetorical skills, he suffers from logophobia, a fear of words that is consistent with his denigration of the public. His horror of publicizing his wounds by ritually showing them in the marketplace is doubled by a horror of showing them through speech. It is synecdochic substitutions like these that make the miscarriages of Caius Martius's names so appropriate and telling. And it is just such a synecdochic substitution of private for public that gave rise to riots in the Midlands in 1607, which are widely thought to be reflected in *Coriolanus*.[47] The Enclosure Acts resulted in the privatizing of public lands or "commons," a process that began in the thirteenth century but was still continuing in Shakespeare's time. As a result of these acts, tenants were dispossessed of traditional rights to the land, driving them to the towns. Enclosures probably also produced "the fear of suffering and starvation through corn shortage,"[48] reflected in the opening scene of the play. A contestation between private and public is reenacted in so many forms in the play that it seems far from unlikely that Shakespeare might have taken his cue for *Coriolanus* from the conversion of public lands into private ones. *Coriolanus's* topicality, in other words, is reflected at the most minute rhetorical levels, since enclosures were a species of synecdoche, arguably the dominant trope in the play.[49]

The conversion of public into private is also evident in Martius's will-to-fame, that most public of Renaissance objectives, which in his case is driven by an unequivocal allegiance to the private and particular.

34

The First Citizen maintains, "What he hath done famously, . . . though soft-conscienced men can be content to say it was for his country, he did it to please his mother, and to be partly proud, which he is, even to the altitude of his virtue" (1.1.35–39). The privacy of Coriolanus's motivations echoes the privacy of his wounds and body, as well as the privacy, secrecy, or invisibility of the belly, the representation of the patrician class in Menenius's retelling of the fable. Coriolanus also appears to be champion, albeit an ineffectual one, of the particular or private when he requests special amnesty for a private citizen of Corioles who gave him succor (1.9.80–85), then cannot remember his poor host's name. The importance of family connections in *Coriolanus* further exemplifies a conversion of public value to private. In one critic's words, "the notion of a body politic . . . gives way to the notion of a family politic."[50] Echoing her husband's allegiances to the sphere of the private, family and home, Virgilia, anxiously awaiting his return near the beginning of the play, maintains a kind of privacy, resisting her friend Valeria's and mother-in-law Volumnia's repeated injunctions to come "out of doors": "I'll not over the threshold till my lord return from the wars" (1.3.74–75).

Rhetorically, Coriolanus's affiliation with the private manifests itself in his distaste for proverbs. Of the mobs of plebeians demanding "corn at their own rates" at the beginning of the play, Coriolanus snarls,

> They said they were an-hungry, sigh'd forth proverbs—
> That hunger broke stone walls; that dogs must eat;
> That meat was made for mouths; that the gods sent not
> Corn for the rich men only. With these shreds
> They vented their complainings. . . .
>
> (1.1.204–8)

The anonymous and popular authority claimed by proverbial forms of speech, together with the implicit claim of the proverb to be a general and therefore potently representative truth, are mocked by Coriolanus, who implies that proverbial wisdom is had by shredding documents, so to speak. The only access to general truth and authority by the plebeians is a specious one put forth with odds and ends, shreds of wisdom gathered from here and there by equally fragmentary persons. By implying that the people's proverbial wisdom is composed of undigested, unincorporated odds and ends, Coriolanus challenges the proverb's implicit claim to self-sufficiency and integrity—its inherent claims to be able to stand alone, independent of context—as well as its generality.

Consonant with Coriolanus's disdain for "the general" (Shakespeare's sometime name for the people) and for the people's generalizing proverbs is his disdain to *be* general, in two senses of that word: to be military general and to be universal, or at least effectively re-presentative of the Roman populace he loathes. The first is left for Cominius, a man whose name seems to contain a faint echo of "common," as suggested in these lines:

> Com.   Hath he not pass'd the noble and the common?
> Bru.   Cominius, no.   (3.1.28–29)

The echo of "common" (as well as the beckoning "Come," as in 1.1.271, Sic. " . . . Cominius." Bru. "Come") within "Cominius" is appropriate because of the different ways in which the word "common" sounds on Cominius's and Martius's tongues. Whereas Martius speaks disparagingly of "the common file" (1.6.43) and "You common cry of curs!" (3.3.120), Cominius speaks to and of the commons more ingratiatingly: "Hear me, my masters, and my common friends!" (3.3.108). For Coriolanus, "common" signifies "vulgar": "You should account me the more virtuous, that I have not been common in my love," he instructs the citizens who have come to give him their voices (2.3.93–94). Cominius can be "general" in both the more specialized military sense and in the more general sense of that word, because, unlike Coriolanus, he does not seem convinced that he has nothing in common with the commons.

The tribunes cast further light on Coriolanus's failure and unwillingness to be general. When Sicinius wonders at Martius's ability to play a subordinate role to the general Cominius, Brutus responds,

> Fame, at the which he aims,
> In whom already he's well grac'd, cannot
> Better be held, nor more attain'd than by
> A place below the first: for what miscarries
> Shall be the general's fault, though he perform
> To th' utmost of a man, and giddy censure
> Will then cry out of Martius, 'Oh, if he
> Had borne the business!'
>   (1.1.262–69)

Sicinius adds that "if things go well," Martius will attract most of the praise, and Brutus sums up,

> Half all Cominius' honours are to Martius, .
> Though Martius earn'd them not; and all his faults
> To Martius shall be honours, though indeed
> In aught he merit not.
>   (1.1.272–75)

Military honors and blame, at least in the tribunes' view, seem to be no more fairly distributed than corn. The tribunes' deprecation of Martius by providing the most cunning of motives for his willingness to be commanded by a general also makes glancing reference to the tortured problem of representation in the play. Brutus suggests that fame often, if not ordinarily, fails to represent faithfully its bearer. The irony of their observation is that, although the tribunes are presumed to be representative of the will of the people, they (privately, to be sure, for no one overhears their conversation) undermine the representation of authority and impugn the authority of representation, including their own.[51]

Political Parties, Theatrical Parts

Coriolanus's distaste for posturing and role-playing before the people of Rome is another way in which incorporative synecdoches, representational bonds between parts and wholes (as opposed to dissociative synecdoches like the inversion of individual and gens, Caius and Martius, private and public) become obstructed in the play. Menenius urges Coriolanus to play the part that is expected of him and to respect the political rituals that have governed election to the consulship: "Pray you go fit you to the custom" (2.2.142). Coriolanus rejoins, "It is a part / That I shall blush in acting, and might well / Be taken from the people" (2.2.144–46). Before repeated appeals by his mother Volumnia to dissemble for the sake of his own fortunes and his friends', Coriolanus asks, "Why did you wish me milder? Would you have me / False to my nature? Rather say I play / The man I am" (3.2.14–16). The only part he will consent to play is the part that is not a part. A reference to the imperfect and forgetful actor that he has become in the face of appeals from wife and mother not to lay waste all of Rome hints at a disparagement of actors in general (including the actor who is playing or taking his part): "Like a dull actor now / I have forgot my part and I am out, / Even to a full disgrace" (5.3.40–42).

After having donned the gown of humility and entreated the "voices" or votes of five citizens, he resigns himself to finishing the play: "I am half through, / The one part suffer'd, the other will I do" (2.3.122–23). The word "part" in these lines and elsewhere condenses a number of the play's themes. On the one hand it means "fraction or portion of a whole," and evokes the play's endless elaboration of the language of dismemberment and disintegration: for instance, Coriolanus's memorable insult to the plebeians, "Go get you home, you fragments!" (1.1.221); his reference to the plebeians who demand corn as "these quarter'd slaves" (1.1.198); young Martius's "mamocking" or shredding of a butterfly (1.3.65), in some ways an emblem of the disintegration that infects Rome; and Coriolanus's eventual fate among his former enemies, the Volscians. Coriolanus himself suggests, "Cut me to pieces, Volsces, men and lads" (5.6.111), and the Volscians soon echo his language: "Tear him to pieces!" (5.6.120). So much of the language of the play is of wholes being shredded, giving way to pieces, whether it is the natural body of Coriolanus, the political body of Rome, an army, military honors, or a butterfly.[52]

Thus when Coriolanus, standing for the consulship, says he is "half through, / The one part suffer'd, the other will I do," his language also calls up the extensive language of a disintegrated body politic, a unity giving way to parts, parties, factions. The opening of the play especially is replete with such language. Coriolanus jeers at those who stay at home yet presume to know "What's done i'th'Capitol; . . . side factions, . . . making parties strong" (1.1.191–93). The association of the people with party and faction is strengthened by the repeated reference to their being two "troops" or mobs of angered citizens (see 1.1.202f.). Menenius, like Coriolanus, seems to associate party and faction with the people. "Proceed by process," he warns the tribunes, "Lest parties, as he is belov'd, break out / And sack great Rome with Romans" (3.1.311–13). "Part" and "party" belong to the democratic process that the patricians fear and hate: the Third Citizen asks his fellows, "Are you all resolved to give your voices? But that's no matter, the greater part carries it" (2.3.37–38). Menenius's and Coriolanus's distaste for party politics echoes the dominant assumption of Renaissance England. Political parties will not become a fundamental part of the English political process until the end of the seventeenth century.[53] In *Coriolanus,* "party" is an ugly word signaling division and strife, often with legal overtones.[54]

After we are introduced to the language of "party" and "faction" at the beginning of the play, when two mobs of citizens are roaming the streets in opposite sides of the city, it is hard not to hear echoes of that language of political strife in descriptions of the war against the Volscians, including Coriolanus's motives for going to war. The language of "party" casts shadows over what might be called the proud patrician fictions of wholeness and integrity: the parallel fictions that the state would be whole if not for the people's wrangling and the instigations of their tribunes and that the patrician is a "microcosm"—Menenius calls his face "the map of my microcosm" (2.1.62), the only occurrence of that word in Shakespeare—whereas the people are but "fragments." When the question of Martius's motives for fighting is raised, it is in language that suggests that he is himself a divided body, split by faction long before his banishment, when he becomes divided between his loyalty for family and friends and his detestation of Rome as a whole: "though soft-conscienced men can be content to say it was for his country, he did it to please his mother, and to be partly proud" (1.1.36–38). At the end of the play, he remains divided and factionary. Aufidius muses in an aside, "I am glad thou hast set thy mercy and thy honour / At difference in thee" (5.3.200–1). It is a motivationally divided Coriolanus that is somewhat redundantly threatened with bodily division or mutilation in the closing scene.

The battle scenes of act 1 are oddly reminiscent of the mob scenes and equally informed by the language of division, suggesting that the integral life of the resolute soldier bears more resemblance than difference to the fractious divisions, the self-division, the theatrical posturing, the parts and parties of Roman political life. Martius tells Titus to "take / Convenient numbers to make good the city, / Whilst I, with those that have the spirit, will haste / To help Cominius" (1.5.11–14), reminding us of the two mobs of citizens on opposite sides of the city. In the next scene a messenger brings news to Cominius, "I saw our party to their trenches driven, / And then I came away" (1.6.12–13). The reappearance of "party," a word of scorn for the patricians in its political setting, in the context of military maneuvers and heroics is unsettling. It undermines our confidence in Coriolanus's view that the political life and values are opposite to and at odds with their military counterparts. Coriolanus himself applies the language of faction to war: "Were half to half the world by th'ears, and he / Upon my party, I'd revolt to make / Only my wars with him [Aufidius]" (1.1.232–34).[55]

The language of "part" and "party," then, structures political life, military action, as well as individual motivation. The implications of division and disintegration implicit in these words extend to the theater as well, for "part" in *Coriolanus* is several times used in an explicitly theatrical sense. To return to Coriolanus's lines when standing for the consulship—"I am half through, / The one part suffer'd, the other will I do" (2.3.122–23)—the word "part" glances at the theatrical metaphor that is elsewhere invoked far more explicitly. After being warned by Cominius to "make strong party, or defend yourself / By calmness or by absence" (3.2.94–95), Coriolanus balks at having been reduced to a mere actor: "You have put me to such a part which never / I shall discharge to th'life" (3.2.105–6). Volumnia reminds her antitheatrical son that in a sense he has always been an actor, taking direction from his mother:

Come, come, we'll prompt you.
I prithee now, sweet son, as thou hast said
My praises made thee first a soldier, so,
To have my praise for this, perform a part
Thou hast not done before.

(3.2.106–10)

Theatrical "part" joins an ensemble of terms designating partisanship (Cominius's "make strong party"), faction, and divisiveness. Theatrical posturing, or electing to play a "part," an essential part of the Roman political life Coriolanus detests, is sure to be a species of dis-integration, a way of losing whatever integrity one has, because of the division it posits between an essential self and a public persona. Coriolanus fears this parting of the ways of person and persona, which may come about through public and political posturing or through the words of others, which create a second and public self beyond the pale of his governance. Paradoxically, though Coriolanus himself constantly polarizes the public and private through his shifting and fanatical allegiances to each in turn, he fears, far more than he fears the Volscian enemy, the polarizing of his private and public identities.[56]

Especially in light of his references to the fragmentary nature of the people (as in his command to them to "Mend," 1.4.38)[57] and their knowledge (popular proverbs are "shreds," 1.1.207), Coriolanus's refusal to play a part may seem more than a proud patrician's posturing. It may betray a fear of the dis-integration that he repeatedly attributes to the plebs. In other words, in light of the continual threat of fragmentation within both the body politic (through factional fighting) and the figure of the body politic (especially in Coriolanus's taunting rhetoric), there may be equal and parallel dangers in "taking part" (politically) or "playing a part" (theatrically). Without faith in the bodily, organicist rhetoric of incorporation, theatricality, or any election to play a "part," threatens to lead to dissolution: not only of one's "integrity," as some Puritan writers of Shakespeare's day argued, but also of whatever unity obtains in the political body.

Since the Rome represented in the play is that of the Republic rather than the Empire,[58] Shakespeare and his contemporaries might have already brought to the play certain assumptions about an inorganic body public, a body inadequately "incorporated" into a unity by a ruling body. In other words, they might have been automatically suspicious of the venom in Sicinius's speech, "Where is this viper / That would depopulate the city and / Be every man himself?" (3.1.261–63), as they would of a similar speech by Cassius in *Julius Caesar*—another play filled with the language of parts, party, and parting or division—concerning Caesar's construction of a Rome filled with "but one only man" (1.2.155). Sicinius's lines seem a fair description of the genre of tragedy, which often gives the impression of a city or a world represented by a single man who would "be every man himself," as well as of the logic of absolutism. The tragic protagonist, in other words, is representative in something like the same manner that the absolute monarch claimed to be representative of the English people. Among Shakespeare's tragedies, however, *Coriolanus* is anomalous in featuring a protagonist who does not seem fully "representative" in those senses, or as representative as Hamlet, Othello, King Lear, and Macbeth. In spite of his being a habitual generalizer, like his predecessors,[59] most readers and spectators seem to think he is a far less representative tragic figure than those others. Though Coriolanus would deny the people their political representatives, the tribunes, he himself is unable to represent them—and us—as fully as the laws of his genre dictate. Coriolanus's re-presentational deficiency is mocked by Volumnia in her plea to her son to dissemble with the people for the sake of his fortunes and his friends. She claims to speak and stand for all of patrician Rome: "I am in this / Your wife, your son, these senators, the nobles" (3.2.64–65). Hers is a reduced version of the representational power Coriolanus wants but does not achieve: reduced, because it leaves out the most numerous members of the body politic, whom she calls "our general louts" (3.2.66).

Coriolanus's failure to achieve the status of political re-presentative is mirrored by a similar deficiency in the sphere of theatrical represen-tation. The apparent failure of the play and its protagonist to measure up to the universality and representativeness of that famous lineage stretching from *Hamlet* to *Macbeth* seems oddly consistent with the political themes of the play. The play, it may be said, actually predicts its protagonist's representational inadequacies vis-à-vis his audiences. In other words, the apparent deficiencies of Coriolanus and *Coriolanus* may not be deficiencies at all but calculated rather than accidental features of the play. They serve as mirrors of Coriolanus's failure as a political re-presentative of Rome, including its common people. *Coriolanus* is a tragedy that seems to go against the Shakespearean tragic premise of a world nearly filled with and represented by "but one only man," in Cassius's words; a man who would "be every man himself," in Sicinius Velutus's.[60] It is therefore a tragedy that, like the people's demand for representation by the tribunes, would seem to offer or at least to hint at the need for an alternative concept of representation to the one operative in other plays, an alternative understanding of the tragic protagonist's representativeness. With the starkly unsympathetic Coriolanus, a character who is decidedly not representative in the same sense as his immediate theatrical predecessors, Shakespeare seems to be enacting a quarrel within the concept of representation, a quarrel that is enacted on several other levels in the play and that will be replayed continually on political stages throughout the century. The relation of Coriolanus to the play that contains him displays the same quarrels with (and within) the concept of re-presentation that are evident in the people's recent demand for representation by the tribunes.[61] Parallel to the challenges to ideas of political representation in the play, Shakespeare revises his methods of theatrical representation, which largely accounts for the anomalous nature of this play in the Shakespearean canon.

A similar quarrel occurs within the representative function of the world of the play, which ordinarily in Shakespeare, I think it is fair to say, serves as a microcosm of the world at large for the English audiences of Shakespeare's day.[62] Coriolanus's celebrated line as he returns Rome's decree of banishment with an answering banishment of Rome, "There is a world elsewhere!" (3.3.135), suggests a failure of re-presentation analogous to similar failures embodied by Coriolanus himself. Applied to the world of the play as perceived by the spectator, the line would imply a dramatistic failure to represent, through the synecdoche of the play-world, something close to the entirety of the world at large.[63] Coriolanus is deficient as re-presentative of the political body of Rome; Rome for Coriolanus is similarly deficient representationally, he suggests by claiming that there is a "world elsewhere." Overruling Coriolanus's assertion, a direct challenge to Rome's re-presentational powers, is the play's claustrophobia, its implication that there is no elsewhere that is not essentially a repetition of the Roman here. There is so negligible a difference between the three locales of Coriolanus, Rome, Antium, and Corioles, as well as between the Volscian and Roman cultures,[64] that Coriolanus's assertion seems erroneous in retrospect. His claim would be apt for almost any other tragedy of Shakespeare (with the notable exception of Timon of Athens). Even the dark Macbeth offers glimpses of a real and salubrious alternative to medieval Scotland, an England ruled by the saintly Edward the Confessor.

In the uniformity of its play-world, it may appear that Coriolanus ultimately overrules the divisive action and rhetoric of the play. But the uniformity of the play-world, remarkable for Shakespeare (though this aspect will be repeated in his next tragedy, Timon of Athens), may instead, like all the other elements of the tragedy investigated in these pages, signal the superannuation of the very figure of the body politic.[65] That figure is predicated on the notion of variety in unity. When variety (of locale, of rhetoric, of motivation, of class) drops out of the formula, as it does in Shakespeare's last two tragedies, the whole formula begins to smack of obsolescence. In *Coriolanus* and *Timon,* unity (as a criterion if not an actuality) gives way to uniformity, and uniformity does not imply unity, at least in its contemporary senses.

The quarrels between competing senses of representation that would endure throughout the seventeenth century and beyond, and that would help make both literary and political representation such different affairs in the later seventeenth and eighteenth centuries than they were in the Elizabethan and Jacobean eras, are already at a high pitch in Shakespeare's late tragedy *Coriolanus,* which in many respects seems a synecdoche and omen for the century as a whole.

2

PARTIAL TO SYNECDOCHE
(OPHELIA'S RHETORIC)

Now when the first weeks life was almost spent,
And this world built, and richly furnished;
To store heav'ns courts, and steer earths regiment,
He cast to frame an Isle, the heart and head
Of all his works, compos'd with curious art;
Which like an Index briefly should impart
The summe of all; the whole, yet of the whole a part . . .
—Phineas Fletcher, *The Purple Island*, 1.43

Galeatzo.   Well, and what dost thou play?
Balurdo.   The part of all the world.
Alberto.   The part of all the world? What's that?
Balurdo.   The fool.
—John Marston, *Antonia and Mellida* (c. 1599)

R enaissance tragedy's economy of representation reflects a similar
economy in the system of absolutism, where the king was presumed to re-present the body politic. Confidence in the system of
monarchy presupposed confidence in the trope governing part/whole
substitutions. In the era of the novel, where the economy and rules for
representing a life drastically changed, the nature of political representation would similarly shift: MPs would be presumed to represent particular constituencies rather than, as during the Renaissance, the whole
realm, and representation of the whole nation would become a matter
of piecemeal representation of divergent constituencies and opinions.[1]

The most fundamental and enabling synecdoche for Shakespearean
tragedy may be the assumption that a life may be represented by a single
sequence of events, an essential episode that may represent the whole.
Georg Lukács has pointed out modern drama's break with such an
assumption and consequently its departure from the genre of tragedy.

In the modern drama, "The data, actions manifested in the external world, fail to account for the whole man, who in turn is not able to arrive at an action revelatory of his entire self."[2] Such challenges to the rule of synecdoche in drama, however, are already evident in Shakespearean tragedy at the top of its form. That is one reason that these plays seem like the culmination of their form. The vigor of *Hamlet* and its successors owes much to their energetically questioning their own structuring principles, including their dependency on various kinds of synecdoche. *Hamlet* is pivotal among Shakespeare's tragedies in this respect: tropologically, it is a study in the obstructed synecdoche, the part/whole substitution that is either illegitimate like Claudius or ineffectual like Polonius. Obstructed synecdoches complicate the representation of Hamlet's life by means of the play no less than Hamlet's potential representativeness as a Renaissance prince. Since the play as a whole might be characterized as a study in the obstructed synecdoche, our recurring sense of the peculiar elusiveness of this play whose many parts are notoriously difficult to assimilate to a whole and integrated interpretation seems consistent with, and even predicted by, the rhetoric of the play. Our difficulties as interpreters are prefigured by Ophelia's anxieties about grasping the meaning of the whole of the inner play through the ordinarily synecdochic dumb show and prologue.

I will begin with the assumption that the concept of impartiality— whether of characters or playwrights, magistrates or sovereigns—is synecdochic, presupposing legitimate exchanges or substitutions be- tween parts and wholes, wholes and parts. The impartiality of political outlook that Coleridge imputed to Shakespeare—though the imputa- tion may spring more from Coleridge than from Shakespeare—seems consistent with the ascendancy of various other kinds of synecdoche helping to structure Shakespearean drama, both character and plot: an ascendancy that is challenged by many of Shakespeare's so-called "mature" tragedies, beginning with *Hamlet*.[3]

Impartial Playwrights, Whole-hearted Sovereigns

For the Lawes of Nature (as *Justice, Equity, Modesty, Mercy,* and (in summe) *doing unto others, as wee would be done to,*) of themselves, without the terror of some Power, to cause them to be observed, are contrary to our natural Passions, that carry us to Partiality, Pride, Revenge and the like.

—Hobbes[4]

The wonderful philosophic impartiality in Shakespeare's politics.

—Coleridge[5]

45

Much of the political rhetoric of Renaissance England suggests that the perfect sovereign is also the perfect synecdoche: a part of the body politic that stands for, re-presents, or quasi-mystically makes present the whole;[6] and an embodiment of the whole that will override party and faction and, because of his or her impartiality, be trusted to take the part of any of that body's wronged members. King James was especially concerned to present himself as impartial, given suspicions that he would be partial in his acts and decrees to the Scotsmen many English feared would impoverish their own country. Discussing the Union of the Kingdoms in a speech to Parliament in 1607, James declared that, as for "limitations and restrictions" on the naturalization of the Scottish, "you may assure your selues I will with indifferencie grant what is requisite without partiall respect of Scotland."[7] Of the English fear that the Scots "shall eate our commons bare, and make vs leane," James assured his audience, "By Law they cannot, and by my partialitie they shall not."[8] Such assertions would have been tacitly supported by the prevalent notion of the body politic, which James frequently invoked in his writings and speeches. Implying an already existing whole subdividable into parts, the organicist metaphor of the body politic tacitly supports claims to impartiality by the sovereign, the part (namely, the head) that stands for or re-presents the whole. In a speech to the Lords and Commons of 1610, James employed the organic analogy to suggest that the notion of a partial and injudicious king is illogical, since such a monarch could only be self-wounding and self-defeating: "And it were an idle head that would in place of physic so poison or phlebotomize the body as might breed a dangerous distemper or destruction thereof."[9]

James had cause repeatedly to assert his impartiality before Parliament, whether through the organic analogy or other related rhetoric of parts and wholes. The favor he showed the Scotsmen he brought with him on accession to the throne, the patronage and perquisites he lavished upon them, together with his corresponding failure to forge strong social links to the English nobility, left him vulnerable to charges of partiality. Though he implied otherwise, it was James more than his subjects who had reason to find comfort in representing himself in rhetorical terms as a potent synecdoche:

> All foreigne Kings that haue sent their Ambassadours to congratulate with me since my comming, haue saluted me as Monarch of the whole Isle, and with much more respect of my greatnesse, then if I were King alone of one of these Realmes: and with what comfort doe your selues behold Irish, Scottish, Welsh, and English, diuers in Nation, yet all

walking as Subjects and seruants within my Court, and all liuing vnder the allegiance of your King."[10]

The anxieties masked by this rhetoric, including the anxiety that he too may be a "foreigne King" in his own kingdom, are also addressed by his frequent recourse in speeches to Parliament to the rhetoric of "parts." For instance, "The actual Naturalizing [of the *Post nati,* those Scots born after James's accession to the throne of England and therefore after the theoretical union of the kingdoms] . . . is already graunted to by your seluues to the most part of such particular persons as can haue any vse of it heere"; "without partiall respect of Scotland"; "nothing before heard or seen in those parts [the border between England and Scotland] but bloodshed, oppressions, complaints and outcries"; "the inconueniences that are feared on England's part"; "my partialitie"; "yet were [the Scots] euer but vpon the defensiue part, and may in a part thanke their hilles and inaccessible passages that preserued them"; "And for my part": the sampling is taken from a page of James's address to Parliament on the Union issue.[11] This insistent rhetoric of "parts" may simultaneously betray a fear of disunion, raise the phantom of a fear of disunion among the MPs who were his audience, and work to suggest a whole—indivisible and headed by an impartial monarch—whose parts are uniformly tied to and suggestive of the meaning of the whole. Such a rhetorical dance around the family of words related to "parts" may have been designed precisely to show members of Parliament the suppleness of an impartial king capable of taking any part but inflexibly committed to none.

When Elizabeth or James wished to mask their partiality in the granting of monopolies to court favorites, or when James wished to mask his partiality to his fellow Scotsmen, they could draw on a powerful and well-entrenched tradition according to which the sovereign symbolically embodied the whole realm. The multiplicity of a people can be made one, can become a unified body only through the unity of the sovereign's person. Without re-presentation by a sovereign, a people do not constitute a political body, but only an unorganized multiplicity. The unity guaranteed by the sovereign's person promises to negate "partiality" in two senses: the incoherence of unrelieved particularism, the chaotic coexistence of a multitude of parts without a whole;[12] and, even after the people are mystically united into a body politic through monarchical representation, the partiality or bias of individual members of that body, who may from time to time forget that their own welfare is organically united with the welfare of the whole body.

Whereas James could deploy a whole rhetoric of "parts" and "wholes" to suggest (or dissemble) impartiality, Locke stressed that the supersession of partiality is a strenuous process, for magistrates and philosophers as well as ordinary people, so many are the obstacles placed in the way of the human understanding's efforts to rise above its biased and partial perspectives. Locke was the thinker who arguably influenced the early development of the English novel more than any other, and in a way, the eighteenth-century English novel makes a virtue of what appears to be a Lockean necessity. In the early phases of the development of the English novel, partiality—especially a feeling of partiality toward certain characters at the expense of others on the part of both author and reader—is often painted as a virtue. Fielding and Sterne were fond of openly confessing to their readers their partiality toward certain characters. The genre of the sentimental novel popular in the eighteenth century seems designed to give readers an education in partiality. Shakespearean drama, by contrast, seems on many levels closer to the political rhetoric of Elizabeth and James, which repeatedly insisted on the monarch's impartiality and function of symbolically representing the whole realm.

In his "Conduct of the Understanding," an incomplete treatise originally conceived as an additional chapter to the *Essay Concerning Human Understanding*, "a sort of practical appendix" to the *Essay* according to its editor Thomas Fowler,[13] as in James's speech to Parliament of 1607, the words "parts," "partial," and "partiality" are scattered throughout. Locke held that we can rise above our partiality to a degree through the exercise of our natural potential for rationality. But the overriding "distinctive feature of the collective predicament of man" remains his partiality, from the early, conservative *Two Tracts on Government* to his later works on civil government and on religious toleration, according to the editor of the *Tracts*, Philip Abrams.[14]

For Locke "no man is free" from the defect of shortsightedness, since all "see but in part, and know but in part, and therefore it is no wonder we conclude not right from our partial views."[15] Partiality is a ubiquitous condition, one that sets limits on our understanding as well as determines the far from perfect conduct of magistrates. As the passage from *Conduct of the Understanding* continues, it becomes clear that the word "parts," a kind of banner of human frailty and prejudice, is intended to have several meanings, as it ordinarily has in Shakespeare:

> This might instruct the proudest esteemer of his own parts, how useful it is to talk and consult with others, even such as come short of him in capacity, quickness and penetration: for since no man sees all, and we generally have different prospects of the same thing, according to our different, as I may say, positions to it, it is not incongruous to think

nor beneath any man to try, whether another may not have notions of things which have escaped him, and which his reason would make use of if they came into his mind.[16]

Reason for Locke is the faculty by means of which we progress, by difficult paths, from our naturally partial positions to more judicious, comprehensive, total or "impartial" ones, in at least two senses of that word. Locke juxtaposes two senses of the word "part." In the phrase "the proudest esteemer of his own parts" the word has the meaning, as it commonly does in Shakespeare, of "qualities," "capacities," or "talents," but that meaning squares off against its predominant meaning in Locke, who ordinarily employs the word and its derivatives mainly in contexts that imply the limitations our predispositions impose on our understanding. Men are "partial to themselves."[17] What seems missing from the context surrounding the phrase "proudest esteemer of his own parts" is any suggestion that the parts of a nobleman add up to a whole greater than the fragmentary and partial selves of members of the lower classes.[18]

Locke's intention in the phrase "proudest esteemer of his own parts" is to bring down a notch or two the pretensions to superiority of men of parts. For Locke men are "of equal natural parts."[19] Inequality in the development of parts or capacities arises through practice: "most even of those excellences which are looked on as natural endowments will be found, when examined into more narrowly, to be the product of exercise, and to be raised to that pitch only by repeated actions."[20] In the process of deflating "men of parts," Locke also deflates the value of "parts" as well, which becomes a term designating some kind of obstacle, unlike in James's speech where it is employed to help conjure the image of an impartial monarch. In Shakespeare, the word, whether it is used in a theatrical or political sense or used to suggest an individual who is more comprehensive than the norm owing to a multiplicity of "parts" or qualities, generally does not threaten the assumption that parts—whether of an individual, a state, or a theatrical performance— are superintended by a comprehensive whole to nearly the degree that Locke's writings do. But Shakespeare's tragedies challenge the trope of part/whole substitutions that is fundamental to most forms of representation in the Renaissance, both dramatic and political: a challenge that would be widespread in a century in which political and literary forms of representation were to be extensively refashioned and redefined.

What distinguishes Locke's later writings from his earlier, Philip Abrams contends, is the disappearance of the gulf that in the earliest speculations separated the wise, knowing, and presumedly impartial magistrate from the partiality and ignorance of those of little or no education. Partiality becomes more and more an ineluctable circumstance of our condition. Abrams writes in his commentary to the *Tracts*, "unlike the *Tracts* of 1660 his later works recognize [partiality] as the only thing that can be reliably said and empirically demonstrated about human knowledge."[21] He cites 1667 as a watershed year in Locke's thinking on the problem of partiality: "after 1667 the gulf between rational and irrational man is narrowed and bridged by the linked notions of actual ignorance and possible rationality. All are by nature partial but some few manage to approach a modest rationality. And the way in which they do so is open, in theory, to all, even to 'very mean people'—for 'the original makes of their minds is like that of other men.' "[22]

The belief that we are all born to be rational creatures led to Locke's growing interest in and commitment to education as a way of alleviating our equally natural partiality. Still, a belief in the ubiquity of partiality remained the dominant theme of Locke's mature ethical reflections, as his belief in a nonsubjective and impartial knowledge faltered. Abrams writes, "As he became more and more doubtful about the objective availability of moral knowledge, the equal status and partial nature of every man's subjective knowledge destroyed for him the authority of all possible forms of moral discipline. Believing now in a discoverable but perpetually undiscovered order, Locke found himself unable to offer any safe guide through the 'endless maze' of private perceptions: 'I think we may as rationally hope to see with other men's eyes as to know by other men's understandings.' "[23] It is a predictable residue of partiality that makes toleration so necessary, and it is the inevitable partiality of human knowledge that, according to Locke's *Letters Concerning Toleration* (1689–92), causes magistrates to be no more qualified than ordinary citizens to determine what the true religion is or to have access to knowledge of objective moral standards. Such nonpartial knowledge is restricted to the angels and their Superior: "Endowed with more comprehensive faculties," Locke writes, they can, "in the twinkling of an eye, collect together all [merely finite beings'] scattered and almost boundless relations."[24]

Locke's interest in the *Second Treatise on Civil Government* in the separation of powers, in "ballancing the Power of Government, by placing several parts of it in different hands,"[25] bears a close relation to his speculations on partiality. For Locke it is impossible for the judicial responsibility to reside in the absolute monarch in whom are concentrated "all, both Legislative and Executive Power in himself alone."[26] If such responsibility were to reside in the monarch, "there is no judge to be found, no Appeal lies open to any one, who may fairly, and indifferently, and with Authority decide, and from whose decision relief and redress may be expected of any Injury or Inconveniency, that may be suffered from the Prince or by his Order."[27] Locke argues that the absolute monarch cannot serve as a legitimate political authority because the concentration of legislative and executive power in one figure prevents that individual's being a separate, impartial, and indifferent judge. Such an argument rests not a little on suspicion of the rhetorical trope by means of which absolute monarchs of the Renaissance could claim or feign impartiality. By contrast, according to the eminent Elizabethan common lawyer Sir Edward Coke, the function of the "plenary and entire power" concentrated in the king as head of the body politic was "to render justice and right to every member of this body . . . ; otherwise he should not be a head of the whole body."[28] Coke's lines suggest that there is no inconsistency in the king's wielding sole and undivided power, his constituting a *part of* (though the head) the body politic, and his judicial *impartiality*. In rhetorical terms, Coke's absolute sovereign is an ideal synecdoche, a part of the body politic that also embodies or represents the whole; Locke's is a dangerous synecdoche, a (necessarily) partial member of the body politic who may impose his partial understanding and interests upon the whole.[29]

In the Shakespearean theater the spectator has many models of impartiality to emulate. There is the Fool, often a "disinterested truth-teller" as Enid Welsford notes,[30] the "learned judge" Portia, and Friar Lawrence, who, though at some level clearly partial to Romeo, helps him marry Juliet because of something closer to impartiality: his desire to patch up the ancient quarrel between two houses. And then there are Shakespeare's kings, who, like Queen Elizabeth when discussing the issue of monopolies and King James when masking his favoritism toward his fellow Scots, often put on a good theatrical show of impartiality. The Shakespearean monarch frequently needs to mask his partiality because he is presumed to represent the whole of the body politic. Richard II pretends to have no personal stake in the quarrel between Mowbray and Bolingbroke. King Lear only partly, and exceedingly briefly, masks his partiality toward Cordelia in the division of the kingdom, blurting out a confession of what everyone knows—that he is partial to his youngest daughter—in his anger at her recalcitrance. Shakespeare's plays certainly did not and do not presuppose audiences not stacked with countless Bassanios (and Antonios, for that matter), audiences capable of refraining from hissing or spitting at Shylock, instead of showing the judicious restraint of a "wise judge." But his plays do in many ways attempt to promote disinterest to a degree that novels, which above all are concerned with promoting the specific feeling of sympathy,[31] do not. The partiality of a monarch frequently marks the beginning of calamity in Shakespeare. And even when we share a monarch's partiality—Lear's for Cordelia, for instance—that very partiality helps reinstate the ideal and criterion of impartiality, for that is what Cordelia and her advocates represent, as against the rampant self-interest and particularism of the opposing factions. The endings of his tragedies, though not the beginnings, favor figures of sovereign impartiality, a Richmond or Cordelia, though at times such impartiality is dissimulated, like Mark Antony's, which is a poor imitation of Brutus's.

In *Hamlet,* impartiality and disinterestedness receive what is perhaps their most complex Shakespearean treatment. The sovereign figure of disinterest is not a sovereign at all but a subject, the stoical Horatio. Furthermore, what would seem a virtue in a prince appears in the subject a defect. Horatio's impartiality paradoxically makes him seem limited, partial, fragmentary. The two senses of "impartial"—unbiased, and integral or whole—that seem mutually reinforcing in the case of a prince become competitive in the case of a subject. Paradoxically, in order for Horatio to seem less limited or partial in the sense of incomplete, he would have to show more partiality than he does. Though Hamlet repeatedly praises Horatio for his stoic disinterestedness, even he seems to be able to smell a fault in his friend's gift for detachment.

Hamlet praises Horatio as one who is virtually without "business and desire" (1.5.136):

> Since my dear soul was mistress of her choice,
> And could of men distinguish her election,
> Sh'ath seal'd thee for herself; for thou hast been
> As one, in suff'ring all, that suffers nothing,
> A man that Fortune's buffets and rewards
> Hast ta'en with equal thanks;
>
> (3.2.63–68)

Hamlet is partial to Horatio because of his impartiality, even toward "Fortune's buffets and rewards." The words "one," "all," and "nothing" suggest one who remains integral and indivisible through a cultivated indifference toward rises and falls in fortune. The placement of the immoderately unimpassioned Horatio in "my heart's core, ay, in my heart of heart" (3.2.73), the seat of emotion, is paradoxical, and suggests something more than a stoical mastery of emotion installed in emotion's own domain. The overall effect is to suggest trouble at the heart of the dramatic (and monarchical) value of impartiality.

Hamlet's praise of Horatio is informed by a complex of political as well as private motives. First, it may reveal a wish on the part of this highly dissociative character for the "impartiality" of the sovereign, in both senses of that word: the integral nature of one who is presumed to embody or re-present the whole of the body politic, and the sovereign's nonpartial perspective from which he could collect in a single totalizing gaze the partial and fragmentary views of his subjects. Second, Hamlet has been disappointed by a political system that, in contrast to the hereditary monarchy in England, is dependent on the direct expression of partiality but whose electors have not been partial to him. That the historical Denmark as well as the Denmark of this play had an elective monarchy lends an important edge to Hamlet's recurring praise of Horatio's impartiality. Monarchical impartiality presumably couldn't flourish as well under the Danish system as it could in England's hereditary monarchy, since the nobles surviving a monarch's death were called upon to voice a preference for a successor.

Hamlet's use of the word "election" in his warm expression of admiration to Horatio almost amounts to a paradox: he says in effect that he has "elected" Horatio to membership in his own party, the party of the partyless or impartial. But unlike his counterpart Brutus in *Julius Caesar,* Horatio is no figure of essential soundness or reintegration: he is merely another among several shards in the play, including Laertes and Fortinbras. His opening line, though probably intended to suggest a wholeness beyond a supervening fragmentary condition, may also be taken to forecast that the cultivation of a godlike "impartiality" will not work this time, in this place, to produce a perspective that other characters and onlookers alike can regard as integral:

> Barnardo.   Say, what, is Horatio there?
> Horatio.   A piece of him. (1.1.21–22)

By the end of the eighteenth century, when monarchical power was being challenged if not toppled on a massive scale, not only the possibility of an impartial sovereign but the very idea of such impartiality seemed quaint. In one of the most influential English political treatises of the period, *An Enquiry Concerning the Principles of Political Justice* (1793), William Godwin systematically raises objections to all forms of monarchical government, including a limited monarchy. The latter

> might be executed with great facility and applause, if a king were, what such a constitution endeavors to render him, a mere puppet regulated by pullies and wires. But it is among the most egregious and palpable

of all political mistakes, to imagine that we can reduce a human being to this neutrality and torpor. . . . Is any promotion vacant, and do we expect that he will never think of bestowing it on a favourite, or of proving, by an occasional election of his own, that he really exists? This promotion may happen to be of the utmost importance to the public welfare; or, if not—every promotion unmeritedly given, is pernicious to national virtue, and an upright minister will refuse to assent to it.[32]

The very nature of a limited monarchy, according to Godwin, is to perform the impossible task of making the king entirely neutral and impartial, an idea he describes using the unflattering image of a puppet whose every action is regulated by pullies and wires. It is clear that Godwin, like Locke, regards impartiality as beyond the pale of human possibility. But even more radically than Locke, Godwin demotes the ideal of the impartial sovereign, now captured in an image of absolute torpor and immobility, a lifeless marionette.

Taking Part

One possible response open to a Shakespearean character such as Horatio or Hamlet who is particularly sensitive to the threat of social or personal dis-integration is to resist theatricality, to refuse to play a part. In comedy such a tack seems sheer perversity: either a lack of comic faith that the various "parts" of the play will eventually yield or (re)constitute a dramatic and social whole or else an unnatural lust on the part of a character for the integrated perspective beyond perspective of the playwright. Such is Jaques's refusal to play any part except that of fool—the most synecdochic of parts, "the part of all the world," according to Marston's Balurdo in my epigraph. In the later tragedies, refusals to play a part like those of Horatio or Coriolanus seem a bit wiser, and justified sometimes as a last line of defense against the psychosocial and political disintegration that surrounds the hero. Horatio's antitheatricalism, his refusal to play a part, is part and parcel of his refusal to take part in courtly intrigues. Even Coriolanus's refusal to play a part in either sense of the phrase—to don the gown of humility, a gesture that would implicate him in pretense and playacting, or to show any interest in party politics and their faction, squabbling, pleading, and entreating—may seem something more than a haughty patrician's posturing, or the ultimate pretense to be beyond pretense, above both part and party. It might very well be a desperate defense against the malfunctioning of synecdoche in the play, including the degeneration of the very figure of integration, that of the body politic, by means of which the patricians have manipulated and tamed the wills of the plebeians for so long. The failure of that figure in *Coriolanus* necessitates other measures to help maintain integrity, whether personal integrity or the integrity and soundness of the body politic. One such measure is Coriolanus's effort to conjure the simulacrum of wholeness or impartiality—if I may stretch that term a bit—by refusing to play a political or theatrical part.

Another possible response to dis-integration for a tragic character is the comic or antic one: to try to play *every* part. It is a strategy that puts Hamlet in the same company as Hal, Rosalind, and many of Shakespeare's fools. But beginning with *Hamlet,* whichever path one follows, the way of Hamlet or the way of Horatio, playing every part or playing none, seems to bespeak a falling confidence in the various kinds of social, psychological, and aesthetic forms of integration promised by synecdoche. The middle and later tragedies of Shakespeare become skeptical in intriguing ways of this trope that promises to cure madness, cancel partisanship and faction, and ensure that all or most forms of theatricality, all elections to play parts, will serve larger theatrical and political purposes. The earlier tragedies, by contrast, seem far more confident of the legitimacy of what is in many ways their most fundamental organizing trope.

The centrality of the part/whole relationship in *Titus Andronicus* is indicated by its obsession with the human body and its mutilation.[33] Tamora's son Alarbus is hewn and offered as a sacrifice to the ghosts of the Roman soldiers killed in battle, Lavinia loses tongue and hands, her father is cheated of one of his hands, and Chiron and Demetrius lose their heads in more ways than one. These acts of disfigurement— wholes giving way to dissociated parts—are checked by the opposite synecdochic substitution: following their mutilation, characters are re-membered (or re-collected) by the parts they have lost, toward which we form something like a fetishistic and synecdochic attachment.[34]

Bodily disfigurements are in turn related to the play's many instances of moral disfigurement, the obverse of Marcus Andronicus's life of "uprightness and integrity" (1.1.51). Both these forms of personal disfigurement, bodily and moral, in turn reflect a larger process of political disintegration, similarly imagined as a sundering of the body. The play begins with a "headless Rome" seeking a "head" (1.1.189) and political fractiousness, three rival candidates seeking to fill the post of emperor: "Princes, that strive by factions and by friends" (1.1.18). The moderate Marcus says to the citizens of Rome following the successive slayings of Tamora by Titus, Titus by Saturninus, and Saturninus by Lucius, "O, let me teach you how to knit again / This scattered corn into one mutual sheaf, / These broken limbs again into one body" (5.3.69–71).

That the political body of the state and human bodies participate in a common process of mutilation bodes well for the eventual reintegration of the "broken limbs" of the state "into one body." Even at their most dissociated, natural and political bodies never really become dissociated from one another, since their fates remain so inextricably linked and mutually reflective.

The silent sway of synecdoche, which may even account for (rather than being challenged by) the anatomical mutilations that produce some gruesome theatrical results, is evidenced by Titus's raging over Lavinia's grief after parting with his hand; he does not yet know that by literally lending a hand he has not purchased the heads of his sons:

> I am the sea. Hark how her sighs doth blow;
> She is the weeping welkin, I the earth.
> Then must my sea be moved with her sighs,
> Then must my earth with her continual tears
> Become a deluge, overflow'd and drown'd. . . .
>   (3.1.226–30)

Titus's anatomy of himself as earth and sea, grounded in the Renaissance analogy of the world as body, is immediately followed by the entrance of a messenger bearing the heads of his sons and his own hand. The timing of the messenger's entrance does not so much discredit the official Elizabethan synecdoches called up in Titus's speech. For the very strength of those synecdoches are responsible for the peculiar fascination attached to losing a part of the body in this play, and indeed throughout Renaissance drama. Those mutilated parts, rather than challenging or qualifying the dominance of the trope of synecdoche over Titus's Rome, actually testify to its sovereignty: though the leadership of Rome changes twice in the course of the play, synecdoche silently continues its rule. It is not until the middle and later tragedies that its sovereignty will begin to be challenged.

In another early tragedy, *Richard III,* threats to the welfare of the state are similarly conceived as the splitting apart of a whole into pieces or fragments, the inevitable result of partiality and faction. Just as the Renaissance didn't ordinarily conceive character as a loosely organized complex, neither did it conceive of political entities that are loosely organized wholes. Division is almost always imagined as absolute, like the severing of a limb, rather than conceived along a spectrum of gradually increasing or decreasing organization. Within such a set of assumptions, faction becomes the preeminent political evil. Chastising Elizabeth, Dorset, and Buckingham, King Edward charges,

"You have been factious, one against the other" (2.1.20). Political health is ordinarily signaled in Shakespeare by images of factious parties reuniting to form an indivisible whole, like the unification of the White Rose with the Red at the end of *Richard III*.[35] A more fragile image of unification appears earlier in the play: following news of Edward IV's death and before the accession of his son, Buckingham addresses the princes and peers of the realm, "The broken rancour of your high-swoll'n hates, / But lately splintered, knit, and join'd together / Must gently be preserv'd, cherish'd, and kept" (2.2.117–19). Imagining state or country as body, as in Buckingham's "The noble isle doth want her proper limbs" (3.7.124), suggests that no rebellion by a party or faction is ever anything but provisional.

Though the related word "party" usually suggests threats to unity and integration in *Richard III* as throughout Shakespeare, "part" may be used to suggest either integration or its opposite. As in Hastings's lines, "And in the Duke's behalf I'll give my voice, / Which I presume he'll take in gentle part" (3.4.19–20), it may serve as a reminder that even the most self-seeking egotist belongs to and bears responsibility toward a whole, both a political entity and a play in which s/he takes part. In other words "part" in Shakespeare generally implies a whole that embraces, contains, and will eventually overturn the mutiny of a single part or party. On the other hand, the word "part" not infrequently bears a subversive potential. Buckingham addresses Richard, "Had you not come upon your cue, my lord, / William Lord Hastings had pronounc'd your part— / I mean your voice for crowning of the King" (3.4.26–28). Buckingham retracts the word "part" and sheathes it as if it were a dangerous weapon. The implication of the speech is that "part" is now inappropriate to designate Richard, no longer a part and party but a re-presentation of the whole realm (though his deformity would suggest to audiences steeped in synecdochic forms of thought a maladjustment of parts and whole that in itself would indicate what kind of sovereign he will prove to be, how distorted a re-presentation of the political body). Buckingham's retraction of the politically loaded word attests to the subversive potential of "pronouncing one's part"—speaking for one's part, belonging to a party, taking part, even playing a part. The very word "part" therefore needs to be resuscitated at the end of *Richard III*, which celebrates an end to the long period of faction and party politics that was the War of the Roses. Richmond's use of "part" in his oration to his soldiers retrieves it from association with Richard and makes it serve the cause of reunification rather than faction: "But if I thrive, the gain of my attempt / The least of you shall share his part thereof" (5.3.268–69).

Whether their immediate effect is subversive or conservative, the uses of words like "part" and "party" to articulate political relationships in the early plays of Shakespeare attest to the power regularly exercised by various forms of that trope of integration, synecdoche. That power, though continually asserted in early plays like *Titus Andronicus* and *Richard III*, is abdicated by the later tragedies.

Dashing Figures

The powerful sway that synecdoche (in its part/whole, whole/part forms) exercised over the Renaissance theatre, akin to its sway in the political sphere, is evidenced by the frequency with which the death of an individual and the destruction of a political body are imagined as acts of dismemberment. One might recall the multiple mutilations and decapitations, for instance, in early plays like *Henry VI, Part II* or *Titus Andronicus;* Henry V's vow to bend France "to our awe, / Or break it all to pieces" (1.2.225–26); the soldier Williams's speech to his monarch in disguise on the eve of the battle of Agincourt, in which he imagines that if the King's cause is not just, "all those legs and arms and heads chopped off in a battle, shall join together at the latter day and cry all 'We died at such a place,' some swearing, some crying for a surgeon, some upon their wives left poor behind them, some upon the debts they owe, some upon their children rawly left" (*Henry V,* 4.1.135–41); or Hotspur's response to news that his father Northumberland has taken ill on the eve of battle, "A perilous gash, a very limb lopp'd off" (*1 Henry IV,* 4.1.43).

Imagining destruction as the shattering of a whole into pieces is especially characteristic of the Roman plays, where moral integrity appears to be a species of integrality involving the coordination of complementary parts. The concern with moral integrity is in turn reflected by a concern with physical integrity and by the retribution of dismemberment. A popular chorus of "Tear him to pieces!" erupts against Coriolanus in the final scene of that play (5.6.120). Responding to Cassius's refusal to supply him with gold to pay his soldiers, and insisting in the same speech on his own integrity, Brutus inveighs, "When Marcus Brutus grows so covetous, / To lock such rascal counters from his friends, / Be ready, gods, with all your thunderbolts, / Dash him to pieces!" (4.3.79–82). "Tear him to pieces!" cries an anonymous plebeian of Cinna the poet (3.3.28). That the demand for Cinna's destruction comes from an unnamed character is significant. If lacking a name is a form of theatrical disenfranchisement, then what this cry represents is a form of "nominal" envy by the unnamed of the named character. But in Cinna's case, the ordinarily synecdochic and integrative proper name[36] helps rather than hinders his physical dis-integration. The demand for his dismemberment is based solely on the accident of the poet's bearing the name of one of the conspirators. Cinna's "integrity" is therefore threatened in two ways: by the act of physical mutilation and by the unmooring of the proper name from its synecdochic relation to this particular man.

The theme of mutilation reveals much about the way character is organized in Shakespeare. Not only are bodies natural and bodies politic conceived as careful coordinations of parts and wholes (making the loss of a part, limb, or member an event of considerable danger), but characters too seem to be conceived largely in terms of part/whole relationships ideally leading toward a totality. In one of his tedious verses, Orlando describes Rosalind ("of many parts") as a composition of the best of Helen, Cleopatra, Atalanta, and Lucretia (*As You Like It,* 3.2.146). And in *Cymbeline,* Cloten describes Imogen, whom he both loves and hates, as of "all courtly parts . . . compounded" (3.5.72–74).[37] The sense of the noble character as composite, as incorporating the best "parts" of a larger class (women, Roman men, humankind) or as composed of literary and mythological archetypes, echoes the political notion of the sovereign as re-presenting in the sense of embodying, symbolizing, or making present an entire political body.

Paul Goodman has argued that novels, by contrast with plays, show characters in rather loose states of organization who crystallize into more fixed and stable patterns in the course of the novel—unless it is a novel like Sterne's *A Sentimental Journey,* "founded on the principle of avoiding fixing the character or generating a single action."[38] "A dramatic character is a relatively fixed complex"; the "sentimental" character common to novels, by contrast, is "a relatively loose complex, and a sentiment is the rearranging of the loose structure by adding new elements. . . . In the kind of novel we have been discussing the rearrangements are progressively more fixed; they are stages toward commitment, or rejection, a final rearrangement permanently including or excluding certain parts."[39] Novelistic rearrangement of character may also proceed in the other direction, "from the more fixed to the more loose and sentimental."[40] In either case, unlike the sudden change of a dramatic character, in which "one abiding structure gives way to another related one," the novelistic "fixing of character" takes place as "a sequence in relatively freely varying responses."[41] The process by which a novelistic character's parts eventually yield a whole is an arduous one, one that does not allow for clarifications of the whole by an individual part or parts along the way.

The relation of dramatic plot to character also seems more synec-dochic than that of their novelistic counterparts. In many novelistic plots, Goodman writes, "the actions of the persons do not essentially engage them; that is, formally, the persons have a scope and career greater than these particular actions; the persons respond to the events rather than being completely in them."[42] It is not that the novelistic occasion has "a comically accidental or again a merely random relation to him, for it belongs to a sequence that, as a whole, will define him."[43] It tends to be the case in novels that no occasion within the whole sequence has a synecdochic or summarizing relation to character, though it may have a looser representative function of not fully summing up but typifying the character. The novelistic character can be fully defined only by the entire sequence of episodes, which in turn maps more or less onto the whole of the character's life. If the powerfully synecdochic relation of plot to character on which Renaissance dramatists depended obtained in novels, their plots would seem a needless journeying.

In other words, novelistic characters, unlike their dramatic coun-terparts, seem to resist description by means of synecdoche. Their authors refrain from coordinating parts that may too easily, or too early on in the narrative, crystallize into stable patterns. In general, novels show characters undergoing transformations that are also acts of progressive integration; Renaissance plays show characters *presumed to be already integral* constantly threatened with disintegration or else undergoing sudden reorganization into different though equally fixed patterns. Corresponding statements hold true, I believe, for political representation in the Renaissance and its aftermath. In an essay "Of the Parties of Great Britain" (1741), David Hume observed, "Were the BRITISH government proposed as a subject of speculation, one would immediately perceive in it a source of division and party, which it would be almost impossible for it, under any administration, to avoid. . . . However the nation may fluctuate between them, the parties themselves will always subsist, so long as we are governed by a limited monarchy."[44] If a party is a type of obstructed synecdoche—a part that, though it may strain to do so, cannot adequately represent the whole without a significant, unrepresented remainder—then it is no wonder that the rise of party politics in England coincides with the rise of the novel, the genre of the obstructed synecdoche.

In the Renaissance understanding of political representation, ac-cording to Raymond Williams, an assumed "whole state or condition" was represented by a particular institution or monarch; "the 'represen-tative' quality came from the whole state outwards, rather than from the scattered and diverse opinions brought together and, in a more modern sense, 'represented.' "[45] In the aftermath of the Renaissance, representation of character as well as political representation will be increasingly a matter of scattered and dislocated parts brought together and "represented" to form a composite that is loose by the standards of absolute monarchy. The shift away from the monarch's mystical representation of a presumed whole to an interest in piecemeal or part-by-part representation is perhaps nowhere more apparent than in a manifesto drawn up by Leveller army officers in October 1647, the first article of which reads, "That the People of England being at this day very unequally distributed by Counties, Cities, & Burroughs, for the election of their Deputies in Parliament, ought to be more [fairly] proportioned, according to the number of the Inhabitants: the circumstances whereof, for number, place, and manner, are to be set down before the end of this present Parliament."

The Renaissance imagination, rigorously synecdochic as it was, didn't seem to countenance the novelistic possibility of character as a loosely organized complex (nor of political entities as loose complexes). The alternatives regularly conceived to the sound, integrated character in Shakespeare are the fragmentary one; the temporarily unbalanced character, or humor (the usurping Duke Frederick in *As You Like It* or Hamlet, for instance); the madman or madwoman, also imagined as fractured or dashed to pieces, echoing the way that physical destruction is most often conceived; and the character who is thoroughly disorganized because s/he is every character and no character, as in Portia's description of her protean suitor Monsieur le Bon. None of these alternatives approaches by a single step the conception common to many novels of characters as a loosely constituted complex.

Hamlet Before His Father's Death

Complications in the various kinds of synecdoche operate at nearly every level of *Hamlet*. Though it is no less obsessed with imagery of body parts than is *Titus,* unlike the earlier play, it spares us the actual mutilations. In *Hamlet* bodies are symbolically mutilated through the metonymies and synecdoches in which limbs wag, wiggle, jostle, wave, step, kick, and bend their way through various speakers' rhetoric.[46] But such symbolic dismemberment is not compensated for by a political "incorporation" such as the one conjured by Marcus Andronicus. The faith of the earlier play that the reassembly of "these broken limbs again into one body" (5.3.71) will be accomplished is ratified by Emillius's comment, "well I know / The common voice do cry it shall be so" (5.3.138–39). No such general political voice is heard at the end of *Hamlet,* certainly not that of Fortinbras, who has highly particular motives for seeking the Danish crown.

In this respect *Hamlet* resembles many of Shakespeare's Jacobean tragedies in which social and political reintegration fails to take place. At best, the endings of the later tragedies provide instances of the consolidation of power, a poor substitute for reintegration.[47] Given King James's interest in political integration, his overriding interest in his Project for the Union of the Kingdoms to form Great Britain, it is especially telling that the later tragedies refuse to enact such scenes.[48] Earlier figures such as Lucius in *Titus Andronicus,* Prince Escalus in *Romeo and Juliet,* Bolingbroke in *Richard II,* Richmond in *Richard III,* and even the dead Brutus in *Julius Caesar* all stem the tide of, and usually reverse as well, psychosocial disintegration, if only in the final minutes. In Shakespeare's Jacobean tragedies, acts of reintegration are far more tentative. In *King Lear* the initial division of the kingdom is not exactly confidently revoked by the search for someone to hold sway in the play's final exchanges. In *Othello,* power in Cyprus is transferred to one dubious in strength and experience. *Antony and Cleopatra* inverts the pattern of *King Lear,* a triumvirate's rule of three giving way to rule by one. But what the ending of *Antony and Cleopatra* enacts is not so much the reintegration of empire as the consolidation of power. The same may be said of the ending of *Macbeth,* where Malcolm seems less concerned with reintegrating the kingdom than with consolidating his personal power.[49]

Closely related to the deficiency in rhetoric of reintegration at the end of *Hamlet* is critics' tendency to regard the play's characters as puzzles with pieces missing. This is as much true for Ophelia as it is for Hamlet. One critic notes, "Her character is marked by an incompleteness which tempts critics to add some dimension, ranging from inexperienced demureness to the physical condition of pregnancy and the depravity of one who 'was not a chaste young woman.' "[50] Hamlet's incompleteness is apparent in what many critics perceive as the maddening tendency in nineteenth-century and even some twentieth-century commentary to show an interest in Hamlet as he was before his father's death. Often Shakespeareans chalk up that supposed error to the misplaced emphasis of romantic criticism on character. It may also be blamed on a novelistic age's showing far more interest than did the Renaissance in the *genealogy* of character.[51] In the particular case of Hamlet, however, novelistic archaeologies of Hamlet's prehistory seem motivated by the widespread malfunctioning of synecdoche in the play, a malfunctioning that will also make *Hamlet* (no less than Hamlet) notoriously resistant to totalizing explanations.

Goethe, speaking through his character Wilhelm Meister, may have inaugurated the interest in Hamlet's prehistory. Wilhelm Meister speaks of the need to investigate "every trace of Hamlet's character, as it had shown itself before his father's death" in order to make sense of the play as a whole.[52] A. C. Bradley especially has been taken to task for his tendency to make such novelizing excursions. Bradley of course was writing at the end of a century whose sensibility was overwhelmingly novelistic, not dramatistic. Bradley proposed, "Let us first ask ourselves what we can gather from the play, immediately or by inference, concerning Hamlet as he was just before his father's death."[53] His lectures on the play are peppered with references to "the Hamlet of earlier days."[54] To reconstruct from the slender evidence we possess of any dramatic character the full-blooded person who develops in time is apparently the procedure that all dramatic interpretation must follow, according to Bradley. More recently and cautiously, J. E. Hankins has written,

> While the dramatist is necessarily limited to a few scenes from the lives of his characters, to portray them consistently he must think through their actions before the play opens and also during the intervals between their appearances on the stage. Indeed, some attention to these periods *in absentia* is absolutely necessary to an understanding of the scenes actually shown.[55]

The New Critical orientation of much twentieth-century criticism has made such critical time-travel seem entirely misguided to a majority of critics. But rather than dismissing such approaches as completely off the scent of Shakespearean characterization, or debating whether such excursions may be productive or should be allowable, it would be more valuable to speculate whether the rhetoric of the play's construction itself motivates such excursions. The play enacts the obstruction of various synecdoches at the level of character as well as of the state. The failure of the body politic to be properly knit together in the play may reflect and be reflected by the malfunctioning of synecdoche in the articulation of both Hamlet and Ophelia. Such malfunctioning, always with enormous political interest and ramifications, may be the most reliable thing that can be said about this play whose various strands are so maddeningly difficult for the critic to weave together or synthesize.

Ophelia's Rhetoric

Even though her fate is to become one of the most dissociative characters in the play, it is Ophelia who demonstrates the greatest fidelity to the trope of integration and the greatest interest in fashioning and sustaining synecdochic relationships and orders. One particular outcome of this reading of Shakespearean tragedy based on the trope of synecdoche is the partial resuscitation of Ophelia, who has suffered oblivion once, in being bullied into silence by her brother and father; twice, by having part of her past erased by Hamlet (whose own significant past seems under erasure to the critics cited above); a third time, by drowning; and a fourth, by the "silent treatment" she often receives at the hands of male critics and painters.

Male critics have tended to dismiss Ophelia. One eminent Shake-spearean ably represents what was until recently the majority opinion of twentieth-century critics toward her: "Ophelia is cast for the part of Juliet, but in the test is revealed only as a timid daughter tamely obeying a foolish father."[56] According to Elaine Showalter, "Though she is neglected in criticism, Ophelia is probably the most frequently illustrated and cited of Shakespeare's heroines."[57] That she has been so popular a subject of painters and illustrators (particularly in the Victorian period) seems perfectly consistent with her treatment within the play, for the painter by the nature of the craft necessarily repeats other characters' gestures toward silencing her.

Though "Ophelia" and "rhetoric" are not two words that ordinarily go together in criticism of the play, Ophelia is in an important sense well qualified to serve as Elsinore's court rhetorician. Given the extent of psychological, social, and political disintegration in the play, Ophelia's interest in articulating synecdochic relationships should be of consid-erably more interest than the criticism has allowed. Keeping in mind her wholehearted commitment to synecdoche will help to account for some of the speeches that for many critics mark her as a creature of considerable simplicity, even simplemindedness.

Following a ruthless assault by Hamlet's rhetoric designed to shatter her composure, Ophelia says in soliloquy, "O, what a noble mind is here o'erthrown! / The courtier's, soldier's, scholar's, eye, tongue, sword" (3.1.152–53), revealing all the while a strength that shuns self-pity. Synecdoche operates on at least two levels in this speech. The various fragments of Hamlet's personality—courtier, soldier, scholar— are represented by means of synecdoches (eye, tongue) and a metonymy (sword). Second, Hamlet represents a wholeness that gathers and unites the attributes of a host of comparatively partial characters: Horatio the scholar, Osric[58] and Laertes the courtiers, and Fortinbras (and perhaps Old Hamlet) the soldier. That unity is partly reconstituted through the difference between the general and collecting phrase "noble mind" and the careful dissection or anatomy of that noble unity in the line that follows. The metonymy and synecdoches in Ophelia's lines both collect and disperse, for although they describe the disintegration of Hamlet's personality and prefigure the end of the play when Hamlet will be survived only by fragments of himself (Horatio, Fortinbras, Osric), they may also be seen as a benevolent attempt to gather the shattered pieces of her lover: if not to reassemble them, then to hold them lovingly in the cupped hands of her soliloquy.

Ophelia's questions to *Hamlet* during the staging of *Gonzago* suggest a synecdochic interest in grasping the meaning of the play as a whole. Dumb show, prologue, and "chorus," three means of conveying the general meaning of a dramatic action, all evoke questions or comments from her. "Belike this show imports the argument of the play," she remarks after the Dumb Show miming the murder of the King and the courtship of his widow by the poisoner (3.2.136). When Hamlet identifies the role of the actor playing the King's nephew upon his first entrance, Ophelia notes, "You are as good as a chorus, my lord" (3.2.240). The chorus traditionally has a synecdochic function, placing particular events in a more general and unifying framework (like the "Chorus" that opens *Romeo and Juliet*). And when Ophelia asks Hamlet of the actor delivering the Prologue, "Will a tell us what this show meant?" (3.2.139), rather than betraying a fear that her intellect will lose the thread of the narrative midway through the play without her lover's assistance, she is displaying her characteristic (and especially in Elsinore, necessary) interest in part/whole relationships.

Her attraction to synecdoche persists even after the onset of her madness. Distributing emblematic flowers to Laertes, Gertrude, Claudius, and herself that serve to characterize or typify their recipients, Ophelia bestows fragrant synecdoches, signs of particular attributes that summarize and may stand for the whole person. The recipients of these flowers are in several instances disputable. But there seems to be little disagreement among critics that each is the sign of a particular character, rather than suggesting the arbitrary and meaningless raving of a disordered mind.[59] That the identity of each flower's recipient has been and remains such a point of contention seems part of the point of the speech. So many synecdoches, including these floral ones, no longer function in a reliable way in this tragedy:

There's rosemary, that's for remembrance—pray you, love, remember.
And there is pansies, that's for thoughts. . . . There's fennel for you, and
columbines. There's rue for you. And here's some for me. We may call
it herb of grace a Sundays. You must wear your rue with a difference.
There's a daisy. I would give you some violets, but they withered all when
my father died. They say a made a good end. (4.5.173–75, 178–83)

Ophelia begins her liberal dispensing of these emblematic flowers
with one that signifies a highly synecdochic mental faculty, memory.
In fact, most of the flowers Ophelia mentions are more or less directly
connected to memory, which because of its highly selective nature, customarily relies on part-whole substitutions. We ordinarily "re-member"
a person, place, event, or thing by a selection of attributes or details that
may stand for the whole. What Ophelia's speech enacts is not so much
important instances of re-membering as forgetting, or the suppression
of differences of various kinds, including the difference between brothers, fathers, and lovers, and the difference between the two contexts
evoked by the herb rosemary, funerals and love-thoughts. Here as well
as in her mad songs of lamentation earlier in the scene, the distinctions
between brothers and others on the one hand, and between brothers
and fathers on the other (the distinction on which so much of the play's
political intrigue and interest rest)—the differences, in other words,
between Laertes, Hamlet, and Polonius—are suppressed. Laertes, as
the recipient of a sign frequently exchanged between lovers, is confused
with her former lover. In the songs she confuses a lover's and a father's
loss, as she does, Jenkins argues, in her gift of the rue, daisies, and violets.[60] In Ophelia's madness there occurs an explosion of resemblances
that overwhelm unity and order. This explosion takes place within the
very trope, synecdoche, that in Renaissance thought generally serves to
integrate resemblances into larger unifying structures.[61]

That Ophelia maintains an interest in part/whole relationships
even after suffering a shattering of her own mind and personality
is particularly affecting if not effective and signals her wholehearted
partiality to synecdoche and to the unities it promises. No one, however,
is capable of putting Ophelia back together again. No synecdoche can
succeed in reassembling the parts of her disarticulated self. It is a favor
she herself tried to bestow, ineffectually, on her lover earlier in the play,
in her reference to him as "The courtier's, soldier's, scholar's, eye, tongue,
sword" (3.1.153).

It may be that Gertrude is trying to bestow a similar favor on her
in her lengthy account of Ophelia's drowning, so notoriously decorated
with references to flowers:

> There is a willow grows askant the brook
> And shows his hoary leaves in the glassy stream.
> Therewith fantastic garlands did she make
> Of crow-flowers, nettles, daisies, and long purples,
> That liberal shepherds give a grosser name,
> But our cold maids do dead men's fingers call them.
>
> (4.7.165–70)

The succession of three names (the second merely alluded to) for a single flower has frequently been seen as a distracting elaboration in the midst of Gertrude's report. But those long purples, so susceptible as they are to metaphorical elaboration, are far from distracting and irrelevant to Ophelia's death. They occasion the same profusion of resemblances within a flower, a synecdoche, that occurred in Ophelia's flower scene. The multiplication of resemblance here is entirely appropriate to the description of the death of a mad person, since as Foucault has shown, madness, especially toward the end of the Renaissance and after—his prime example is Don Quixote—is understood as the uncontrolled proliferation of resemblances.[62]

The profusion of resemblances in the line about cold maids and dead men's fingers is prepared for by the innuendo of the "grosser name" bestowed by "liberal shepherds": presumably the part that is most often *mistaken* for the whole, a form of synecdoche that is decidedly reductive (or usurping, like Claudius) rather than integrative. Within the chaste maids' name for the flower, "dead men's fingers," there blossoms a second metaphor, since "dead men's finger's," especially when it occurs within clutching proximity of "cold maids," cannot but have a phallic thrust to it. Those dead men's fingers, by virtue of their coldness (a feature they share with the cold maids), are warmed and revived by our imaginations, which make them figures of a threatening sexuality. The chain of resemblances unleashed by these lines is long and complex, extending roughly from chastity, coldness, death, orgasm (for there lies beneath this description an echo of the favorite Elizabethan metaphor of orgasm as "dying"), and sexuality. Besides being a combined synecdoche and metonymy for death—they are a synecdoche for the corpses that metonymically, through a reversal of cause and effect, represent death— those dead men's fingers are also a metaphor for the instrument by means of which the owners of those maidenheads will be dispossessed. The general effect of Gertrude's lines is to suggest an untended garden of unwanted metaphors adjacent to, or beneath, Ophelia's flowers. The fecund and uncontrolled proliferation of resemblance upon resemblance within these flowers, the "dead men's fingers," also spells the decay of

67

the trope of synecdoche associated with Ophelia, which in many ways dis-integrates with her.

Among other things, Gertrude's lines suggest a resemblance between enforced loss of chastity (one form of "death") and orgasm. The vehicle of one form of death is yet another kind of death, suggesting the conversion of a causal and narrative sequence into something like a mad and deathly repetition of the same.[63] Thus, the several narratives suggested by the flower with the multiple and suggestive names—chastity giving way to its enforced loss or chastity eluding the grasp of those chilling fingers, for instance—translate into one form of repetition or another: one form of coldness yielding to another form of coldness or one form of death (loss of chastity, and perhaps madness as well) succeeding another (orgasm). As in *Macbeth,* there is in Gertrude's description a powerful though unstated association between madness and repetition, madness and the collapse of successive orders. The flowers resembling dead men's fingers mock in the manner of Yorick's grinning skull. One of the things they mock, in addition to the mind's pride in establishing or discovering sequential orders, is the integrative function associated with flowers in Ophelia's mad scene.

That Ophelia, who is partial to the trope of integration, becomes herself the most dissociated of selves in the play may be a sign of a dis-integration deep within the trope throughout the play: so that no character and no critic is able to summarize its meaning even as effectively as do, say, Friar Lawrence or Prince Escalus at the end of *Romeo and Juliet;* so that the play seems to be constructed in such a way as to suggest that, despite its extraordinary length, it remains partial.

A Trope Deserving Its Turn

Metaphor and metonymy have for some time now really cut a figure in contemporary criticism. Synecdoche, however, is a trope that deserves its turn. Estimates of the importance of synecdoche relative to other tropes range widely, with the following remarks from Geoffrey Leech's *A Linguistic Guide to English Poetry* representing the low end of the spectrum: the "rule which applies the term for the part to the whole . . . is of little literary interest, but is found in proverbs."[64] Representing the high end, Kenneth Burke was the first modern critic to make large philosophical claims for synecdoche, in pieces like his remarkable "Four Master Tropes," which only a prolific mind like Burke's could afford to consign to "Appendix D" of *A Grammar of Motives* (1945), and in the essay "The Philosophy of Literary Form" (1941). In the latter essay he muses, "The more I examine both the structure of poetry and the structure of human relations outside of poetry, the more I become convinced that [synecdoche] is the 'basic' figure of speech, and that it occurs in many modes besides that of the formal trope. I feel it to be no mere accident of language that we use the same word for sensory, artistic, and political representation. A tree, for instance, is an infinity of events—and among these our senses abstract certain recordings which 'represent' the tree."[65] Synecdoche for Burke is the fundamental trope of all forms of representation, including so-called perception or "sensory representation." And in subsequent pages from the same essay Burke identifies fetishes, scapegoats, proper names ("as fetishistic representative of the named"), and causation all as species of synecdoche.[66] In many ways this chapter has been nothing more than a postscript to Burke's suggestive pages on synecdoche, though I hope the relations between the various parts of my chapter and the whole are more transparent than they ordinarily are in Burke. I have tried also to be more historical and genre-specific than Burke. My purpose has been to locate various dependencies of Renaissance dramatic form on synecdoche and to show how those dependencies are not only asserted but also interrogated and challenged by Shakespeare's middle and later tragedies.

Shakespeare's notorious disregard for the classical unities of space, action, and time, alluded to in the Choruses to *Henry V,* constitute an area of Shakespeare's dramatic practice in which it is particularly difficult to disentangle the reliance on synecdoche from challenges to it. No less duplicitous than Henry, who masquerades as "the mirror of all Christian kings" (2 Chorus. 6), the Chorus cloaks himself in a false humility, constantly pointing our attention to the inadequacy of the Renaissance theaters' resources and methods of staging. Pleading with those who have read Henry's story "to admit th'excuse / Of time, of numbers and due course of things / Which cannot in their huge and proper life / Be here presented" (5.0.3–6), he pretends to dismay that they "shall much disgrace, / With four or five most vile and ragged foils / Right ill-disposed in brawl ridiculous, / The name of Agincourt" (4.0.49–52). Just as Henry's frequent references to his temperateness and Christian humility should not distract us from recognizing his fierce will-to-power, so should the Chorus's repeated references to the shortcomings of "this wooden O" (1.0.13) not cause us to forget that these apparent inadequacies are also forms of power. Synecdoches of nearly the same representative potency as the Renaissance sovereign empower those wooden "O"s to "hold / The vasty fields of France" (1.0.11–12). "Oh for pity!" (4.0.49), and "O, pardon" (1.0.15): these requests for pity and pardon make punning reference to the representational inadequacies of that "wooden O," site and scene of oh, so much moaning in affairs of love and war. The Chorus's suggestion that by its very form the stage is sighing about its own representational powerlessness is as duplicitous as any speech of Iago or Richard III.

What has struck classically minded critics as Shakespeare's wild expansiveness in the dimensions of space and time and his inattentiveness to the dramatic need for a single unified action might be understood more profitably as a consequence of synecdoche's dominance in every aspect of his stagecraft. His violations of the unities may express not so much a brave or reckless disregard for constricting laws of theatrical practice as a law-abiding allegiance to the fundamental trope of Renaissance political order. A playwright working under the aegis of synecdoche can afford to take liberties with more explicit forms of unity, since temporal and spatial gaps can be made irrelevant by the ubiquity of synecdochic forms of organization. Indeed, it would be plausible to argue that the greater the apparent liberties with space, time, and action, the greater the confidence in and reliance on the trope of synecdoche.

Conversely, a later age's resuscitation of the classical unities, while costumed in rhetoric applauding its own civility relative to the barbarous Elizabethans, may result less from a positive attraction to purer theatrical forms than from an untraversable distance between the late seventeenth and eighteenth centuries and the synecdochic discourses and representational economies of the Elizabethans: economies that are already being dismantled in the most celebrated of Renaissance texts, the tragedies of Shakespeare.[67]

Part II

Generalizing

3

Generally Speaking:
The Rhetoric of Shakespearean
Tragedy and Modern Criticism

> For as a Parliament is the honourablest and highest judgement in
> the land (as being the Kings head Court) if it be well used, which
> is by making good Lawes in it; so is it the in-justest Judgement-seat
> that may be, being abused to mens particulars: irrevocable decreits
> against particular parties, being given therein under colour of generall
> Lawes . . .
>
> —King James, *Basilikon Doron* (1599)[1]

At the time of Shakespeare's childhood, the north of England was
the stage for a dispute—a "final showdown," historian Lawrence
Stone calls it—between a particularist culture governed by "lineage
loyalties, kin networks, and the ties of 'good lordship,'" and the "new
universalist culture of the nation state."[2] That showdown was the
Northern Rebellion of 1569. The disordered and confused rebellion
was triggered by the flight to England of the Catholic Mary, Queen
of Scots, and centered on the great houses of the north, including
the Percies, whose ancestors are key players in Shakespeare's history
plays. There was discontent with Elizabeth both at court and among
the northern Earls, particularly Westmoreland and Northumberland,
who hoped to recover some of their lost prestige by championing Mary
and Catholicism. The Earls allied themselves with the Duke of Norfolk,
who planned to marry the Catholic Queen and have her recognized as
heir to the English throne.

According to Stone, the defeat of the Northern Earls marked the end
of the "particularist system of values"[3] of the fifteenth and early sixteenth
centuries. According to this older set of values, "personalized loyalty and
lordship was the highest and most prized of qualities, taking precedence
over those of obedience to the Ten Commandments, of submission to

the impersonal dictates of the law, and of deference to the personal authority of the King."[4] A world where men were bound together primarily by a network of patronage, this "highly localized, highly personal world . . . had yet to be affected by wider notions of loyalty to more universalistic codes and ideals."[5] The Northern Rebellion of 1569 showed that the old particularist culture was "already hollow, and no longer able to sustain the challenge of outright rebellion against the sovereign."[6]

The conflict between a particularist culture united by a network of patronage and mutual interest and the universalist culture of the nation-state is signaled throughout Shakespeare's history plays and tragedies. It is perhaps most visible in *Hamlet,* where the Ghost stands for the older culture driven by particular loyalties, ties, and interests, in this case with revenge; Hamlet, for the newer culture of the nation-state. One of the more interesting manifestations of the conflict between the two cultures is the universalizing rhetoric issuing from, and often applied to, his tragic protagonists. For various reasons that I suggest below, criticism has rarely paid attention to the political implications of such rhetoric, implications that I propose to explore over the next two chapters.

The Immodesty of Generalizing

"To generalize is to be an Idiot," Blake scribbled in the margins of a copy of Joshua Reynolds's *Discourses on Art* sometime between the years 1798 and 1809.[7] During those years of romanticism's heyday, it would be hard to characterize Blake's position as a marginal one, as it might have been in 1779 when he entered the Royal Academy Schools as a student. Neither would his rejoinder to Reynolds and Neo-Classicism—effective, it is hard to overlook, because of its startling simplicity and generality—meet any serious opposition today, when many of our critical watchwords sport prefixes like "hetero-," "multi-," and "poly-." Such prefixes seem designed both to show the would-be generalizer the door, like an unwelcome drunk at a party, and to establish the critic's credentials in a community of very "particular" people.

A rhetoric of the particular runs throughout the old New Criticism as well as the now dominant school of criticism that still polemicizes against New Criticism, the new historicism. Shakespearean criticism, however, frequently serves as a haven for what often still comes across as a more old-fashioned generalizing rhetoric. Congregants of the Shakespearean Universalist Church—those for whom Shakespeare is "Not of an age, but for all time," in Ben Jonson's words—have, despite the prevailing critical winds, brandished a rhetoric of the general and universal throughout this century's criticism. Both prominent critical rhetorics, the particularizing rhetoric of New Criticism and new historicism on the one hand and the universalizing rhetoric of much humanist Shakespearean criticism on the other,[8] similarly fail to appreciate the degree to which and the ways in which generalizing is situated by Shakespeare in scenes of conflict, struggles over sovereignty, power, and representation. The quarrel over the people's representation by tribunes in *Coriolanus,* for instance, is fought in tandem with a less explicit quarrel over the prerogative to generalize. Hamlet's celebrated practice of generalizing is an important instrument in his bid to achieve sovereignty or access to the potent generalizing signs of kingship. In fact, in many of Shakespeare's tragedies the pursuit or maintenance of sovereignty is closely related to questions of the authority and legitimacy of general statements. *Timon of Athens* plays two modes of generalizing against one another, each highly politicized: one linked with Renaissance notions of sovereignty, the other with a democratic levelling or confounding that the play fails to expunge. Both the particularizing and generalizing forms of criticism tend to overlook generalizing as a site of conflict in Shakespeare.

My second contention in this chapter is that Renaissance tragedy has a high stake in the legitimacy of various modes of generalizing. Everyone acknowledges the importance of the category of the general for comedy, with its preference for stock types. I want to contend that Shakespearean tragedy, with its singular and irreplaceable heroes, is equally committed to generalizing tropes and practices. Renaissance tragedy is in many quite specific ways a genre that depends as much for its success on generalizing rhetorics as did Renaissance notions of sovereignty. The rhetoric of the particular that predominates in twentieth-century literary criticism is strangely incongruous with the generalizing rhetorics of the Shakespearean theater. One of the most widespread (or general?) anachronisms of twentieth-century criticism is its tendency to assume that "general" and "particular" have always been in more or less the same relation, and therefore subject to the same interpretive and evaluative schema as our own. In other words, we often tend to overlook the prestige and importance of the category of the general for the Renaissance: in part, because of our modern tendency to associate generality with banality and attenuation of rhetorical power; and in part because of the association that drove the New Critics toward the haven of a particularizing rhetoric: namely, the association of generality with the scientific discourses perceived as dominant in the modern world, and against which literary critics have raised the banner of a countergeneralizing literature and criticism. Such anachronistic critical assumptions have caused a whole range of questions concerned with the activity of generalizing in Shakespeare's plays to be largely ignored.

I will first examine some instances of modern critical rhetoric of the particular, then proceed to support my second claim about Shakespearean drama's generalizing resources. I will then contrast critical rhetoric with that of two tragedies, *Romeo and Juliet* and *Julius Caesar,* which I believe exhibit something like a normative faith in and reliance on generalizing. Finally, I will show how *Hamlet* registers a departure from the norms of the earlier plays. It may be that, coming immediately after the nationalistic decade of the 1590s,[9] *Hamlet* registers a strain within the increasingly universalist discourse of the nation-state.[10]

We Critics Are Very Particular

During the era of the New Criticism it was common to view works of art and general statements as virtual enemies. Cleanth Brooks exemplified this view:

> The poem seemed to be best described as a verbal context whose meaning resisted expression in any simple proposition—and indeed resisted complete expression in any abstract statement whatsoever. . . . It was not so much a "statement" of a generalization as a dramatization of a particular situation.[11]

Brooks was responding to what many New Critics perceived as the tendency of the naive reader to construe the poem as a statement of general truth, as well as advancing the already widespread conviction that poetry served a countergeneralizing mission in resistance to the ever more dominant generalizing discourses of science.

General statements that occur within a poem or play would seem to present a special problem. Yet for Brooks they too are reducible to dramatizations of particular situations. Poetic statements, no matter how general they appear, are inextricable from the particularities of their contexts. This view of poetic language was commonly described and legitimized by New Critics using the analogy or metaphor of drama: statements in poems—"including those which appear to be philosophical generalizations—are to be read as if they were speeches in a drama."[12] It seems curious that the New Critics would have relied so heavily on the metaphor "poems-as-dramas" to build a case for a countergeneralizing view of the work of art, given the heavy dependency of Renaissance drama, and arguably the drama of most ages, on generalizing rhetoric of various kinds (the subject of the next section of this chapter).

Though not a practitioner of New Criticism himself, M. H. Abrams, for a generation the foremost critic of English romanticism, was an ally of the New Critics in their assault on generality. In "The Correspondent Breeze," an essay of 1957 that discusses the recurrence of a pervasive romantic metaphor, Abrams attacks archetypal critics (led by Frye in the area of literary criticism, Jung in that of psychology):

> A mode of reading that persists in looking through the literal, particular, and artful qualities of a poem in order to discover a more important ulterior pattern of primitive, general, and unintended meanings eliminates its individuality, and threatens to nullify even its status as a work of art. . . . A procedure which ingeniously contrives to reduce all—or at least a great many—serious poems to variations upon a timeless theme is not so much to the purpose of the literary critic, whose chief concern is with the particularity of a work; nor is it more useful to the literary historian, despite his greater interest in establishing literary types and the general qualities of a literary period.[13]

Abrams's parenthetical qualification—"all—or at least a great many"—resembles some of Hamlet's misgivings about his own generalizing habit: for instance, his immediately qualifying the generalization, "That one may smile, and smile, and be a villain—" with the afterthought, "At least I am sure it may be so in Denmark" (1.5.108–9). Both Abrams and Hamlet seem a little uneasy about belonging to the community of idiot-generalizers, and therefore exercise a greater than ordinary vigilance over whatever covert generalizing practices threaten to infiltrate their own discourses. Six years later the enemy has apparently changed, though the critic is firing from the same box of ammunition. Now it is not the archetypalists but a collection of economist-critics who are responsible for generalizing the individuality of literary works out of existence. In an essay of 1963 on the importance of the French Revolution to romantic poetry, Abrams complains of a recent collection of critical essays on romanticism that "the few essays which give more than passing mention to the French Revolution do so to reduce the particularity of Romantic poems mainly to a distant reflection of an underlying economic reality."[14]

The New Critics have been a favorite polemical target of the new historicists, yet the newer critical practice shares with the older a considerable hostility to generalizing rhetorics and strong allegiance to the rhetoric of particularity. Usually relying very heavily on anecdote, a form of discourse at the opposite end of the rhetorical spectrum from the generalization, and on detailed description of a particular incident or scene, and working always within the assumption that literary texts are embedded in highly localized contexts, new historicism seems as concerned as any criticism has been with expunging generality from its own discursive practices. Words like "particular" and "local" serve almost a ritual, exorcistic function in much recent criticism, banishing the specter of generalizing as Hamlet himself so often does. For instance, in a generally and justly admired essay on how authority in the Renaissance produces subversion as a means of containing it—an argument that has become paradigmatic and general in one vein of new historicist research—Stephen Greenblatt writes that this means of containing potential opposition "is not a theoretical necessity of theatrical power in general but an historical phenomenon, the particular mode of this particular culture."[15]

The New Critics were generalists in spite of themselves. In the process of lending an ear to the highly nuanced voices within particular poems, they effectively generalized poems by viewing them outside of time, place, and historical circumstances. That much, I am sure, would meet with almost universal agreement among critics today. From our vantage point it is more difficult to appreciate that many new historicists are as susceptible as the New Critics to becoming generalizers in spite of themselves. In what many critics have noted is an unwillingness to theorize about their methodological assumptions, new historicists often write from what must seem a generalized, unlocalized discursive space. Another tendency in recent cultural criticism, of which the new historicism is one instance, is to enthrone general terms like "culture," "history," "politics," "hegemony," and "power." It strikes me as a paradox of this vigorously and insistently particularizing mode of critical discourse that it has helped an array of general terms to assert their dominance over the field of criticism. Also, as Jean Howard has noted in an article surveying the field of Renaissance new historicism, essays cast in this mode tend to "sketch a cultural law" from a "painstaking description of a particular historical event, place, or experience," without considering "a culture's whole system of signifying practices" that "would allow one to assess, relationally, the importance and function of the particular event described."[16]

In the work of Michel Foucault too—a thinker who is in many ways the presiding genius of the new historicism—conventional philosophical totalizing gestures are avoided, temporarily at least, through the intense concentration on a single institution or event. In the course of Foucault's analysis, such events and institutions often become the

78

slender bases on which to rest enormous generalizations. As Edward Said writes in an appreciative essay written on the occasion of Foucault's death, like many benefactors of Nietzsche, Foucault preferred "all that is specific and special . . . to what is general and universal."[17] But paradoxically his pursuit of archival oddities that have escaped the gaze of sanctioned forms of history writing perhaps necessitated a stronger reliance on generalizing than a more conventional scholarship: "At the same time that he was immersed, perhaps even immured, in archives, dossiers, and manuscripts, Foucault seems paradoxically to have stimulated himself and his audience to a greater degree of sovereign authority, as if to illustrate his own thesis that power produces resistance, and resistance, new forms of power."[18] In the later stages of his career, Said notes, Foucault "had a tendency to venture comically general observations."[19]

My point here is not to show in a general way that we critics are all unwittingly one species or another of generalizing comedians. Critics with an unshaken faith in critical rhetoric of the particular may very well share with Shakespeareans of the universalizing, humanist variety a largely unexamined faith in the rhetorical trope that governs both their critical practices—namely synecdoche, involving a substitution of particular for general or general for particular, of part for whole or whole for part. But more significantly, they may also share a tendency to overlook generalizing in Shakespeare as a political act that often issues from and generates conflict. Thus, for Bernard McElroy, an able spokesman for the universalizing trend, Shakespeare's characters and their author work toward a common goal of harmonizing the general and the particular. Shakespeare's manifest superiority, McElroy maintains, is owing in large part to his ability to universalize the particular and to particularize or flesh out the universal. Shakespeare broadens both the intellectual scope of his heroes and "the horizons of his own plays, making it possible to deal with the most universal ideas and issues without being heavy-handed or sententious."[20] Moreover, his general-minded characters—a tendency to universalize is one of five principal qualities of mind that his mature tragic heroes share in common—work in cooperation with their maker's larger project, like apprentices to a master. "It is largely through this character trait in the hero that Shakespeare achieves the effortless coalescence of the universal and particular which is one of the hallmarks of his tragedy."[21] An unchallenged faith in Shakespeare's mastery of synecdoche like that exhibited by McElroy may make a non-issue of the clashes between generalizing and countergeneralizing rhetorics of Shakespeare's plays—both those employed by his characters and those that inform the *structure* of the plays. A more rhetorically and historically based criticism may help show, for instance, the several ways in which the clash between plebeians and patricians in *Coriolanus* takes place within the context of a continual reinterpretation of the generalizing act, a reinterpretation that may help account for the strange spareness of the play as a whole; or how the extreme modes of generalizing in *Timon of Athens* implicate and indict many of the generalizing practices of Renaissance drama itself. Such a criticism might demonstrate the parallel ways in which Renaissance drama and absolutism invested heavily in various forms of generalization, depending on the legitimacy of generalizing practices for many of their own claims to authority.

Generality and Drama

In the course of discussing the historical novel and its other, the historical drama, Georg Lukács implies that in all its phases drama is an inherently generalizing genre:

> By concentrating the reflection of life upon a great collision, by grouping all manifestations of life round this collision and permitting them to live themselves out only in relation to the collision, drama simplifies and generalizes the possible attitudes of men to the problems of their lives. The portrayal is reduced to the typical representation of the most important and most characteristic attitudes of men, to what is indispensable to the dynamic working-out of the collision.[22]

Since this description appears in a discussion of the historical novel, it might be mistaken for a belittling gesture toward drama, conceived as a less complex genre because of its interest in the typical or representative.[23] But in fact, Lukács's Marxist orientation results in a word like "generality" being marked quite positively. Associating tragic drama as he does with revolutionary periods and periods of ideological collapse, he is eager to maintain that, in socialist societies, where the element of tragic downfall wouldn't have the same importance as it would for pre-socialist societies, a function for tragic drama remains, a function tied to its capacity for generalizing and thereby intensifying the typical. Dramatic collisions persist even in the most advanced forms of social organization, though such collisions are no longer predicated on class antagonisms or tied to the notion of a tragic downfall:

> Today [Lukács was writing in 1936–37] it is specially important to stress this side of the tragic collision, to see how dramatic form generalizes

a typical fact of life and makes of it an intense experience. And this human side of the dramatic collision, which is by no means necessarily linked with tragic downfall, is present, too, as a fact of life, in Socialist society and can thus become the basis of a significant dramatic work.[24]

That the rescue of tragic drama for a socialist age is tied to, and perhaps largely motivated by, a desire to rescue the intensely generalizing capabilities of drama is made clear by Lukács's contrast of novel and drama. As in most other accounts the novel comes across as a much more tentatively generalizing form, which for Lukács would mean "less concentrated and economical."[25] "While the dramatic character must be directly and immediately typical, without of course losing his individuality, the typical quality of a character in a novel is very often only a tendency which asserts itself gradually, which emerges to the surface only by degrees out of the whole, out of the complex interaction of human beings, human relations, institutions, things."[26]

Lukács's remarks seem useful as an antidote to the frequently unexamined assumption in twentieth-century criticism that literature has a countergeneralizing function,[27] especially because they are genre-specific, associating drama as they do with particularly concentrated forms of generalizing. Lukács's characterization of the drama seems to me a useful starting point for investigating Shakespearean tragedy as a series of inquiries into the rhetoric of dramatic form. I stress starting point for three reasons.

First, what makes the issue of general and particular in Shakespearean tragedy seem especially vital is the inclusion in those tragedies of critical reflections of (and on) their own generalizing practices. One of the principal forms such reflections take is the plays' tendency increasingly to favor characters who are themselves not merely general (in the senses of comprehensive and representative) but also set apart from others by being more habitually generalizing in their discourse. The generalizing practices of tragedy are thereby made a more integral part of the tragic protagonist and his fortunes and at the same time are foregrounded, situated in a place where they can be made visible and subject to contestation.

Second, by no means do the tragedies embrace the generalizing practices of the genre to which they belong with the same confidence or fervor. Many key differences among the tragedies can be related to differences in the ways they represent their generalizing practices. The vigor of the middle and later tragedies derives in large part from their growing tendency to question those practices and other key aspects of dramatic form. In later tragedies like *Coriolanus* and *Timon of Athens* the generalizing practices of Coriolanus, the citizens, Timon, Apemantus, Alcibiades, and others are taken to such extremes that the very impulse to generalize, in so many respects native to Renaissance drama, is placed on trial. Shakespeare seems increasingly fond of casting shadows over the generalizing habits of his protagonists. The plays' growing suspicion toward the generalizing turn of mind of their characters was shared by many voices in what Hiram Haydn has characterized as the Counter-Renaissance, voices that, in opposition to the tradition of Renaissance Christian humanism, display "a militant antagonism to the concept of comprehensible universal law."[28] His preeminent examples—Montaigne, Agrippa, Bruno, and Machiavelli—all reach a point he characterizes as "the ultimate desertion of the universal for the particular."[29] Montaigne's warning about the futility of seeking man in general, choosing instead to "represent a particular one";[30] Agrippa's claim that "justice depends upon the fairness and honesty of a particular judge"; and Machiavelli's insistence on the "importance of a single individual to the formation of the state," a state having no prior foundation on universal principles of law or justice: all are instances of a broader trend "away from the science of the universal to the consideration of the particular."[31]

Third, such reflections by Renaissance tragedies of their own generalizing practices need to be situated in the context of Renaissance assumptions about sovereignty, about the sovereign as universal. A certain confidence in generalizing rhetorics may be necessary both to the flourishing of Renaissance drama and to the security of the monarchies under which Shakespeare wrote. Accepting that premise doesn't preclude that Shakespearean tragedy may go a long way toward critically examining and even reproving or censuring its own generalizing policies and practices.

In Renaissance tragedy, devices and practices serving the cause of generality include dumb shows, choruses and choric elements, the use of emblems or emblemlike scenes, generalized scene setting, typological handling of character, the rich background of communal language that found its way into Renaissance drama in the form of proverbs, and large summarizing similitudes like Ulysses' great chain of being, in addition to the general and generic tendency of drama to concentrate "the reflection of life upon a great collision." In the middle and later phases of its development, Shakespearean tragedy increasingly foregrounds generality, including its own generalizing procedures, as a problem. Earlier Shakespearean drama, by contrast, appears much more confident of the legitimacy of its own generalizing practices. For instance, choric elements, so prominent in an early Renaissance tragedy like *Gorboduc* and to a lesser degree in Shakespeare's earlier plays, are reduced in his later tragedies. The dumb show, which in early Renaissance practice sometimes opened an act, "allegorically stages what will happen in the act proper, and the allegory is so codified, even proverbial, that it will be immediately understood. . . . The moral precedes the tale, and the general model anticipates the particular case."[32] A play like *Hamlet* complicates in many ways the presumed relation of general to particular, the precedence and governance of general model over particular case, and one such way is the inability of the dumb show to govern the unruly meanings it unleashes, let alone those issuing from the play that follows, which it pretends to summarize. In addition, large summarizing icons are much more likely to go unchallenged in Shakespeare's earlier plays than in the later ones, where the more massive similitudes like Menenius's fable of the belly or Ulysses' great chain of being are more closely interrogated and often subjected to iconoclastic treatment.[33]

Nevertheless, in all its phases Shakespearean drama shared a certain confidence in its own generalizing practices: for instance, its ability to represent large social bodies or communities by a few of their members or its ability to represent a life by means of one or at most a very few adventures from it. Bernard Beckerman writes that it was typical of Elizabethan scene setting to specify "a place at large but not a particular section of it": for instance, "Rome as a whole rather than some portion of it is often the setting of *Coriolanus* (I,i; IV,ii; IV,vi)."[34] He goes on to claim that the generalized setting often serves to add to the dramatic power of a scene. Frequently "dramatic impact proceeds from the general rather than the specific nature of the locale."[35] Too often are observations like Beckerman's lost amidst a choral chant of twentieth-century criticism's rhetoric of the particular: a critical rhetoric that assumes that great literature, of whatever historical milieu and in whatever particular cultural or political climate, serves a countergeneralizing function.

The typological handling of character in Shakespeare is often overlooked or underplayed as well, largely due to a romantic stress on individual motivation. But Shakespeare's was an age for which "character" meant conformity to a certain type, as required by decorum. A late play like *Timon of Athens* may answer to and participate in the growing Jacobean vogue for character writing, collections of sketches of character types.[36] Though it may be true that Shakespeare laid more stress on individual motivation than did any of his contemporaries, it would still be necessary to confront a second order of generality informing character in his plays, one defined by the ubiquitous notion of man as microcosm, or as reflection of the universal.

Another way in which drama seems to have negotiated ancient treaties with generality (treaties that Shakespeare's middle and later plays are busy renegotiating) is that drama seems to rely on a relatively stable and widely held system of beliefs. Kenneth Burke writes in his early *Counter-Statement* of that perennial pair of critical terms, "objective-subjective":

> In the "great ages," when drama flourishes, art is "objective." That is, the artist gets his effects primarily by the exploitation of the current ideology. In the society of the times there are many implicit judgments, a general agreement as to what is heroic, what cowardly, what irreligious, what boorish, what clever. . . . This dramatic or objective method (of composing one's symbols from the standpoint of the effect desired) is weakened in proportion as the ideology which the dramatist relies upon is weakened. And in time an ideology must weaken, either through processes of exhaustion, or through the encroachment of new material which the ideology cannot encompass.[37]

In certain highly suggestive remarks about *Hamlet*, Burke claims that Shakespeare's method in that play is more "essayistic" than "dramatic," the essayistic according to Burke being "the least dramatic of all ways of thinking": "The essayist, in contrast to the dramatist, can dispense with a maximum of certainty in ideology. If a code is crumbling he can, with all the convenience in the world, say so. Whereas the dramatist exploits beliefs, the essayist can devote himself precisely to the questioning of beliefs."[38]

Burke takes *Hamlet's* deviation from a "dramatistic" and "objective" method to be a temporary departure by an author who could still rely on a fairly intact ideology, had he chosen to do so, but for some "great personal stress." Such a crisis, hypothetical of course, caused Shakespeare to depart from the drama's characteristic reliance on an ideology or generally held beliefs. Burke writes, "We may suppose that a skilled dramatist, writing at a time when an ideology was intact, could be induced only under pressure of great anguish to symbolize a specific pattern of experience—whereas this readjustment could be accepted by artists of a later age with almost no discomfiture whatever, since they had never found the ideology powerful enough for them to build a method upon its full utilization."[39] But I want to contend that what Burke and countless other critics since the romantic period (including T. S. Eliot) have characterized as the "subjectivity" of *Hamlet* is not an isolated incident in Shakespeare's career, the unique production of an author in a time of great personal stress who allowed matters of momentous personal concern to infiltrate his normally objective art. The notorious subjectivity of the play, and more broadly the construction of the modern subject that Joel Fineman has recently attributed to Shakespeare,[40] take place, I propose, within the matrix of a growing suspicion toward generalizing practices shared to some degree by all of Shakespeare's tragedies. Furthermore, the suspicion toward generalizing is at least as much a rethinking of the terms of political representation as it is the marking of a new phase in the construction of modern subjectivity. *Hamlet* may show the first, but certainly not the last, explicit signs of strain in those relations between drama and the generalizing rhetoric that was of as great importance to monarchs as to playwrights of the Renaissance.

"Another General Shout?"

A play nearly contemporary with *Hamlet, Julius Caesar* shares a suspicion of generalizing rhetoric, particularly that of Antony and Brutus. But *Julius Caesar* conducts its inquiry on a narrower scale. In some respects, *Julius Caesar,* together with *Romeo and Juliet,* may be used to exemplify something close to a normative confidence in certain generalizing discourses and practices of Renaissance drama.

Like several later Shakespearean tragedies, *Julius Caesar* features military leaders who go by the title "general" but who are not general enough in the wider sense of the word, who fall short of the high standards of comprehensiveness and representativeness set by the heroes of tragedies. It is hard not to hear that wider meaning of "general" behind the more specific military use of the word, in light of locutions like Brutus's question, "Another general shout?" (1.2.130) or Hamlet's " 'Twas caviare to the general" (2.2.432–33). The sudden intrusion of a second and anonymous, generalized Poet in act 4 (the other, particularized in a minimal way by being endowed with a proper name, Cinna, that leads to his destruction, his nondifferentiation from one of the conspirators) seems almost a dramatic poet's chastisement of his bickering generals, whose fractiousness makes them something less than "general" in the broader sense of the term. One of the two squabbling generals, Brutus, is a clear contestant for the honor of most general general.

In death Brutus appears to achieve the universality falsely claimed by Caesar and simulated for him by Marc Antony in a funeral oration sprinkled with phrases like "the general coffers" (3.2.91), "the commons" (3.2.132), and "every several man" (3.2.244). The loss of Caesar, the man who would be "universal landlord" (as Mark Antony says of Octavius Caesar in *Antony and Cleopatra*), is more than compensated for by Antony's celebration of Brutus as the single man able to subordinate private, particular end to the general good:

> This was the noblest Roman of them all.
> All the conspirators save only he
> Did that they did in envy of great Caesar;
> He only, in a general honest thought
> And common good to all, made one of them.
> His life was gentle, and the elements
> So mix'd in him, that Nature might stand up
> And say to all the world, "This was a man!"
>   (5.5.68–75)

The speech echoes Brutus's own admission, "And for my part, / I know no personal cause to spurn at him, / But for the general" (2.1.10–12). By contrast, the announcement of Antony's approach in the preceding scene, "Here comes the general" (5.4.17), seems inappropriate insofar as the man it announces is considerably less general than the general (Brutus) whom Antony's soldiers mistakenly think to have captured.

Antony's speech accords Brutus the extraordinary honor customarily reserved for the tragic hero: a singularity ("save only he," "He only") expressive of the highest generality. In rhetorical terms, he is the most synecdochic of characters; like the ideal Renaissance sovereign, he is also the perfect synecdoche, the part that can best stand for or represent the whole, and at the same time a representation of the whole capable of taking the part of wronged parties. The singular or particular and the general do not represent separate phases in the unfolding of character. In Brutus, the mediation of particular and general interest is complete and (seemingly) seamless: the salient feature that sets him apart from his fellow Romans is his singular concern for the general. What is particular about Brutus is his ability to subdue the particular or private. Of all the conspirators, only Brutus "made one" of them "in a general honest thought." Conversely, and equally synecdochally, it is the collective minus one—"All the conspirators, save only he"—that is subject to the isolating influence of "envy."

The eulogy proceeds by mentioning the only particular attribute ascribed to him: "gentle," a word linked etymologically to "general" and "gentility" as well as to the Latin "gens," a grouping of families constituting a clan and sharing the same nomen, the most general of the four divisions of the Roman name. "Gentle" derives from the Latin *gentilis,* "belonging to the same gens or race" (*O.E.D.*). The single attribute "gentle" seems well chosen to particularize Brutus in such a way as not to remove him from the sphere of the general, since that attribute, both in its Latin root and its contemporary meanings, is a word of class or kind. It belongs to a class of words denoting class, including "genus," "gender," "gentility," "gentry," and a host of others (all engendered from a root meaning "to engender"). Also, "gentle" is an adjective with both a special and a general sense. The Elizabethan audience of *Julius Caesar* would have recognized the more specialized meaning of "well born" in "gentle."[41] For all these reasons, the attribution of "gentleness" to Brutus helps him remain something of a gateway between general and particular interests as well as meanings.

Antony's speech then broadens by proceeding through the synecdoche of man as microcosm, a whole consisting of harmoniously balanced "elements" or parts ("the elements / So mix'd in him"), to the general terms "world" and "man."[42] Those last three lines build quickly and economically from the particular to the general via the intermediary of the arch-synecdoche of the Renaissance, one that illustrates an easy commerce between parts and wholes and between particular and general: that of man as microcosm. This synecdoche is perhaps the most powerful and authoritative instance of generalizing in Antony's speech and the play as a whole, and examining its operation in another speech of Brutus's illustrates the importance of generalizing in Shakespeare, its links to authority and control.

A speech like the following establishes Brutus's kinship with Hamlet, his membership in the Shakespearean fraternity of habitual generalizers, though what this speech lacks of Hamlet is a suspicion of the generalizing turn of mind:

> Since Cassius first did whet me against Caesar,
> I have not slept.
> Between the acting of a dreadful thing
> And the first motion, all the interim is
> Like a phantasma, or a hideous dream:
> The genius and the mortal instruments
> Are then in council; and the state of man,
> Like to a little kingdom, suffers then
> The nature of an insurrection.
>   (2.1.61–69)

The generalizing rhetoric of this speech subtly counteracts the problem it describes. The speech likens the psychological effects of a state of suspension between intention and action to a political insurrection within the microcosm or little world of man, a battle between the mind or guardian spirit ("genius") and its corporeal agencies ("mortal instruments") directed to carry out the deed. Because the speech as a whole is an instance of generalizing—like Hamlet's famous soliloquy on suicide, Brutus's soliloquy describes the *characteristic* effects of a state of suspension, not its effects on his particular "little kingdom"—it is implicitly an attempt to restore equilibrium in the microcosm, to reassert the sway of genius over mortal instruments. If a general statement is analogous to a sovereign exercising control over the multitudes of particular contexts to which it may apply and which it in some sense commands, then even a generalization about instability will be potentially stabilizing. Brutus's generalization about "insurrection" within the human actor in an indirect way works to quell that insurrection and restore order.

In a way, the subject of Brutus's generalization is generalizing itself, or a certain way of conceiving the relation between general and particular, one suggested by the commonplace correspondence of the microcosm man to the universe. The microcosm/macrocosm pair, one of the most durable fixtures of Renaissance thought, implies a relation between general and particular in which the general term has the same elaborated and diversified structure as the particular term it embraces and comprehends. The general term is not a pale or simplified version of the particular but rather a model for it. Since the person conceived as a little world contains all the important features of the macrocosm after which s/he is presumed to be modeled, no important features of the particular are lost in the process of being generalized or linked to the more general term. Later in the century, after the microcosm/macrocosm analogy together with many other furnishings of Renaissance thought will have been discarded, Locke will regard generalizing as "a movement away from the object and a subtraction from it,"[43] thereby establishing what is perhaps still our primary way of understanding generalization. In a parallel development in the theater, Restoration characters will accede to a generality unlike that of Shakespeare's generalizers. Like a Lockean species name, which gives a common identity to a group of objects sharing certain arbitrarily and uncertainly chosen secondary qualities, but which in the process abstracts only a few qualities from the objects designated by that name, a character in Restoration comedy is "general" in the sense of being a simplified version of a person, with only a few qualities of a person represented. Like the Lockean species name, the Restoration character seems a movement away from the object (person) and a subtraction from it. By contrast, Shakespeare's most "general" comic characters—a Hal or a Rosalind—are general precisely because they are comprehensive and able to play almost any part.[44]

The main difference between the rhetorical strategy of generalizing in *Julius Caesar* and in subsequent tragedies like *Hamlet* and *Coriolanus* is that in the former it seems as cool and self-possessed as Brutus himself. Hamlet, who shares many character traits with Brutus, including a penchant for generalizing, maneuvers throughout the play for a position of centrality, and perhaps his primary rhetorical means for doing so is the generalization. But Hamlet generalizes in a climate of suspicion toward generalizing, which often comes across as a vehicle of repression and censure. Furthermore, unlike Brutus, Hamlet generalizes so insistently not because of any felt centrality or representativeness but rather out of a sense of deficiency in the universality claimed for, if not by, his father. Generalizing seems far more desperate in *Hamlet* than it does in *Julius Caesar*. Rather than an eminently cool, detached, philosophical means of expression, generalizations in *Hamlet* often seem "wild and whirling" words (1.5.139): not an antidote to the mad speeches or manic wordplay but rather a kinsman to those deviant modes of discourse. *Hamlet* is more self-conscious and critical of the impulse to generalize than are any of its predecessors. Within range of its suspicion, and possible targets for it, are the generalizing practices shared by Renaissance drama and a monarchy ensconced in the universalist culture and language of the nation-state.

In her "Golden Speech" of 1601, delivered to about 150 members of Parliament assembled at Whitehall on the afternoon of November 30, 1601,[45] Queen Elizabeth asseverated, "Since I was queen, yet never did I put my pen to any grant, but that upon pretext and semblance made unto me that it was both good and beneficial to the subjects in general, though a private profit to some of my ancient servants who had deserved well."[46] Elizabeth's remarks responded to the uproar at the time over the issuing of monopolies, grants she often either issued as rewards for service or sold to raise income. Her line shows the importance to a monarch of asserting the semblance of a perfect compatibility between general and particular interests, when she was accused of using this indirect form of taxation during a time of scarcity, inflation, and deficit spending to line the pockets of court favorites. In his speeches to Parliament, James—who, because of his Scottish background and the many nobleman he brought with him on his accession to the English throne, was far more vulnerable than Elizabeth to charges of particularism, performing acts of favoritism that harmed the general welfare—repeatedly stressed the importance of that body's members maintaining the "generall weale" uppermost in their minds. In the course of a discussion of the difference in status of the *Antè nati* and *Post nati,* those Scotsmen born before and after the accession of James to the throne of England, he asserts, "For, my rewarding out of my Liberalitie of any particular men, hath nothing adoe with the generall acte of the Vnion, which must not regard the deserts of priuate persons, but the generall weale and conioyning of the Nations."[47] He insisted in a manner like Elizabeth's that his rewards to particular men never contradicted or went against the general welfare, but he was also trying to divorce the particular question, the rewarding of particular persons, from the general, which alone (according to James) it is Parliament's proper place to discuss. In a speech two years earlier, James maintained, "Now the matters whereof [members of Parliament] are to treate ought therefore to be generall. . . . It is no place then for particular men to vtter there their priuate conceipts."[48] The same constriction might be said to apply to Renaissance plays and playwrights, who were forced to comment on matters of topical interest that frequently touched particular persons (for instance, Essex, or Elizabeth herself) under the guise of speaking generally.[49] In the political rhetoric of the time, the right of speaking generally was everything from a monarch's privilege to a limitation on the range of questions considered by Parliament, whom James enjoined to consider only general questions, implicitly leaving the field of "priuate conceipts" and "the rewarding of particular persons" the sole domain of the sovereign.

The generalizing and countergeneralizing rhetoric of Shakespeare's plays would seem to be implicated in questions of the precedence of general welfare over private interest and the ability of the monarch to represent (or dissemble) a generality that, even when it does grant "a private profit" to particular individuals, always gives precedence to the general welfare. The precedence Brutus customarily gives to the general welfare would make him well suited to occupy the place of Renaissance absolute monarch. Perhaps the supreme irony of Antony's eulogy for Brutus is its implication that this representative of an anti-monarchist position would make the perfect monarch. A countervailing irony is Antony's tendency to use the form of the universalizing eulogy, both Caesar's and now Brutus's, to further his own particular political ends. Though teaching suspicion toward universalizing rhetoric (through Antony), the play also restores the ideology of absolutism (through Brutus) following the murder of Caesar, within the circle of the conspirators themselves. Because of his unique concentration on the general at the expense of particular (or private) gain, Brutus would seem to fulfill the monarch's qualifications of "but one man" who may stand for or represent the whole of the body politic. Thus, Cassius's anger over the dissimulated universality of Caesar[50] would have an even more appropriate target at the end of the play in Brutus. Cassius declaims,

When went there by an age, since the great flood,
But it was fam'd with more than with one man?
When could they say, till now, that talk'd of Rome,
That her wide walks encompass'd but one man?
Now it is Rome indeed, and room enough,
When there is in it but one only man.
(1.2.150–55)

But of course Cassius is wishing against the current not only of absolute monarchy but also the genre that contains him, since Renaissance tragedy very frequently if not usually gives the impression of a world filled with, and synecdochically represented by, "but one only man."

Antony's largely phony oration over the corpse of his defeated enemy Brutus, the uncontested supreme generalist in the play, nevertheless helps reassert the prerogative of princes, and indirectly the playwright, to stand for, represent, speak to and on behalf of "the general."

Generality and Closure

Turn back a few more years in Shakespeare's career and questions of the authority and legitimacy of the plays' generalizing rhetorics become less complicated. In *Romeo and Juliet,* the choric "Prologue" to act 1 (providing an abstract of the play, both its action and meaning), Friar Lawrence's lengthy choric summary at the end of the play (in spite of its emendations and omissions), and the Prince's relatively terse summary and promise to serve as "general" of the affected parties' "woes," all serve to frame and contain the particulars of the story and their meaning, guarding the narrative itself from the threat of the same riot and disorder that destroy Mercutio and Tybalt. Friar Lawrence's stream of rhyming *sententiae* while walking in his garden (2.3.1–26) has nothing like the qualities of Polonius's. Even though all three voices of generality—Prologue, Friar, and Prince—seem inadequate to honor Shakespeare's richly particularized lovers, the predominant tone of generalizers in this play is one of temperateness and sobriety gained from years of observation, not one of authoritarianism, the sign of a hand used to directing and controlling and of a reckless and laughable detachment from the singularity of any occasion over which the sententious generalizer pretends to exercise dominance and control.

As in *Hamlet,* it is nearly impossible to differentiate the generalizers from the non-in *Romeo and Juliet.* Romeo himself belongs to the

91

community. He generalizes himself by speaking in bookish, Petrachan terms, at least until Juliet teaches him to do otherwise. Friar Lawrence and the Prince, spiritual and worldly power, undoubtedly stand out as the most general or encompassing voices in the play. But nearly everyone gets into the generalizing act, each in a particular way. The old nurse Angelica, in a conversation designed to test Romeo's sincerity, calls on the authority of popular proverbs:

> But first let me tell ye, if ye should lead her in a fool's paradise, as they say, it were a very gross kind of behaviour, as they say; for the gentlewoman is young. And therefore, if you should deal double with her, truly it were an ill thing to be offered to any gentlewoman, and very weak dealing. (2.4.162–67)

The apparent incongruity between the self-assertiveness of "but first let me tell ye" and the retreat to a safer and less exposed position marching in the ranks with the refrain of "as they say" argues a need for a more general or culturally based authority by the particular speaker. That authority may be of a populist kind—the "general" with their ever handy proverbs—or of a monarchist or clerical variety, the authority of a figure of sufficient generality and comprehensiveness (and comprehension) to represent the "general."

Juliet generalizes in quite another key altogether, closer to that most favored by her playwright at this stage of his career. When she hears from her disconsolate nurse of Tybalt's death and mistakenly believes that Romeo too is slain, she cries out, "Then dreadful trumpet sound the general doom, / For who is living if those two are gone?" (3.2.67–68). After garnering more particulars of the fight and learning that Romeo lives, she persists in universalizing him, but not in the more commonplace way of crowning him "sole monarch" among lovers and honorable men. Rather, she makes him the stage upon which honor will be crowned:

> He was not born to shame.
> Upon his brow shame is asham'd to sit,
> For 'tis a throne where honour may be crown'd
> Sole monarch of the universal earth.
> (3.2.91–94)

In one sense Juliet allegorizes Romeo, making him a walking emblem of "honor." She generalizes him further by enlarging the dominion of honor until it includes all the world, "the universal earth." In addition, by making Romeo the *scene* of honor's coronation rather than Honor himself, Juliet adds to the honor by generalizing him one step further. He is a throne on which Honor may sit, something like a stage set for Honor. She keeps him "general" in the sense of not encompassed by any single attribute, even one so general as honor. By demurring or holding back a step from allegory, Juliet reserves for Romeo a broader form of generality than reification into an abstract term. Romeo thereby remains general in the same sense that the bare stages of the Elizabethan public theaters were general. They were always potentially a particular locale. Though to some degree allegorical, the generalized or indefinite spaces of the Elizabethan stage invited particularizing in a way that the more fully emblematic medieval stages did not. Unlike medieval stages, and like Renaissance constructions of the sovereign, the Elizabethan stages bespoke fairly equal and reversible relationships between the general and particular. Similarly, Romeo retains his singularity even at the highest pitch of Juliet's encomium.

The summarizing gestures of the Friar and the Prince at the end of the play register quite different effects than the rather ineffectual attempts to summarize by generalizing at the end of *Hamlet, Othello, King Lear,* and *Macbeth.* Unlike the Friar's detailed summary of events, where a rehearsal of the story's particulars are balanced against the summarizing and generalizing conclusions of the Prince, Horatio's promised summary, described in the most blandly general of terms, looks to be highly deficient, a case of generalizing by default or in the absence of particulars. By contrast, Fortinbras overparticularizes Hamlet by casting him in his own (limited) image as a soldier.[51] Rhetorically, Hamlet immediately after his death is pulled in two directions simultaneously: in two equally inadequate accounts he and his story are overgeneralized (by Horatio) and overparticularized (by Fortinbras). He is victimized by the very trope, synecdoche, that failed to serve him both as a prince and as a dramatic character who should be adequately summarized or represented by the play's action, a small segment of his life. By contrast, Brutus following his death is particularized and generalized simultaneously, in one seemingly indivisible movement.

Stephen Booth demonstrates how again and again the ending of *King Lear* "violently aborts the ceremony of theatrical conclusion."[52] Albany's speech to Edmund (5.3.40–46) "starts out in the standard fashion of victorious generals putting final touches to plays."[53] In a speech to Edgar later in the scene, "Albany sounds like one of dozens of rejoicing personages tying off the ends of a play by inviting narration of the events leading up to the hero's epiphany."[54] Any generalizing summation at the end of *King Lear* would likely seem inadequate, as it would have to compete with Lear's many sovereign instances of generalizing in acts 3 and 4. No movement to a register of greater generality is possible at the end of *Lear.*

The ending of *Othello* provides a more satisfying sense of summation, somewhat closer to that of *Romeo and Juliet.* Because it lacks a tidy narrative in the manner of Friar Lawrence's, *Othello's* summation must be pieced together by the auditor from the shards of information supplied by letters found in Roderigo's pockets after his death and by testimony from Cassio, Emilia, and others. Nevertheless, Othello's summary statement would seem far more conclusive than Horatio's, Fortinbras's, or Edgar's:

> Soft you, a word or two:
> I have done the state some service, and they know't;
> No more of that: I pray you in your letters,
> When you shall these unlucky deeds relate,
> Speak of them as they are; nothing extenuate,
> Nor set down aught in malice; then must you speak
> Of one that lov'd not wisely, but too well:
> Of one not easily jealous, but being wrought,
> Perplex'd in the extreme; of one whose hand,
> Like the base Indian, threw a pearl away,
> Richer than all his tribe: of one whose subdued eyes,
> Albeit unused to the melting mood,
> Drops tears as fast as the Arabian trees
> Their medicinal gum; set you down this,
> And say besides, that in Aleppo once,
> Where a malignant and a turban'd Turk
> Beat a Venetian, and traduc'd the state,
> I took by the throat the circumcised dog,
> And smote him thus.
>
> (5.2.339–57)

Several circumstances qualify this speech's efficacy as summary. First, the summarizing gives way to a postscript, a supplemental narrative ("And say besides") that retreats from the generalities with which the speech begins. Rather than leading from particulars to generalities, the speech moves in the opposite direction, from summary to (particularizing) narrative. In addition, the details of the narrative not only fail to illustrate and confirm the general account of himself he has just given: they qualify or even discredit that summary. The narrative, which almost instantly climaxes in the suicide of its teller, provides an alternative explanation of events, one grounded not in a lover's jealousy but in the deeper layer of anxieties about race and exclusion. Speech as well as speaker self-destructs.

Finally, the general account at the end of *Othello* is delivered by a general who is anything but general to the cultures represented in the play. Because of his racial and religious background he is not easily universalized by the white, Christian culture represented on stage and seated in the galleries. Even Desdemona is fascinated less with her general's generality than with his exoticism.

Macbeth's is the tidiest conclusion of any among Shakespeare's great quartet, but it ends twice: once with Macbeth's unforgettable "Tomorrow, and tomorrow, and tomorrow," and again (and more legitimately) with Malcolm's eminently forgettable concluding speech.

> We shall not spend a large expense of time
> Before we reckon with your several loves,
> And make us even with you. My Thanes and kinsmen,
> Henceforth be earls; the first that ever Scotland
> In such an honour named. What's more to do
> Which would be planted newly with the time,
> As calling home our exiled friends abroad
> That fled the snares of watchful tyranny,
> Producing forth the cruel ministers
> Of this dead butcher, and his fiend-like Queen
> Who, as 'tis thought, by self and violent hands
> Took off her life—this, and what needful else
> That calls upon us, by the grace of Grace,
> We will perform in measure, time, and place:
> So thanks to all at once, and to each one,
> Whom we invite to see us crowned at Scone.
> (5.7.90–105)

Macbeth's great speech, which strikes many as the last word on last words, polarizes historical or universal time, which creeps in a petty pace, and the horribly abbreviated personal, particular time of us poor players. The dramatic effect of Macbeth's speech is largely achieved by the stark contrast between temporal background and foreground. By contrast, Malcolm's closing speech, with its references to the immediate future—a kind of temporal middle ground between the vast deserts of historical time and the pitiful foreground antics—represents an attempt to close the gap between the two senses of time opened up by Macbeth's speech.

The whole of Malcolm's speech, leisurely in pace, with its lengthy period, resembles one of those seventeenth-century Claudean landscapes that gently lead the beholder's eye from foreground to middle ground to background, often with the aid of a meandering river, gently rolling hills, and a diffused light. Malcolm begins by rescinding the sobering attention to temporal background lavished by Macbeth's speech: "We shall not spend a large expense of time / Before we reckon with your several loves." He thereby abruptly returns those of us who have been unwisely tempted to loiter in that impressive but depressing and expansive time opened up by Macbeth's speech back to a contracted present, a temporal foreground. The effect is something like a loudspeaker announcement at an airport: Will all passengers please return to the present tense immediately. Through a classic example of a performative speech act, with no delay between expression of intent and its realization, Malcolm makes the first Scottish earls. The speech then proceeds from this temporal foreground to the middle ground of two specified, soon-to-be performed actions, trying Macbeth's ministers and calling back friends and allies who remain in exile. This middle ground in turn gently fades into a temporal background of unspecified future acts, all to be performed in "measure, time, and place." Whether that repair of the rupture between private or particular time and general, public, historical time is anything more than sleight of hand is open to question.

What is beyond question is that Malcolm and Macbeth are generalizing in two entirely different registers at the end of the play. Malcolm attempts to assert a sovereign's authority over the succession of moments and events, as present, immediate future, and distant future succeed one another in his speech in as orderly a manner as James could hope for the line of Stuart kings. That sense of mastery may be said to be caricatured in Macbeth's speech, where, rather than an orderly succession of three dimensions of time we encounter one dimension repeated in an idiotic stammer of three, "Tomorrow, and tomorrow, and tomorrow." Furthermore, the movement of Macbeth's speech is regressive, moving from those tomorrows to all our yesterdays, perhaps through the intermediary of "today" couched in the phrase "from day, to day." Malcolm is concerned to establish sovereignty over immediate business, and he modulates smoothly and effortlessly from the particular affairs of state he manages at the beginning of the speech to the abstractions of "measure, time, and place" at the end. But Macbeth's generalizations are wider than Malcolm's by several miles. Furthermore, Macbeth's superbly generalizing speech has the opposite effect of most generalizing at the end of a Shakespearean tragedy. Rather than effecting closure, Macbeth's speech seems designed to deprive every one of us of the sense of an ending, whether of the play or of our lives, besides disturbing from beyond the grave the new sovereign's efforts to effect closure.

Macbeth offers us two generalizing endings. We are implicitly asked to choose one toward which to show our loyalties: that is, to decide whether Macbeth's climactic speech on anticlimaxes (which alone would ensure that he and his play would have many theatrical tomorrows, and tomorrows, and tomorrows) is as sovereign as it appears to be, whether it is as general in its applications as it claims, or whether instead it merely reflects the particular circumstances and eccentric position of its speaker. Macbeth himself might very well have become a juggling fiend, like the witches he blames for his demise. Now it is he who is tempting us. He invites us to embrace his prophecy—one that, curiously unlike the witches', erases rather than announces our legacies, our futures—with unmeasured approval rather than with the more skeptical response of a Banquo.

No matter how hard we struggle to resist the implications of Macbeth's speech, that speech casts an immense shadow over Malcolm's last words. This is especially true insofar as one of the subjects of Macbeth's speech, the futility of any sense of an ending, issues a direct challenge to the aim of Malcolm's speech. The usurper upstages the legitimate sovereign in the end, making it perfectly legitimate for us to question whether Malcolm indeed comes into full—i.e., symbolic as well as actual—possession of the kingdom. Since sovereignty is so often linked in Shakespearean tragedy to the mastery promised by a generalizing rhetoric, it would not be exaggerating to say that Malcolm's sovereignty is indirectly circumscribed or impugned by his unequal performance with Macbeth in the generalizing contest Shakespeare stages at the end of the play.

A relation between generalizing and the pursuit of sovereignty is nowhere more evident than it is in *Hamlet,* the subject of my next and final section. Both *Hamlet* and the subject of a subsequent chapter, *Timon of Athens,* stage confrontations between two modes of generalizing: one linked to the representation of sovereignty in Shakespeare's plays; the other, which may be described as levelling or confounding, issuing a challenge to sovereignty and offering glimpses of contemporary political challenges and turmoil written in the margins of Shakespearean tragedy.

Generality and Sovereignty

It is the one of Shakespear's plays that we think of the oftenest, because it abounds most in striking reflections on human life, and because the distresses of Hamlet are transferred, by the turn of his mind, to the general account of humanity. Whatever happens to him we apply to ourselves, because he applies it so himself as a means of general reasoning. He is a great moraliser; and what makes him worth attending to is, that he moralises on his own feelings and experience. He is not a common-place pedant.

—William Hazlitt[55]

This aversion to personal, individual concerns and escape to generalizations and general reasonings a most important characteristic [of Hamlet].

—Samuel Taylor Coleridge[56]

Of Shakespeare's inveterate generalizers, Hamlet is most famous. Unlike the philosophical hero beloved of Coleridge and Hazlitt, the generalizing Hamlet I will represent is one for whom generalizing is a political measure, closely tied to the pursuit of sovereignty, as well as a highly particular or personal one, an attempt to accede to the potent generalizing signs of kingship he associates with his father. It is also a sort of fool's gold, or worse, a specious solution that generates more problems than it resolves.

Hamlet seems the first of Shakespeare's tragedies critically to question on a large scale the generalizing tropes of the Renaissance stage, tropes intimately connected, I have suggested, to the formation of what Stone describes as the new culture of the nation-state. It is especially concerned to differentiate various styles of generalizing: for instance, the "great moraliser" from the "commonplace pedant," as Hazlitt calls them in my epigraph. Probably not as certain as Hazlitt of his difference from the pedantic Polonius, Hamlet periodically censures his own generalizing habit. Both Polonius's foolishness and his claims to authority are so closely tied to his taste for glib generalities that, unless one adopts Coleridge's rather sympathetic view of him, it is difficult to ignore that in *Hamlet* generalizing practices—among which we should have to number the play's own—are targets of suspicion.

The impulse to generalize in *Hamlet* is so general that it "must give us pause" (3.1.68). Harry Levin writes, "The habit of generalization is strong, not merely in Hamlet but in all the others, from the sententious Polonius to the earthy Gravedigger," "all the others" sounding like Levin's self-conscious surrender to the ubiquitous generalizing habit.[57] Less self-consciously, A. C. Bradley noted, "Again and again we remark that passion for generalization which so occupied him, for instance, in reflections suggested by the King's drunkenness that he quite forgot what it was he was waiting to meet on the battlements,"[58] apparently unaware of the complicity of his own "again and again"—that is, the generalizing passion the play cunningly reduplicates in readers and viewers—and of Hamlet's own generalizing attitudes.

Sometimes characters not overly inclined to generalize are required to do so owing to a lack of information: the dearth of clarifying details, for instance, in the hazy atmosphere of act 1, scene 1. Of the appearance of the Ghost on the battlements, Horatio acknowledges, "In what particular thought to work I know not, / But in the gross and scope of my opinion, / This bodes some strange eruption to our state" (1.1.70–72). It is about precisely such a lack of information—for instance, the lack of information about Hamlet before his father's death—upon which Bradley more than once remarks in his reading of the play, and which ensures that we auditors/spectators will both participate in the play's rampant generalizing and feel uneasy about generalizing conclusions, the gross and scope of our opinions, made in the absence of details. But for the most part, generalizing in *Hamlet* is not a makeshift, a provisional exercise to fill in gaps until the particulars of the case become known. Very frequently, it is motives of a political nature that compel the play's characters to generalize.

This is indirectly implied by Hamlet and Horatio's description of Hamlet's father, a description that implies a link between generality (or universality) and sovereignty. Conversing with Horatio and the sentinels before receiving news of the Ghost, Hamlet says of his father, "A was a man, take him for all in all: / I shall not look upon his like again" (1.2.187–88). This in response to Horatio's "I saw him once; a was a goodly king" (1.2.186). Horatio's description is impersonal and starkly general, attributing to his friend's father only a single quality, and a general one at that, "goodly." Hamlet, true to his generalizing habits, takes Horatio's already broad term and broadens it further, as if to enlarge the scope of his father's sovereignty: "A was a man." By demurring from identifying particular attributes, Hamlet is able to suggest that his father was comprehensive and universal. And he ends the line with a phrase that is a signature of the broadening generalization, "all in all." As Empson has noted, clearly Hamlet intends to suggest by the general term "man" some particular attribute, and presumably one lacking in most creatures that go by the name of "man."[59]

In other words, Hamlet's remark particularizes by generalizing: it is impossible even to disentangle the particularizing and generalizing threads of Hamlet's praise of his father. That is certainly not true of Hamlet's discourse generally, where we can frequently watch the particularizing and generalizing threads of his speech in the process of becoming unraveled; where the generalization often wears the mask of the censor, radically suppressing differences; where he repeatedly has to dodge the generalizations that are aimed in his direction like so many slings and arrows; and where, generalizing, he more than once retreats in apparent embarrassment at inconsistencies in his own generalizing rhetoric. The irony of Hamlet and Horatio's universalizing Hamlet's father is that the latter doesn't show the ghost of an interest in universal categories. His is instead an ethos of personal loyalties. Old Hamlet apparently was monarch over "a bounded, localized, highly personal world, which had yet to be affected by wider notions of loyalty to more universalistic codes and ideals."[60] The old particularism and the new universalism, Old Hamlet and young Hamlet, are the real mighty opposites in the play, and for reasons broader than (though not inconsistent with) the heritage of Oedipus.

Generalizing as Suicide or Withdrawal

If generalizing is Hamlet's attempt to establish his distance from the older particularism of not only his uncle but also his father (in spite of Hamlet's universalizing descriptions of him), it still holds no fixed, stable position in the kingdom of Old Hamlet's successor. The activity of generalizing in *Hamlet* is as mercurial as Hamlet's moods, and as difficult to characterize. The generalizing impulse is compatible with (and perhaps responsible for) three of Hamlet's principal aspects: melancholy, in which mood he reduces all to a low common denominator; altruism, a possible antidote to the general and poisonous pursuit of private (or in Shakespearean parlance, "particular") interests everywhere at court; and ambition, his desire to emerge from the shadows and become the universal and representative man he thinks his father was. It is no wonder that the issue of Hamlet's generalizing is a confusing one, since he alternately generalizes both to pursue worldly power and to renounce it.

Most obviously, a generalizing turn of mind seems consistent with the first of Hamlet's images, the "romantic": distracted (Bradley accuses him of becoming so absorbed with generalizing that he "quite forgot what it was he was waiting to meet on the battlements"), dreamy, escapist (Coleridge in my second epigraph speaks of his "escape to generalizations and general reasonings" from "personal, individual concerns"). One of the most spectacular instances of protracted generalization—"To be, or not to be"—is a speech about withdrawing from the shocks of this world into a hypothetical hereafter. The speech is also an instance of that escape. To adopt J. L. Austin's terminology, Hamlet's soliloquy is a "performative utterance" that brings about a state of affairs rather than merely describing one.[61] Viewing it as performative must qualify our first impression of it as a hesitating speculation about escape from the world that steps back from the brink of action. Simply because it is a general reflection, capable of applying to a multitude of contexts beyond Hamlet's own, the speech transports Hamlet beyond the pale of immediate action, motive, or context. That the general reflection on suicide is also delivered in a soliloquy and set speech only enhances the aspect of withdrawal and helps simulate the appearance of a relatively context-independent statement.

Withdrawal is enacted at the discursive level in this soliloquy by the suppression of the first-person singular pronoun. Grammatically, two of the most prominent features of this soliloquy are the preference for the infinitive, which tends to suspend time and action in a manner fully appropriate to the meaning of the speech, and also, since this is a meditation on suicide, the marked absence of the "I." The first-person singular pronoun does not enter until Hamlet's musings are interrupted by the appearance of Ophelia. Hamlet has committed grammatical suicide by rubbing out the "I." The careful avoidance of the fully anticipated pronoun accomplishes or realizes the suicide fantasy in a manner of speaking.

The suppression of the "I" not only in Hamlet's soliloquy but in all or most instances of generalizing may be understood in a less somber way. Though Hamlet's generalizing fervor suggests to Coleridge an escapist aversion to personal concerns, that apparent aversion might be interpreted more generously, as the mark of a generous mind. In altruistic fashion, Hamlet habitually generalizes outward from his own circumstances, refusing to take himself as a particular case. Of course, Hamlet's altruistic generalizing is rooted in highly particular motives: it seems an attempt on the part of a character isolated by madness, melancholy, and a host of other circumstances to emerge from that isolation and discover by means of a generalizing discourse a common place with others. Because he is a prince, such an emergence is colored if not governed by political motives, since to be an ideal king in the new universalism of the Elizabethan age is to be general in the sense of universal: one who represents the whole political body of the nation. If considered in the light of Hamlet's political motives, "To be, or not to be," ostensibly a speech about faltering will, may be seen to possess a strong will of its own and a vaulting rhetorical ambition. A meditation on the most private of themes couched in impersonally general terms, even this speech about renunciation secretly pursues the sovereignty of the father. "Never alone / Did the King sigh, but with a general groan" (3.3.23), the obliging Guildenstern delivers. The dilated sigh that is Hamlet's soliloquy, you might say, subscribes to the same theory of kingship as does Guildenstern's flatulent bit of flattery. By means of a generalizing rhetoric, Hamlet's soliloquy aspires to deliver both the princely sigh and the "general groan" that echoes it.[62]

Generalizing as Censure and the Censure of Generalizing

But generalizing in *Hamlet* wears more sinister masks as well. Generalizing suits Hamlet in his misanthropic and misogynistic moods. "Frailty, thy name is woman" (1.2.146), he charges, criminally generalizing from his mother's instance to the whole gender. He is guilty of the same crime in his violent words to Ophelia: "I have heard of your paintings well enough. God hath given you one face and you make yourselves another. You jig and amble, and you lisp, you nickname God's creatures, and make your wantonness your ignorance" (3.1.144–48). That the second-person pronoun is identical in its singular and plural forms may have induced Hamlet to think he can get away with assuming a perfect continuity between his singular lover and a plural womankind. Or at least that potential confusion makes it difficult for us, the members of the jury, to decide whether to charge him with generalizing in the first or the second degree.[63]

Given the potentially censorious effects of generalizing instanced here, it is not surprising that Hamlet should more than once try to withdraw a generalization in midstream. This is the case in the following instance, where, as Levin notes, Hamlet is "generalizing about the tendency of human beings to generalize."[64] On the battlements, awaiting the appearance of his father's ghost, Hamlet in a general way—that is, he doesn't seem to be directly addressing either his father's situation or his own—decries "general" or popular judgments on "particular men":

> So, oft it chances in particular men
> That for some vicious mole of nature in them,
> As in their birth, wherein they are not guilty
> (Since nature cannot choose his origin),
> By their o'ergrowth of some complexion,
> Oft breaking down the pales and forts of reason,
> Or by some habit, that too much o'erleavens
> The form of plausive manners—that these men,
> Carrying, I say, the stamp of one defect,
> Being Nature's livery or Fortune's star,
> His virtues else, be they as pure as grace,

As infinite as man may undergo,
Shall in the general censure take corruption
From that particular fault.

(1.4.23–36)

Editors have tried to correct the passage by making the pronouns
consistent, undoing the sudden and agrammatical shift from the plural
"their," "they," and "these" to "His" in line 33. As Harold Jenkins notes
in the New Arden edition of the play, it is unlikely that the incongruous
singular suggests that Hamlet really has his own particular case in the
back of his mind. Jenkins proposes that the shift from plural to singular
may simply "be due to the influence of the singular *defect.*"[65] The sliding
from plural to singular strikes me as more than a grammatical slip. It
would be more accurate to say that he is trying to give grammar the
slip, as it pursues his criminally generalizing steps. In the process of
decrying generalization from a single "vicious mole of nature" to the
whole man, Hamlet catches himself generalizing, and for the sake of
consistency and scrupulousness opts toward the end of his speech for
the singular. The speech, after all, champions "particular men" who are
seen as the prey of a tendency to generalize.

Though the speech censures the generalizing turn of mind for its
censoriousness, Hamlet himself has been generalizing at several levels
in the course of the speech. First, he chooses to single out what is already
a general category rather than a particular individual and to designate
that category by a plural rather than a singular: "particular men," not a
particular man. As Levin notes, the speech moves in a progressively
generalizing direction. Hamlet begins the speech with observations
on Claudius's alcoholism, proceeds to the Danish reputation for hard
drinking, and ends with the human tendency to generalize from "the
stamp of one defect" to the whole man.[66] Finally, in choosing to regard
the opinions of the people as a unified body—that is, in choosing to
consider them generally—Hamlet of necessity generalizes. The very
phrase "general censure," harboring a fugitive generalization, may itself
be deserving of censure. In the process of describing it, Hamlet commits
the very crime he condemns, producing one of those instances of
specularity that are so common in the corridors of Elsinore, like the
avenger becoming too much like the murderer who is the object of
his revenge. The phrase "the general censure" generalizes in another
dimension as well. Jenkins observes that it may refer to either "public
opinion" or "the appraisal of the man as a whole, the overall estimate,
in contrast with the 'particular fault.' "[67] Hence, the phrase may refer
to either the censurer or the censured, or to both. Its range of reference

is too general. It may not be injudicious, therefore, to see that phrase as a miniature of the speech as a whole or in general.

To avoid resting general conclusions on a single instance, let me cite another speech from the first act of the play, in which the general again reappears soon after its banishment, like a return of the repressed, and in which Hamlet also catches himself red-handed in the act of generalizing. Following the departure of his father's spirit, an impassioned Hamlet vows,

> Remember thee?
> Yea, from the table of my memory
> I'll wipe away all trivial fond records,
> All saws of books, all forms, all pressures past
> That youth and observation copied there,
> And thy commandment all alone shall live
> Within the book and volume of my brain,
> Unmix'd with baser matter.
>
> . . .
>
> My tables. Meet it is I set it down
> That one may smile, and smile, and be a villain—
> At least I am sure it may be so in Denmark.
> (1.5.97–104, 107–9)

Of this passage Coleridge noted, "Shakespeare alone could have produced the vow of Hamlet to make his memory a blank of all maxims and generalized truths that 'observation had copied there,' followed by the immediate noting down the generalized fact, 'That one may smile, and smile, and be a villain.'"[68] The philosophical Coleridge, an adept himself when it came to generalizing, was amused at the brevity of Hamlet's conquest of *his* addiction—to generalizing. The important last line, caustic though it is, seems to me the equivalent of the sudden shift from "they" to "his" in the speech on the "vicious mole of nature": the narrowing of a broad generalization that surfaces, like an unwelcome guest, in the context of a speech overtly hostile to generalizing. The speech moves from a vow to let his father's spirit's *particular* injunction usurp the place in his memory of all the carefully collected and preserved generalities gleaned from both books and experience; to the immediate resurrection of a general statement that should need no limitation (it is hard to pick a quarrel with); to the limiting of that statement's range of reference, in order to express disgust with his own country and countrymen, to be sure, but also to reenact the far from gratuitous limiting of his own habit of generalizing.

In reviewing those last three lines about Claudius, we might recall Hamlet's line about his father, "A was a man, take him for all in all: / I shall not look upon his like again." When describing his father he aims to evoke the singular by means of the general; his father was a paragon because of his generality or comprehensiveness. In abbreviated form, it is the same praise Antony bestows on Brutus at the end of *Julius Caesar.* Hamlet's father is generalized in an honorific way, suggesting that under ideal circumstances generalizing has (or had) the function of investing particulars, relatively weak signs, in the more regal and dignified cloak of a generalization, making the weak sign the token of and partaker in a potent generality. Just as appropriately, in the lines about Claudius, the particular and general remain squared off, vying for ground, as if one of the things wrong with Claudius's Denmark is a dislocation of the relations between general rules and particular cases, as well as between general or public interests and private or particular ones.

Where Hamlet seems false in his rhetoric about his father, which to most critics seems incongruous with the Ghost, is in his suggestion that relations between public and private, general and particular, were once harmonious in his father's kingdom: that his father, Brutus-like, was a political embodiment of the concrete universal, the sole universal man in the kingdom. What seems to be the case is that the particularist system of values of Old Hamlet's Denmark largely circumvented the distinctions that were to trouble the reigns of both Elizabeth and James, dramatized in *Hamlet* by the ghostly confrontation between those mighty opposites, a particularist political order and the universalist order of the nation-state.

Generalizing as Snake Oil for the Melancholic

Nowhere is this confrontation more apparent than in the figure of Hamlet himself, who might be characterized rhetorically as an obstructed synecdoche, a prince for whom, in the new universalist culture, the ideally smooth and unforced substitutions of general and particular interests are impeded.[69] Often accused of advancing particular interests at the expense of the general welfare, James directed the same criticism at Parliament. In *Basilikon Doron* (1599), an advice book for his son Prince Henry written four years before James succeeded to the throne of England, he exhibits a suspicion of general rhetoric—in this case issuing from Parliament in the form of legislation—as do Shakespeare's plays from the same years. To his son he characterized Parliament as "the in-justest Judgement seat that may be, being abused to mens particulars: irrevocable decreits against particular parties, being given therein under colour of generall Lawes,"[70] a view that was reinforced repeatedly during his reign in England.

By contrast with the official rhetoric of James and Elizabeth, Hamlet finds the poles of his tropological being continually at odds. "Why seems it so particular with thee?" Gertrude asks her son about what seems to her an uncommonly keen response to his father's death (1.2.75). The question, like nearly every line in the play, reverberates with meanings more general than those intended. For Hamlet remains particular in another sense: he has been denied access to the potent generalizing signs of kingship. "Particular" is a word that frequently attaches to Hamlet. "Then if he says he loves you," Laertes instructs his sister, "It fits your wisdom so far to believe it / As he in his particular act and place / May give his saying deed" (1.3.24–27). "His particular act and place" serves nicely as a diagnosis of Hamlet's malaise: his place and deeds remain too particular and may not attain to what he perceives as the monumental, heroic generality of his father's.

Reversing his customary bent toward generalizing, Hamlet some- times particularizes in self-defense, to refuse the glibly consolatory generalities of his mother and uncle: "Thou know'st 'tis common: all that lives must die, / Passing through nature to eternity" (1.2.72–73). Though Hamlet is soon to strike a generalizing pose countless times, on our first meeting with him he is placed in a position where he must resist it, even to the point of playing on the very word that might designate a shared or general attitude: "Ay, madam, it is common" (1.2.74)—that is, a commonplace. If we concede that words, proper names excepted, can better deliver general categories than particulars, then wordplay might be, if not a positive step in the direction of a more particularized language, at least a refusal or corrosion of the glib generalities of ordinary language. Or, to view things from a slightly different angle, if the ordinary use of language and its commonplaces entails a "common place" or common ground, then Hamlet's wordplay in this scene and elsewhere refuses a common place, takes the common ground out from ordinary language. It divides the word from itself and makes it uncommon in the sense of new or fresh but also in the sense of not shared in common. The very word "common" suffers such a fate in Hamlet's third line in the play. Its fracturing reverberates across this scene featuring a son who is convinced that he has little in common with those who surround him: a son who is also a prince, for whom the sensation of having nothing in common translates into erosion of his representational power and potential.

Hamlet also fends off generality—the very index of his father's power in his eyes—because it seems to be tied to his melancholia.[71] A tricky thing to manage or control, generalizing may either gain for him a sense of sovereignty and centrality or, if it misfires, have the effect of canceling differences and flattening degrees, eventually producing a melancholic indifference. Though it is what one might call a necessary instrument in Hamlet's bid for sovereignty, generalizing frequently has the look of a snake oil cure or worse, a prescription that will exacerbate his symptoms rather than eliminate them.

The speech of the melancholic in many ways parodies the aspirations of the universalizing generalizer. The melancholic's speech already realizes, although in deflated form, many of the effects aspired to by generalizers in the play. The generalization by its very nature aims for a measure of independence from any particular and limiting context. To some degree, it may always be a dissimulating form of discourse insofar as the speaker of a generalization pretends that his or her speech is relatively independent from motives. The generalizing speaker's aim to transcend the limitations of contexts, to aspire to a speech not formed (or malformed) by ordinary pressures from motives and contexture, is already registered in the melancholic's relation to his speech. Hamlet's response to Polonius's query about the material he is reading, "Words, words, words," may qualify as the most extreme instance in the play of a denial of contexture. The positive disinterestedness of the generalizer, in other words, is mimicked by the indifference of the melancholic. The melancholic's speeches, the wild and whirling words that seem to have drifted to the most distant of contexts or otherwise to be without an anchor in a particular context, are frequently marked by a detachment from (and perhaps nostalgia for) the particularity of contexts. The melancholic's is (or seems) a verbal homelessness. The generalizer ordinarily aspires to a universal validity and *positive* independence from contexts for his or her speech. Sometimes it is difficult to distinguish the two, in this play that is so laden with set speeches, epigrams, and proverbial forms of speech: the enlarged vision and higher moral ground promised by the generalizing statement in *Hamlet* frequently turns out to be the verbal equivalent of a "sterile promontory," as Hamlet calls the earth in a speech before Rosencrantz and Guildenstern. That is certainly true of nearly all of Polonius's myriad generalizations. Hamlet's phrase about the great globe aptly characterizes the view from the general in this play: what the world too frequently looks like from the perspective of the universal.

It seems to me the supreme irony of the play's relation to its critics that, while perhaps troubling the generalizing impulses more than any other Shakespeare wrote, it has been subjected to those impulses more than any other work of literature. Setting aside the question of its universality, it is almost indisputably the most *universalized* of any literary work. Legions of critics have claimed for it a universality that the play itself, through its main character in relentless pursuit of a substitute and supplemental discursive sovereignty, seems to whisper to us is beyond reach of anything so provisional, moody, and malleable as a play.[72] Moreover, critical discourse almost universally fails to grasp the particular or local meanings of *Hamlet's* universalizing rhetoric, the clash of particularist and universalist political cultures.

And yet, given the play's multitude of epigrams, it is plausible to argue that the play, like its main character, pursues the sovereignty of a general truth. No less than the prince, this play that according to Hazlitt "abounds most in striking reflections on human life" is burdened with high aspirations that, again, are achieved in part by the instruments of generalizing modes of discourse. The play may even be said to be closer to the sovereignty of a general truth than any other work of literature, in no small part because of its abundance of epigrams. At times seeming openly to mock the epigrammatic style of much Seneca-inspired Elizabethan drama, *Hamlet* is notable even among Shakespeare's plays for having delivered a multitude of epigrammatic sayings into the language. According to Sister Miriam Joseph, "The quality of thought which distinguishes *Hamlet* is due in part to the large number of proverbs and sentences in the play, more than in any other by Shakespeare."[73] Shakespeare's relation to the epigram seems as ambivalent as Hamlet's to all forms of generalizing. Polonius attracts our scorn for his pretentious epigrams, by means of which he claims to be the master of particular situations. And yet, given the "epigrammatizing" in which many readers and spectators of the play indulge—that is, our tendency to remember pithy lines independently of their contexts, such as Polonius's "This above all, to thine own self be true"—it would be wrong to view the play as entirely divorced from, or merely condescending toward, Polonius's epigrammatism.

We tend to epigrammatize Shakespeare more than any other dramatist, contemporary or otherwise, even after we have factored in his enormous popularity. Critics tend to blame this habit on the carelessness of readers or the general reader/viewer's failure to grasp that all speeches in drama rely for their validity and meaning on the contexts in which they are embedded. But it is Shakespeare's frequent recourse to an epigrammatic style that is largely responsible for what we are prone to hastily dismiss as a tendency of naive readers. "Shakespeare's preeminence in sententious utterance was recognized in his own day," Sister Miriam Joseph assures us. Selections from his plays figured prominently in collections from contemporary poets such as *Belvedere* and *England's Parnassus,* both dating from 1600, the year in which Shakespeare in all likelihood began writing *Hamlet.*[74] Furthermore, Katherine Lever has demonstrated that when Shakespeare appropriated proverbs for his plays, he often reworked them to make them more compelling.[75] Such care suggests that there may be an entirely unexpected alliance between Polonius's foolish maxims and the twin aspirations of the prince and the play. And so there is. Generally speaking.

In pursuing the universality he attributed to the king his father, Hamlet has difficulty keeping distinct a species of generalizing that universalizes and one that levels or confounds. Maintaining a proper relation between these two species of generality is of the utmost importance for universalizing the heroes and monarchs of the histories and tragedies. As I shall argue in my next chapter, Shakespearean tragedy regularly makes levelling serve the purposes of its opposite, a stable hierarchy presided over by the pinnacle figure of the universal monarch. Shakespeare's last tragedy *Timon of Athens,* even more than *Hamlet,* complicates the Shakespearean paradigm for universalizing. It does so by confounding the very difference between a universal, hierarchical generality on the one hand and a levelled or confounded one on the other. Unlike *Hamlet,* which in a period of growing nationalism looks backward to an older particularist culture, *Timon* looks to the future and to another challenge to the universalist political culture of the English nation-state: a levelling or confounding form of generalizing whose political implications will be revealed in the English Civil War.

4

The Shadow of Levelling

How little connection there is between money, the most general form of property, and personal peculiarity, how much they are directly opposed to each other was already known to Shakespeare better than to our theorising petty bourgeois.

—Karl Marx[1]

For if you from nobles once take their great possessions . . . you shall in process of years confound the nobles and the commons togidder, after such manner that there shall be no difference betwyx the one and the other.

—Thomas Starkey[2]

In 1649 the Ranter Abiezer Coppe, adopting the posture of the prophet Ezekiel,[3] wrote,

> The very shadow of levelling, sword-levelling, man-levelling, frightened you, (and who, like your selves, can blame you, because it shook your Kingdome?) but now the substantiality of levelling is coming.
>
> The Eternall God, the mighty Leveller is comming, yea come, even at the door; and what will you do in that day.[4]

Coppe's lines seem suggestive for a reading of *Timon of Athens,* and not merely because he implored "rich people to give their possessions to the poor."[5] The shadow of levelling fell over England long before the fateful year that saw the beheading of an anointed English king. In 1607, shortly before the probable date of composition of *Timon of Athens,* famine had resulted in uprisings of Levellers in Northamptonshire and of Diggers in Warwickshire.[6] Though *Timon* makes less explicit reference to these events than does its nearly contemporaneous *Coriolanus,*[7] it is suffused with the idea of levelling, the play's dominant trope.

The idea of social levelling, if only as a distant possibility or phantasm, can be found in early Tudor texts as diverse as Sir Thomas Elyot's conservative treatise *Book Named The Governour* (1531) and Thomas Starkey's *Dialogue between Cardinal Pole and Thomas Lupset* (1533–36), with its frank expression of reformist ideas. But *Timon* makes a very different use of the trope of levelling than Elyot's *Book,* or even than an earlier Shakespearean play like *Henry V.* It may be historically premature to say that in 1608, to paraphrase the famous opening of Marx and Engels's *The Communist Manifesto* (1848), a shadow was haunting England—the shadow of levelling. Still, the unruly behavior of the trope of levelling in *Timon,* in comparison with its operation in works like *Henry V* and Elyot's *Book,* suggests a link between a contemporary social revolt and certain unusual features of *Timon's* rhetoric.

How Shakespearean Is It?

Timon of Athens is sometimes regarded as Shakespeare at his most unshakespearean. The play strikes many as uncharacteristically abstract, containing as it does numerous characters identified only by the profession, class, or kind to which they belong. More than one critic has labeled it "schematic."[8] To several others *Timon* is an "allegorical" play and evidence of the influence of the moralities on Shakespeare's dramatic practices.[9] It is also indisputably rough-hewn, like the Poet's "rough work" he awaits to present to Lord Timon (1.1.43).[10] Almost universally giving critics the impression of being unfinished, a draft that for no known reason Shakespeare never bothered to revise—a play, in other words, in need of fine brushwork—*Timon* may be its author's most thoroughgoing inquiry into Renaissance tragedy's generalizing practices and the relation of those practices to notions of sovereignty. Though Timon holds no office, his play is arguably as political as any that Shakespeare wrote.[11] And it may offer the most thoroughgoing challenge to Renaissance sovereignty to be found in the Shakespeare canon.

The allegorical qualities of *Timon,* like the imaginative spareness of *Coriolanus,* has seemed to many critics hard to reconcile with Shakespeare's earlier practice of tragedy, particularly the "infinite variety" of speech and characterization that has been praised throughout the critical tradition from Dryden onwards. What makes these two plays seem less than anomalous to me as the final development of Shakespeare's practice of tragedy is the extremity of their critical reflection on the related generalizing tropes of Renaissance tragedy and Renaissance sovereignty. They merely take to extremes an interrogation begun in the famous quartet of tragedies stretching from *Hamlet* to *Macbeth.*

A confrontation between two opposed sorts of generality was not uncommon in English Renaissance political rhetoric: one associated with the levelling of degree and the dissolution of social order, the other instituting and supporting a hierarchical order. One is confounding, the other universalizing. After glancing at two works—the beginning of Sir Thomas Elyot's *The Book Named the Governour* and Shakespeare's *Henry V*—which illustrate how the phantom of a social levelling is employed in the services of absolutist monarchy, I will try to show how in *Timon of Athens,* the confrontation between universalizing and levelling modes of generality becomes considerably more unruly and ungovernable than it is in Elyot's treatise or the earlier play. Elyot expunges the levelling mode of generalizing; *Henry V* employs it more subtly in the service of a universalizing mode of generality having clear affiliations with Renaissance sovereignty. *Timon* complicates both these patterns, not only by allowing levelling to run riot, in almost carnivalesque fashion, throughout the play, but also by confounding the very difference between the two modes of generalizing in the opening exchange between the Poet and Painter. In *Timon of Athens,* the confrontation of two modes of generalizing, levelling and hierarchizing, that are no longer sharply differentiated fails to yield a clear image of social order.

Opposing Generals

In *The Book Named the Governour* (1531), Sir Thomas Elyot imagines a confounding of all social rank that *Timon* speaks to in so many guises. More explicitly than Shakespeare in *Timon,* Elyot raises the specter of ancient Athenian democracy. In the second chapter of the *Book,* Athens makes an appearance as an instance of the orderless republic "where a multitude hath had equal authorite without any soueraygne": "An other publique weale was amonge the Atheniensis, where equalite was of astate amonge the people, and only by theyr holle consent theyr citie and dominions were gouerned: whiche moughte well be called a monstre with many heedes."[12] *Coriolanus,* probably contemporary with *Timon of Athens,* offers another explicit association of Athens with indiscriminating democracy. Coriolanus warns of the drift of Rome toward the catastrophic example of Greece: "Whoever gave that counsel, to give forth / The corn o'th'storehouse gratis, as 'twas us'd / Sometime in Greece— . . . Though there the people had more absolute power—/ I say they nourish'd disobedience, fed / The ruin of the state" (3.1.112–14, 115–17).[13] Shakespeare's contemporaries were notoriously partial to ancient Rome over ancient Greece. The period of Roman history stretching from Julius Caesar to Augustus was frequently cited as evidence supporting the argument for monarchy, as it was by Elyot,[14] and the English of Shakespeare's day claimed to be descended from the Romans. Ancient Greek history could also be so cited, but only in derogatory fashion, as offering an inverted image of order, the misrule that follows when power is given over to the many-headed monster, the people.[15]

Elyot summons the possibility of a confounding of all degrees so as to imply that the sole alternative to monarchy is levelling.[16] Elyot writes of the designation commonwealth or "commune weale," it "semeth that men haue ben longe abused in calling *Rempublicam* a commune weale." At least some who insist on that mistranslation suppose "that every thinge shulde be to all men in commune, without discrepance of any astate or condition," such a supposition being motivated according to Elyot "more by sensualite than by any good reason or inclination to humanite." "Commune weale" is a misnomer implying either an inversion of rank or a confounding of rank and degree altogether: "if there shuld be a commune weale, either the communers only must be welthy, and the gentil and noble men nedy and miserable, orels excluding gentilite, al men must be of one degre and sort, and a new name prouided." A new name besides "commune weale" would be required since the English "commune," like the Latin "*Plebs*," is a word "made for the discrepance of degrees, whereof procedeth ordre." A "publike weale" on the other hand—the accurate translation of the Latin *Respublica* according to Elyot—is "compacte or made of sondry astates and degrees of men, whiche is disposed by the ordre of equite and gouerned by the rule and moderation of reason."[17] The alternative to a social order based on degree and hierarchies is "perpetuall conflicte" and "uniuersall dissolution."[18] Elyot's *Book,* at its outset, performs a representation followed by a ritual expulsion of the "other" of absolute monarchy, the democratic confounding of degree—what Timon calls "the sweet degrees that this brief world affords" (4.3.255).

When King Henry disguises himself on the eve of the Battle of Agincourt in *Henry V,* the two types of generality succeed one another in the same order and to much the same effect as in the opening pages of Elyot's *Book.*[19] In what many critics regard as a supremely democratic moment, Henry, under a borrowed cloak, purports to uncloak himself in a soul-baring rhetoric. But the democratic reflections both in conversation with the common soldiers Williams, Court, and Bates and later in soliloquy are as contrived as everything else in Hal's career from *1 Henry IV* onward. They act as an inoculation against the levelling impulse. To the soldiers the disguised king says, "For though I speak it to you, I think the King is but a man, as I am: the violet smells to him as it doth to me; . . . all his senses have but human conditions; his ceremonies laid by, in his nakedness he appears but a man; and though his affections are higher mounted than ours, yet when they stoop they stoop with the like wing" (4.1.101–8). In the soliloquy that follows, rank is reinstated and safeguarded under the cloak of denying it. "And what art thou, thou idol ceremony? . . . Art thou aught else but place, degree and form, / Creating awe and fear in other men . . . ?" (4.1.237, 243–44). Were the reflection inverted—"What are place, degree, and form but idols?"—the effect of the speech would be quite different. As it is, these lines and the speech as a whole actually enlarge the scope of ceremony. The reflection "What is ceremony but place, degree, and form?" suggests that ceremony is nearly everything, another term for Renaissance Order itself.

Like Elyot in *The Book,* Henry strengthens the claims of place, degree, and form by entertaining the possibility of their levelling. The generality of the king who is but a man is subsumed within the generality of the single man who "must bear all" (4.1.230). The democratic touches in Henry's speeches serve to extend rather than limit the representativeness and therefore the claim to universality of the king. Henry strengthens the legitimacy of his claims to represent common soldiers like Williams, Court, and Bates by temporarily effacing all degrees in rank separating him from them.

With the reinstatement of place, degree, and form under the guise of their erasure, Henry becomes the universal watchman. The peasant's "gross brain little wots / What watch the King keeps to maintain the peace, / Whose hours the peasant best advantages" (4.1.279–81). One type of generality is fully within the orbit of the other. Levelling is made to serve the end of universalizing the central figure of the monarch. Even more than in Elyot's *Book,* the levelling mode of generality is disabled. In Elyot, it is ritually banished but like all banished figures— like Bolingbroke, for instance—remains a threat from the outside. In *Henry V,* it is absorbed into the ideology of absolutism and thus can no longer pose an exterior threat to that ideology.

The threat to order and degree in Elyot and *Henry V* strikes me as a theatrical one: that is, of a kind that the Renaissance stage seems particularly suited to explore. Rather than the gradual rise or slippages of degree explored in novels, Renaissance plays imagine precipitous and absolute shifts of identity—from shepherdess to princess, for example, or from monarch to common man—which are quite unlike the more gradual identity formation explored in novels like Flaubert's *Sentimental Education.* In their suddenness, theatrical changes of identity resemble the many disguisings and removals of disguises on the Elizabethan and Jacobean stages. Similarly abrupt are shifts of identity through levelling of degree, whether in political treatises or in plays, as when Hamlet ruminates on the levelling power of the grave, or Macbeth on the levelling power of the stage ("life's but a poor player"), or Henry in Sir Thomas Erpingham's cloak on the false distinctions conjured by ceremony. The abruptness of such shifts in identity has a lot to do with conditions of performance. The relative brevity of a theatrical performance requires sudden rather than gradual changes of identity, and the ending of a theatrical performance could suggest swift changes of identity on a massive scale, from characters to players.[20]

A tension between two orders of generality similar to the one informing Elyot's treatise or the scenario in *Henry V* on the eve of the Battle of Agincourt also informed the modes of production of Renaissance plays. The generality that empowers a single person to reflect the world at large is equally implicit in the monarch's status as universal representative or symbolic embodiment of the entire body politic and the player's practice of representing, in play after play, a virtual world of characters. Audiences following the season of a company of actors like the King's Men would likely have seen the mode of representation of those actors—a player embodying in play after play a world of parts—as analogous to the only form of political representation they knew, the symbolic re-presentation by the king's body of the body politic. Often in Shakespeare it is within the scope of a single play that such a concept of representation comes into play: Rosalind, Hal, and Hamlet are persons (or personae) of many parts in more ways than one. Each of these figures of Shakespearean theatricality, these brilliant players within Shakespeare's plays, is in part analogous to the comprehensive, representative, and universal figure of the monarch.

But the Renaissance theater bore equally powerful testimony to the levelling type of generality: so much so that the theater could function as a trope for levelling, as it does, for instance, in Macbeth's "tomorrow" speech" or, in more dilated form, in this memorable exchange between Don Quixote and Sancho Panza:

> "Tell me, have you not seen some comedy in which kings, emperors, pontiffs, knights, ladies, and numerous other characters are introduced? One plays the ruffian, another the cheat, this one a merchant and that one a soldier, while yet another is the fool who is not so foolish as he appears, and still another the one of whom he has made a fool. Yet when the play is over and they have taken off their players' garments, all the actors are once more equal."
>
> "Yes," replied Sancho, "I have seen all that."

"Well," continued Don Quixote, "the same thing happens in the comedy that we call life, where some play the part of emperors, others that of pontiffs—in short, all the characters that a drama may have—but when it is all over, that is to say, when a life is done, death takes from each the garb that differentiates him, and all at last are equal in the grave."

"It is a fine comparison," Sancho admitted, "though not so new but that I have heard it many times before. It reminds me of that other one, about the game of chess. So long as the game lasts, each piece has its special qualities, but when it is over they are all mixed and jumbled together and put into a bag, which is to the chess pieces what the grave is to life."

"Every day, Sancho," said Don Quixote, "you are becoming less stupid and more sensible."[21]

This bit of dialogue between the mad knight and his would-be squire, firmly linking the theater to various orders of generality, sets on a collision course two different types of generalizing. Quixote elaborates the medieval and Renaissance commonplace of the world as stage in such a way as to suggest that the theater itself is a potent generalizing instrument in at least two ways. The ending of a life resembles the end of a play in its levelling action, actors becoming again what they were before the play's beginning. No matter how we are particularized in this life, we are "all at last equal in the grave." Furthermore, the ending of every theatrical performance, no matter what its particular and immediate subjects, teaches the same universal lesson about generality. Not only do plays teach their audiences the practice of moral self-generalization, but they themselves embody generalization in a rather extreme form, since each play is implicitly interchangeable with every other, conveying the same ultimate object lesson. Quixote's parable maintains in a rather unstable equilibrium (soon to be upset by Sancho) a democratic levelling and an implicitly hierarchical universalizing.

Quixote invests an idea that could have been sketched more briefly and abstractly (especially since it was familiar even to Sancho) with ample particularity, enumerating the parts of a play whose temporary differentiation gives way to generalized undifferentiation in the end. The effect of such apparently superfluous particularizing is to establish as strongly as possible the sway of the general over the particular, both on stages and on the stage of the world. He is also playing the hypocrite. Like the old counselor Gonzago in *The Tempest,* who imagines himself king of a commonwealth without degree, Quixote aims to reinforce the difference in rank between himself, the master, and his pupil-servant Sancho, by means of a lesson whose very object is the effacement of degree. Like Henry V in a way, Quixote subordinates the levelling trope of the stage to universalizing ends. By imagining the annihilation of place, degree, and form at the end of life as at the end of a play, Quixote resuscitates himself, in Henrician style, as universal watchman of the world's stage.

Against his master's salubrious moralizing, Sancho rejoins that the comparison his master has elaborated has been in general circulation for so long that it has lost some of its patina. The ubiquity of this particular commonplace, Sancho's reply intimates, limits rather than extends its authority. Furthermore, the obtrusion of Sancho's unmistakable voice also serves as a quiet challenge to the sobering generalizing of his master. By rephrasing in his own idiosyncratic and particularizing accents the commonplace to which Quixote has just given rather conventional expression, Sancho unwittingly resists the authority of the commonplace his master has just elaborated.

The most important point for our purposes is that the Renaissance version of *theatrum mundi* could and did frequently impute a levelling and confounding force to the stage. A single performance of a Shakespeare play could therefore suggest to a Renaissance theatergoer two opposed types of generality: one type tending to concentrate representative power, like a monarch; the other tending to efface order and rank. The relation of these two types of generality in individual plays by Shakespeare is usually a good deal more fluid than it is in a monarchist treatise like Elyot's. Plays like *Hamlet, King Lear, Coriolanus,* and *Timon of Athens* grant the levelling or confounding type of generality a greater and more independent voice and make the outcome of the confrontation between the two types of generality more uncertain.

Free Drifts and Eagle Flights

The confrontation between competing orders of generality begins early in *Timon* and underlies the *paragone* of the play's opening, the stylized debate between Painter and Poet over the relative merits of their crafts.[22] The Poet is to present Timon with an allegorical poem in order to curry favor. His work doubles as a piece of flattery as well as a warning to Timon of Fortune's shifts and the effects such shifts will have on his admirers. It is an abstract of the play, encapsulating its argument. It is also general in that its theme is one of the most widely known of all medieval and Renaissance themes, the fickleness of Fortune. And it is delivered by a generalized character without a proper name. In addition, the description he gives to the Painter is fairly sketchy and devoid of visual detail.

Directing the Painter's and our attentions to the groups of anonymous senators amassing onstage (and passing offstage in this instance, to prevent the need for too many actors), the Poet speaks of his "rough work," not unlike the "rough work" that is *Timon of Athens,* in which he has "shap'd out a man" (1.1.43):

> My free drift
> Halts not particularly, but moves itself
> In a wide sea of wax: no levell'd malice
> Infects one comma in the course I hold,
> But flies an eagle flight, bold, and forth on,
> Leaving no tract behind. (1.1.45–50)

The Poet implies that "levell'd" verse—targeted at particular individuals—is of an inferior species. Owen Feltham, in his nearly contemporary *Resolves,* expresses a similar sentiment when discussing jests. One of the two "great errors" of an "offensive truth" or bitter jest is that "we descend to particulars, and by that means draw the whole company to witness his disgrace we break it on. The soldier is not noble, that makes himself sport with the wounds of his own companion. Whosoever will jest should be like him that flourishes at a show: he may turn his weapon any way, but not aim more at one than at another."[23] Feltham's analogy with the actor ("him that flourishes at a show") is telling and suggests an understanding of the theater as an institution that "halts not particularly," though we know of course that much in the plays of Shakespeare and his contemporaries was targeted at particular figures and timely issues.[24] Like the Poet's work, Shakespeare's plays, including *Timon of Athens,* though characteristically riddled with topical allusions and commentary, may give the appearance of trackless eagle flights.

The Poet's use of the word "levell'd" to apply to targeted and topical verse makes the word an equivocating and multilevelled or many layered one, since "levelled" also suggests the erasure of distinction. In 1608, this would have been the primary association of words like "level," "levelled," and "levellers." In 1607, rioters in the midlands protesting enclosures and the subsequent rises in food prices were called "levelers," and their destruction of enclosures "leveling," words which already suggest the radical proposals of the 1640s for social levelling, for the abrupt transformation of a vertical and hierarchal society.[25] The Poet's word "levell'd" therefore manages to suggest at once two opposite but equally unsatisfactory kinds of verse: verse that is highly topical and too particular and verse that is so exceedingly generalizing that, like the social levelling proposed by radicals of the 1640s, it would level all difference. Apemantus and Timon deliver levelled verses in this sense.

The Poet's claim to write untargeted verse soon proves to be misleading, for the work he writes for presentation to Timon has a precise target, namely Timon himself. As frequently was the case with Parliamentary rhetoric, James implied in a speech to Parliament in 1607, general rhetoric may serve as a smoke screen for a particular or private interest. After defining the role of Parliament, stating "the matters whereof they are to treate ought therefore to be generall," James warned, "Nor yet is it on the other side a conuenient place for priuate men vnder the colour of general Lawes, to propone nothing but their owne particular gaine, either to the hurt of their priuate neighbours, or to the hurt of the whole State in generall, which many times by vnder faire and pleasing Titles, are smoothly passed ouer."[26] Like Parliamentary rhetoric, the Poet's work that "halts not particularly" has a decidedly "particular" motive. Not only does the Poet aim at a particular target, the bounteous man he is presuming to warn, but he also has a particular motive: lavish recompense from the munificent Timon. It is no wonder then that he should favor a generalizing poetry that resembles the eagle's trackless flight, since by that means he covers his tracks. The Poet places generalizing discourse in the elevated position and the particularizing discourse—presumably bound to the land rather than moving in a "wide sea" or in the air, crawling and leaving tracks unlike the trackless generalist—in a subordinate one. As the opening scene develops, the hierarchy will be destabilized, hinting at the more massive challenges to be issued to that hierarchy later in the play.

As the conversation develops, a choric cry of "all" can be heard. "All conditions," "all minds," "all kinds of natures" are to be found at the base of Fortune's hill (1.1.53f.), setting the stage for the many "alls" that follow, the tendency of so many of the play's characters to speak and think in terms of "all." In the Poet's lines "all" designates a comprehensiveness embracing, not canceling, a multitude of degrees and ranks. It will be quite otherwise with the levelling "alls" or generalities uttered by Timon and Apemantus later in the play. The Poet includes in the undifferentiated mass of Timon's flatterers a character, Apemantus, who deplores Timon's indiscriminate bounty, and who repeatedly celebrates his own singularity: "—even he drops down / The knee before him, and returns in peace / Most rich in Timon's nod" (1.1.61–63). It is an appropriate fate for the misanthropic Apemantus, who likewise doesn't "halt particularly." Even the generalizer Apemantus, who characteristically exempts himself as a possible subject of his own Cynical generalities, is generalized by the Poet's description of the present scene, the amassing of "all conditions," "all minds." This subduing of one inveterate generalizer by another, Apemantus by the

Poet, shows a clear affiliation of generality with power. By generalizing the generalizer, the Poet disarms him in advance of our acquaintance of him, subverts Apemantus's generalizing rhetoric as an alternate center of authority.

Apemantus and Timon are generalized in the Poet's description and work in opposite ways. Apemantus is confounded, Timon universalized.[27] Apemantus is one of three characters in the play who ought not be confused with the mass of ungrateful and covetous Athenians, the other two being Flavius, Timon's loyal steward, and the general Alcibiades. By contrast, in the process of being singled out from the ranks of men ("all deserts, all kind of natures," 1.1.67), Timon is universalized. The Poet's work eventually makes of him a universal object lesson about the "quick blows of Fortune's" and the human ingratitude those blows serve to reveal (1.1.93).

Twinned with the Poet's claim for Timon's universality is a parallel claim for the universality of his poem, an "eagle flight" that "halts not particularly." But the Painter, who initially seems to be playing along with the Poet, begins to undermine the Poet's claim to universality. He first praises the work not for its wide and comprehensive range of reference but for its specificity, subsequently reinterpreting the generality of the poem as a sign not of the universal but of the common. Interrupting the Poet's description of his work, the Painter affirms,

> 'Tis conceiv'd to scope.
> This throne, this Fortune, and this hill, methinks,
> With one man beckon'd from the rest below,
> Bowing his head against the steepy mount
> To climb his happiness, would be well express'd
> In our condition.
>
> (1.1.74–79)

The word "scope," while embracing our modern sense of "range" and "breadth" (and therefore one meaning of "general"), has as its primary sense in this passage its original meaning of "target," "aim" (Gk. *skopos*, target), as well as its derivative meaning of "aim" in the sense of "purpose."[28] The word connotes precision, accuracy of aim. What the Painter means is that the poem hits our own situations as artists: it is especially apt to describe us. Presumably he also means that the poem has scope in the sense of breadth enough to apply to its maker and his interlocutor as well as to its thinly veiled subject, Lord Timon. "Scope" seems especially well suited to evoking the particular in the general and the general in the particular. Attention to the phrase also raises the question of the "scope" of Shakespeare's play: that is, whether it has breadth enough to comprehend all members of its audience; whether in fact, as many critics have suggested, it was composed for a more specialized and aristocratic audience—a more specific target group—and therefore did not need the broad scope of Shakespeare's other tragedies (it is almost universally held not to possess scope in this sense);[29] and whether the play, like many others he wrote, did not have scope in the other sense, a topical reference or particular target in the contemporary political scene, like the munificent King James, for instance, as Coppélia Kahn has recently argued.[30] Just as the word "scope" may subtly challenge the hegemony of the general in the Poet's work by bringing in the idea of particular "target" or "aim," which the Poet's description conceals, so does his repetition of "this" surreptitiously challenge the Poet's refrain of "all" for the purpose of limiting his rival's claim to universality.

As the colloquy unfolds, the Poet must redefine his "scope" or aim. The Poet's reach for a wide and universal view founders when the Painter inverts the values attaching to particular and general. Having already praised the poem for its precision or scope, he begins to mock it because of what he now perceives to be its commonplace generality. In a way he is thoroughly consistent, but simply working from a different set of assumptions than the Poet's, assumptions that degrade the general and elevate the particular in art. Stressing the emblematic aspect of the poem, the Painter nudges it toward a generality that the Poet is now anxious to deny; the Poet's stress on the narrative element of his poem— wait, there's more besides an all-too-familiar and static moral emblem— is an implicit claim for its particularity. In a way he has retreated from his early claim not to halt particularly. Poet and Painter reverse roles. It is now the Poet who is eager to claim a certain particularity for his work. The Painter, taking the offensive, seeks to limit its importance by insisting on its generality. The role reversal takes place because the "generality" of the poem has been devalued, being no longer the sign of a rare high-mindedness but rather of an all-too-common vision.

Upon hearing the Poet describe that segment of his poem where Fortune, and in turn the fortunate man's suitors or "dependants," spurns the man formerly favored by Fortune, the Painter responds, " 'Tis common. / A thousand moral paintings I can show / That shall demonstrate these quick blows of Fortune's / More pregnantly than words" (1.1.91– 94). With the deflationary phrase " 'Tis common" the Painter shakes considerably the hierarchy of general and particular so carefully established by the Poet. Seeking one kind of generality—a high-mindedness or generosity that flies too high to take note of particulars—he achieves quite another: the crawling, not soaring, generality of platitude. From being the mark of a certain nobility of mind, capable of eagle flights so high that individuals become a blur, generality becomes a sign of the flat or even flatulent. From eagle-ité to égalité, you might say. A second demotion of generality will occupy the latter end of this scene. Following the demotion of the general from poetry to platitude, it falls (as if to presage the fall of the generalist Timon, who in his perfectly indiscriminate generosity at the beginning of the play also "halts not particularly") from commonplace to curse, from ineffectual but harmless platitude to Apemantus's and Timon's indiscriminate raillery.

We have already been prepared for such a demotion of the general and the generalizing turn of mind in the very first lines of the play, in which the Painter's wide and commonplace remark is deflated by the Poet, who is soon to be repaid in kind.

> Poet. Good day, sir.
> Pain.   I am glad y'are well.
> Poet. I have not seen you long; how goes the world?
> Pain. It wears, sir, as it grows.
> Poet.   Ay, that's well known.
>   But what particular rarity, what strange,
>   Which manifold record not matches?
>   (1.1.1–5)

These opening lines set the stage not only for the large-scale generalizing that goes on throughout the play but also for the massive challenges issued to the "general" in this play, including challenges to the authority of the general Alcibiades, to the heady generalizing rhetoric of Apemantus and Timon, to the generalizing tropes of the Renaissance stage itself, nowhere more evident in the Shakespeare canon than in *Timon,* and to the universalizing that helped support Renaissance absolutism.

The latter is challenged most radically by the confounding of the very distinction between a generalizing that levels differences of degree and a universalizing that establishes rather than undoes a hierarchical order in the same manner that the monarch, according to Hobbes, served to give form and order to the (hypothetical) riot of particularity of an ungoverned multitude. Hobbes imagines a people without a sovereign representative, a *universal* figure who will unite the shapeless multitude into a body politic or commonwealth, as a nightmare of unrelieved particularism: "And be there never so great a Multitude; yet if their actions be directed according to the particular judgments, and particular appetites, they can expect thereby no defence, nor protection, neither against a common enemy, nor against the injuries of one another."[31] A similar association of generality with sovereignty and a stable political order lies beneath Sir Edward Coke's pronouncement, in the *Institutes,* "It is to be observed though one be chosen for one particular county, or borough, yet when he is returned, and sits in parliament, he serveth for the whole realm, for the end of his coming thither as in the writ of his election appeareth, is generall."[32] The Poet's privileging of the general would seem consistent with and accommodating to the dominant Renaissance political rhetoric, which likewise tended to privilege the general over the particular and the public over the private.

The other mode of generality is precisely that which sovereignty acts as protection against: without sovereignty, a preacher warned in a sermon at Paul's Cross in March 1642, "the honourable would be levelled with the base, . . . and all would be . . . huddled up in an unjust parity."[33] Or as the *Homily of Obedience* of 1547 imagined the abolition of private property, "Take awaye kings, princes, rulers, magistrates, judges, and such states of God's order no man shal ride or go by the high waie unrobbed, no man shall slepe in his owne bed unkilled, no man shall kepe his wife, children and possessions in quietness, all thynges shall be comon."[34] This second form of generality—generality as the levelled and confounded—is roughly the one familiar to Apemantus the Cynic and to Timon in his misanthropic phase. A memorable and emblematic instance of it is to be found in Timon's instructions to the Lords at the feast in which he serves up warm water instead of food. Immediately before delivering a kind of antigrace, Timon instructs his false friends, "Each man to his stool, with that spur as he would to the lip of his mistress. Your diet shall be in all places alike. Make not a City feast of it, to let the meat cool ere we can agree upon the first place" (3.6.64–67). The abolition of differences of degree is imagined throughout the play, as in Timon's instructing the Senators, "Tell Athens, in the sequence of degree, / From high to low throughout, that whoso please / To stop affliction, let him take his haste, / Come hither, ere my tree hath felt the axe, / And hang himself" (5.1.207–11). But the most disturbing challenge to degree in the play is issued by the Poet, who undoes the very difference between a generalizing that undoes difference and one that helps to support it.

The dialogue between Poet and Painter invites us to make the distinction between two types of generality, even as the Poet's description of his work frustrates that task. Timon, "one man beckon'd from the rest below," is singled out not from a shapeless mass as Hobbes imagines the unrepresented multitude. Rather, he is beckoned from what is already a hierarchically ordered sphere, more Elizabethan than

Athenian: the base of Fortune's mount "is rank'd with all deserts." It is not a chaotic and democratically levelled swarm at the base of Fortune's hill, which is instead "lined in ranks by men of all degrees and worth,"[35] all laboring to improve their states. Conversely, Fortune's beckoning of Timon from the ranks of men threatens to obscure difference, erasing old ones and establishing new differences where there once was parity. When Fortune beckons Timon, her "present grace to present slaves and servants / Translates his rivals. . . . All those which were his fellows but of late, / Some better than his value, on the moment / Follow his strides" (1.1.73–74,80–82). The anxieties these lines would most likely have produced in the men of rank that might have viewed the play (there is no evidence that it was ever performed in Shakespeare's lifetime) would be exactly those produced by the newly wealthy of Shakespeare's day produced by an emergent capitalism. Essentially, Timon in his two phases, philanthropic and misanthropic, speaks to closely related anxieties about rank in Elizabethan England: the fluidity of rank produced by a sometimes impoverished nobility and enriched gentry and yeomanry;[36] and the less and less implausible effacement of rank trotted out in political treatises and sermons alike as a nightmare fantasy that only monarchy can avoid, but soon to be advocated by radical preachers and pamphleteers of the middle of the century, like Gerard Winstanley.[37]

In the Poet's colloquy with the Painter, order (based on rank and degree) and orderlessness (imagined as a confounding of all degree), and the two modes of generalizing rhetoric associated with them, are difficult to extricate from one another's grasp. Like the beckoning of the newly wealthy of Elizabethan and Jacobean England by Fortune's hand, the singling out of one man from a multitude in the Poet's work—on first glance appearing to be a primal scene of the establishment of social order and hierarchy—produces, paradoxically, an effacement of social difference. The difference between the two modes of generalizing (and the two senses in which Timon is general, as universal or a summation of mankind and as a confounder of differences) is both proffered to the reader in the exchange between Poet and Painter and withdrawn, like a hand tantalizingly filled with gold. When Fortune singles him out, making him potentially a figure of some universality, the subject of a poem (or play), she produces a partial levelling of social rank. It is as though the distinction between two opposed forms of generality, hierarchizing and levelling or confounding, is itself in danger of being confounded. Though the scene of Timon's election is decidedly vertical, Fortune's high hill—and "hill and valley were well recognised class symbols in the seventeenth century"[38]—the scenario described by the

Poet hints at the horizontal and levelled. In this respect Fortune's hill is like another promontory, the human nose. Asking Alcibiades' whores Phrynia and Timandra to spread venereal diseases far and wide, Timon inveighs,

> Down with the nose,
> Down with it flat, take the bridge quite away
> Of him that, his particular to foresee,
> Smells from the general weal.
>
> (4.3.159–62)

The rhetoric of the play everywhere exhibits the friction and contestation between two orders of generality enacted in the Poet's exchange with the Painter. The play's predominant style is decidedly epigrammatic. If the epigram is a rhetorical form whose boundaries, far from confounded, are exceedingly clear, then the epigrammatic style, even during Timon's scenes of misanthropic rage, may work to give the impression of order. No discursive form is ostensibly more self-contained and protective of its boundaries than the epigram, which in this respect resembles the greedy members of an atomistic Athenian society. Many of Timon's epigrams, whose aim is to confound or deny differences, assert a kind of order even as they attempt to deny it. The largely epigrammatic *Timon* therefore counteracts at a rhetorical level the confounding that repeatedly takes place at the level of the referent, so that the sense of order restored at the end of the play seems to have been present all along in latent form.

The internal resistance of Timon's epigrams to their own purposes may account for their ceaselessness and energy, their tendency to be emitted in volcanic eruptions—as if Timon were trying to batter down the all-too-distinct boundaries of the epigram. The satirical epigram exhibits very well the difference between two orders of generality: a confounding of difference on the one hand, and an assertion of authority—a centralizing of discursive power—on the other. In a sense, each of Timon's satirical epigrams reenacts the situation described in the Poet's verses: through the epigram, Timon lays claim to an olympian vista, even as the epigram acts to erode or efface the differences of those laboring down below.

A Particular General

When a soldier addresses the practical Alcibiades in the penultimate speech of the play as "My noble general," the phrase has a peculiar ring to it, quite unlike the sound of Brutus's being addressed with the title of "general," both in the sense of military leader and in the honorific sense of the only man among the conspirators who entered upon the action without private or particular cause, but only for the "general good."[39] "Noble general" seems almost an oxymoron in the context of this play, as generalizing is so often connected with confounding and the dissolution of order. Also, Alcibiades is the play's pragmatist, quite unsuited to generalizing or theorizing in the manner of the philosopher Apemantus or the misanthrope Timon.[40] Nevertheless, Alcibiades comes across in the final scene in large measure as an image of the ideal Renaissance sovereign, tempering punishment with mercy, avoiding the excesses of Timon's rage, and above all articulating the strategy so characteristic of the monarchical exercise of power: the reliance on the force of the example, subjected to a spectacular punishment.[41] Those whom the Senator "shall set out for reproof" shall "fall, and no more" (5.4.57–58). His refusal to punish indiscriminately is notable not so much as an expression of mercy but as a promise to reinstate difference, including the all-important differences of rank and degree banished by the satirical generalities of Timon and Apemantus.

But Alcibiades diverges from the Renaissance sovereign in his prominent lack of investment with any symbolic generality or universality. In part he denies himself that universality by his aggressive pragmatistm. It is therefore appropriate, but ultimately disturbing to the ideology of absolutism, that the ending of the play features rhetoric that insists on a return of the banished Particular. Shakespeare's tragedies and histories usually move up to a generalizing register in their final moments, both to impart a sense of closure, of summing up, and also to support the sense of political continuity that the endings of those plays are so concerned to establish through figures like Richmond, Bolingbroke, Malcolm, and Fortinbras.[42] The interests of political continuity and stability are served by a generalizing rhetoric that implies political reunification and an end to faction or particularism under the succeeding sovereign, and that exerts a centripetal force, reversing the dispersions of both accidents and meaning and restoring a strong and centralized rhetorical order.

But the ending of *Timon* lacks anything like a universalizing voice commonly provided at the end of a Shakespearean tragedy or history play. Instead, a sustained campaign is waged on behalf of the particular, or the Exception to general laws or rules.[43] This inversion of the Shakespearean pattern might seem appropriate on the grounds that the setting of the play, ancient Athens, represented the polar opposite of monarchy and civic order for the Elizabethans. Lacking a sovereign, it is also appropriate that such a people lack a sovereign voice. Having no political order mirroring what the Renaissance perceived to be the universal order, ranked in every sphere in all "The sweet degrees that this brief world affords" (4.3.255), ancient Athens may have no figure of universality, no generalizing voice of the universalizing kind, but only two of the levelling kind (Timon and Apemantus).

A more complex way of putting this, consistent with the argument I have been building throughout this discussion, would shift the play's criticism from Athenian democracy to Jacobean absolutism. The play refuses the cathartic expulsion (as in Elyot) or the appropriation (as in *Henry V*) of the democratic levelling of "sweet degrees" by substituting for the orderly and carefully staged confrontation of the two generalizing tropes, levelling and universalizing, their confusion or confounding. The play could then be read as disabling the mechanisms for universalizing that were so important for Renaissance sovereigns and Renaissance stages alike. Indeed, Timon's and *Timon's* lack of a wide appeal may amount to something like a political statement. The play may be said to be about its (apparent) failure as a play. Translated into political terms, Timon's lack of the universal and representative qualities of Shakespeare's other tragic heroes may imply a criticism at the least of other stage representations of the sovereign as universal, though such a lack is also fully appropriate to what most Elizabethans would have perceived as a disordered political context in which sovereignty rested in that many-headed monster, the people.

This play moves so insistently in a generalizing register that it is hard to imagine a movement toward a higher level of generality at the end of the play. Instead of a choric generality (usually invested in a particular figure of authority, such as Prince Escalus, Richmond, or Marcus Andronicus), the ending of *Timon* features solo voices all speaking on behalf of the Exception. Timon's is the first to be heard. Of his faithful steward Flavius he says, "Forgive my general and exceptless rashness, / You perpetual-sober gods! I do proclaim / One honest man. Mistake me not, but one" (4.3.499–501). Similarly, a messenger bringing news of the strength of Alcibiades' army. At the end of his report he provides a personal detail, whose subject is the particular amity that overcame the general enmity of opposed forces:

> I met a courier, one mine ancient friend,
> Whom, though in general part we were oppos'd,
> Yet our old love made a particular force,
> And made us speak like friends.
>
> (5.2.6–9)

And in the final scene, the Senators let go a chant of "not all" to the general Alcibiades, who begins to look like yet another generalist, another Apemantus or Timon, in his hesitation to make the effort to cull out those who have offended. The Second Senator protests, "We were not all unkind, nor all deserve / The common stroke of war," and the First Senator urges, "All have not offended. . . . Like a shepherd, / Approach the fold and cull th'infected forth, / But kill not all together" (5.4.21–22, 35, 42–44). The entreaties on the behalf of exceptions are made in such a way as to respect the sway of the general. "We were not all unkind," the Second Senator says to Alcibiades. In itself, the Second Senator's appeal seems to reverse the expected pattern of generalizing at the close. But it is delivered by a character who is generalized by virtue of his designation only by his position, not by his proper name. And the phrasing itself respects the precedence of general over particular. Besides its obvious meaning, "We were not all unkind" means something like the following: General, we were not all ungeneral, we did not all act in violation of our common nature. (The line builds upon a continual play on the meanings of "kind," that word of category or class that summarizes the play's interest in the kinship between kindness, or benevolence, and "kind"-ness, or general types and universal claims.) In other words, the protests on the behalf of the Exception leave unchallenged the sway of the conquering general, whose power and influence dominate nearly every aspect of this schematic and allegorical play.

Apemantus's Ape

Timon's lack of tragic universality is also apparent in the idiosyncratic way in which Shakespeare employs the figure of the double in this play. Shakespeare's doubling of the figure of the misanthrope exemplifies a common form of generalizing in Shakespeare: the doubling of character, usually tied to a doubling of the plot. Of course, double plots may serve the function of particularizing as well as generalizing. Clearly Shakespeare is at least as interested in the distinctions between Lear and Gloucester or between Hamlet, Horatio, Laertes, Pyrrhus, and Fortinbras as he is in a widening circle of resemblances that helps to generalize the protagonist. But there is no need to decide whether doubling in Shakespearean tragedy is primarily of a particularizing or a generalizing cast. For ordinarily the two form part of a single process: the tragic hero is differentiated from all the others but only to be generalized, to become the exception who is, like the absolute sovereign, most representative. Thus, Brutus is singled out because of his absolute and overriding concern with the general at the expense of the singular and particular: "He only," Mark Antony eulogizes, "in a general honest thought / And common good to all, made one of them" (5.5.71–72). The Elizabethan double plot, with its double suggestion of sameness and difference, its double movement of differentiation and generalization, like two strands of the double plot's double plot, is an effective device for fostering the end of particularizing in the service of universalizing. But *Timon of Athens* doesn't sufficiently differentiate its two misanthropes to serve the characteristic purpose of doubles in Shakespearean tragedy: to help universalize the tragic hero.

In *Timon,* the close working relationship between the generalizing and particularizing functions of Shakespeare's doubles falls apart. Timon (in his misanthropic phase) and Apemantus are too similar in speech and attitude. And rather than reserving for the audience or other characters the task of gauging the degree of their sameness and difference, the playwright leaves it largely to the characters themselves to insist on their difference. Needless to say, they doth protest too much, like the endlessly interchangeable lovers in *A Midsummer Night's Dream.* For Timon, Apemantus isn't the real thing, the authentic misanthrope or true-blooded generalist, because his misanthropy is contingent, conditioned rather than freely chosen. It is caused, Timon maintains, by his *permanently* low social position, which hasn't allowed him to taste other "sweet degrees" or stations and the points of view that frequently go with them (4.3.251–77). For Apemantus, Timon is not the true article because his misanthropy is contingent, caused by the *temporary* and presumably reversible condition in which he now finds himself (4.3.241–44). Each sees the other's misanthropy as enforced by conditions: in the one case stable and more or less permanent, in the other temporary.

The Shakespearean theater as a whole would more likely ratify Timon's understanding of what it takes to have the credentials to generalize. It is implied that Apemantus cannot legitimately generalize because he hasn't played more than one role of the many possibilities open to the human actor. Apemantus's is close to a generalizing by default. He generalizes on a slender foundation, growing out of a dearth, not a wealth, of particulars. For Apemantus, Timon's is a generalizing too conditioned by particulars, the contingencies and accidents of his fallen social condition. For Timon, Apemantus is a leveller, lacking a universal perspective and instead indiscriminately applying the conditions and outlook of his own low degree.

Witnessing two addicted generalizers insisting on their singularity has a comic edge to it. But it is not merely hypocrisy that causes them mutually to insist on the distance between them. For ordinarily in tragedy, the protagonist must be sharply differentiated and particularized before s/he can become general in the sense of widely representative. Of course, neither Timon nor Apemantus wants to become representative in the sense that Richard II or Hamlet or even Lear hungers to do. That is, they express no desire to become universal themselves but only to establish their credentials to generalize. Generality for this latter protagonist of Shakespeare's is a decidedly scriptive or discursive pursuit. Both Timon and Apemantus—and they are similar in this respect to their near-contemporary, Coriolanus—want to be able to represent the people through their general propositions, but decidedly not to function as the people's representatives.[44] In a sense they are striving for the more impersonal, ambitious, and absolute generality of the playwright rather than the generality of a tragic protagonist. Timon, in other words, may not be as different from Prospero as he would at first appear. He may be prologue to the great wizard of Shakespeare's final play.

Timon's specific variation on the theme of the tragic hero as generalist may be traced to differences in Elizabeth's and James's rules. Like Shakespeare's earlier tragic protagonists—Richard II and Brutus, for instance—Elizabeth embodied a sovereign generality through the ubiquitous theatrical pageantry of her reign and in the elaborate Tudor myth woven around her by others. The authority of the more removed James, on the other hand, was established by less theatrical, less bodied, and more discursive or scriptive means, by means of his career as an author. In this respect he is closer to Timon and Coriolanus, for whom the pursuit of generality takes the specific form of a discursive rage to generalize, not the impulse theatrically to embody the general or universal. In a sense, Timon is the symbolic embodiment of the general or universal in his early philanthropic phase; in his misanthropic phase, he becomes more like James, insofar as his persistent claims to universality have a predominantly discursive foundation. Shakespeare's earlier heroes, though skillful enough at speaking generally (a requirement for traversing the boards of the Elizabethan stages), were also the theatrical embodiments of generality. For his later protagonists, the claim to generality resides increasingly in rhetoric, and in a rhetoric that seems monochromatic compared to that of Shakespeare's earlier heroes.[45]

Not only Shakespeare's tragic protagonists but the plays themselves have a considerable investment in the legitimacy of generalizing. This is especially true of a play like *Timon*, which features so many representative characters or types, where every character is a walking generality, and where so much of the expression in the play is formal or conventional.[46] What makes *Timon* a far more estimable play than most critics would allow (the play has a way of making churls of us) is its willingness to take rather extreme measures to interrogate the faith in speaking generally on which its own claims to authority ultimately rest. *Timon* doesn't exactly shake that faith in generalizing, as Hiram Haydn has argued that leading skeptical figures (Montaigne, Machiavelli, Bruno, Agrippa) of what he has termed the Counter-Renaissance were engaged in doing.[47] Rather, it gives surprisingly free reign to a mode of generalizing, levelling, whose shadow once supported monarchical order but would increasingly come to threaten it, especially in the more radical political and religious rhetoric of the seventeenth century. *Timon* comes closer than any other play by Shakespeare—closer even than its nearest kin, *King Lear* and *Coriolanus*—to entertaining the fantasy of a levelled humanity before reinstating difference.

To end, as Shakespeare so often does, where we began: how Shakespearean is it? Those very qualities that have caused many critics to brand the play as unshakespearean seem to me to situate it well within Shakespeare's tradition of writing plays that reflect and comment on the theater, including the ideological underpinnings of Renaissance theater. Though *Timon of Athens* features no magician-playwright in command of the stagelike space of an island, no soused Sly as audience for a troupe of actors, no itinerant players, and no tragical comedy put on by a group of unlettered Athenian artisans, *Timon's* generality and abstractness help make it one of Shakespearean tragedy's most vigorous acts of self-examination.[48] Timon—as well as his doubles in the play, Apemantus and Alcibiades—falls within the tradition of generalizing hero, or hero as generalist, stretching at least from Brutus and Hamlet through Othello, King Lear, and Macbeth.[49] Like its contemporary *Coriolanus, Timon* makes the generalizing practices of the Shakespearean hero suspect and open to contestation, and thereby subjects to close scrutiny what might be called the generalizing tropes of the Renaissance stage. Were we to concentrate less on the striking differences between *Timon's* quasi-allegorical characters and what appear to be the studies in individual motivation in his other tragedies, and more on the generalizing practices shared by playwright and characters in both *Timon* and its predecessors, then the place of this apparently anomalous play in the family of Shakespearean tragedy would I think become clearer.

Part III

❖

Visualizing

5

EYE, CLAUDIUS

... remain / Here in the cheer and comfort of our eye.
                                        —Claudius, 1.2.115–16

oucault writes that, after the Renaissance, in what he calls the
Classical period, "The profound kinship of language with the
world was . . . dissolved. The primacy of the written word went into
abeyance. And that uniform layer, in which the *seen* and the *read,* the
visible and the expressible, were endlessly interwoven, vanished too.
Things and words were to be separated from one another. The eye
was thenceforth destined to see and only to see, the ear to hear and
only to hear."[1] It will be my contention that eye and ear are already
going their separate ways in Shakespeare's middle and later plays, especially the tragedies. The capacity of the verbal to represent the visual,
and vice versa, is regularly challenged and diminished in those plays.
The increasingly strained relations between the visual and verbal will
have enormous consequences at every level of Shakespeare's dramatic
practice, since the rhetorical theater of the Renaissance presupposed a
relative ease of translation between the verbal and visual. In the classical
period, the increasing division of labor between eye and ear will, in the
theatrical sphere, be manifested in the adoption of movable scenery
and the rise of the proscenium arch, to name only the most significant
developments. In the political sphere, such division will issue in the
weakening of the bond between power and visual display. It may be

possible to see—or hear—such developments prefigured in the growing incommensurability of the visual and verbal in Shakespeare's series of tragedies beginning with *Hamlet.*

Hamlet translates the rivalry of the two kings and brothers Claudius and Old Hamlet into a parallel rivalry between eye and ear. By the end of act 1, Claudius has come to be associated with the sense of sight and the Ghost of Old Hamlet with hearing. The strained relation between the visual and verbal becomes so pervasive a concern of the play that the fraternal rivalry on which the plot hinges may seem little more than the initial, unornamented statement of this theme with so many complex variations.

Public Eyes and Private Ears

In the Council Scene, both King and Queen favor visual metaphors. Claudius asks his nephew/stepson to "remain / Here in the cheer and comfort of our eye" (1.2.116): the eye, as Harold Jenkins notes, frequently serving as a "metonymy for the royal presence."[2] The synecdoche toward the beginning of Claudius's speech, "and our whole kingdom / To be contracted in one brow of woe" (1.2.3–4), represents Denmark as an eye. His referring to his own supposedly alloyed feelings as "With an auspicious and a dropping eye" (l. 11) reinforces his association with the sense of sight.

The councillor Polonius similarly favors ocular terms, not only in signature phrases like "Look you" and "Mark you," but also in his lesson in spying to Reynaldo in act 2, scene 1. In general, the family of Polonius holds to what might be called the sovereignty of the eye, although in this sphere, as in that of Danish politics, they may owe their allegiance to the wrong king. It is the ear that is dangerous to Ophelia, according to her brother's warning: "Then weigh what loss your honor may sustain / If with too credent ear you list his songs" (1.3.29–30). And following Laertes' lengthy sermon Ophelia assures him, "I shall th'effect of this good lesson keep / As watchman to my heart" (1.3.45–46), as if the eye were the wise schoolmaster that protects Virtue from the pandering ear. Early associations of the eye with the usually treacherous exercise of power, with the authoritarianism of Polonius, and with the usurper Claudius help prepare for the abundance of auricular metaphors in Hamlet's interview with the Ghost in act 1, scene 5.

Though beginning the first act as a kind of dumb show or speechless picture ("This spirit, dumb to us," Horatio says [1.1.176]), the Ghost becomes by the end of the act a disembodied voice. Tracing the

136

Ghost's progress in act 1 will show him to be a prototype of the many dissociations of word and image in the play, dissociations that mark Hamlet's and Ophelia's madness and that also, according to Hamlet, characterize the vulgar theatrical taste of the groundlings, which runs to "inexplicable dumb-shows and noise" (3.2.12). No one, I think, would accuse *Hamlet* of adding up to dumb-shows and noise, yet the phrase captures the play's widespread verbal-scenic dissociations. During the first two scenes the keepers of the watch repeatedly enjoin the Ghost to "speak." At the end of act 1, the roles have been reversed. No longer a silent illusion but rather a voice sans form, the Ghost commands the sentinels and officers to speak, to "swear" an oath to remain speechless about what they have seen. As the Ghost moves from a figure of pure visibility to one of pure audibility in act 1, the ear itself seems to ascend in position in steps and stages.

At the beginning of act 1, the eye appears sovereign. The sentinels' "watch" will be instrumental, presumably, in defending Denmark. The difficulty of seeing, of piercing through all the darkness and haze, in the opening scene only underscores the importance of the gaze. All the stress is on the wonderment of "what we have two nights seen" (1.1.36), but without the suggestion that there is the ghost of a difficulty translating spectacle into report. Barnardo will "assail" the ears of Horatio, "That are so fortified against our story" (1.1.34–35).

In the space between the two appearances of this "vision," "image," or "sight" in the opening scene, the ear assumes command, in the tales, whispers, and rumors circulating among the watchmen. After the second attempt to make the Ghost speak fails, it is no longer the "approval" of Horatio's eyes that is needed (l. 32), but tales that might be summoned to help explain the vision. The crowing of the cock, which causes the Ghost to start "like a guilty thing / Upon a fearful summons" (ll. 153–54) and disappear, seems a cue for the subsequent dominance by the ear. "I have heard," Horatio begins his story about ghosts returning to their confines at cockcrow (l. 154). The rumor-filled speech that follows, delivered by a character whose very name (Horatio, *oratio*) suggests an allegiance to the kingdom of the ear, is saturated with sounds and syllables that reverberate with the word "ear": "in earth or air, / Th'extravagant and erring spirit hies/ To his confine" (ll. 158–60). Marcellus's rejoinder begins with another ear-tickling rumor, "Some say" (l. 163), and ends with a reference to witches' "charms": a word derived from L. *carmen*, song, indisputably aligned with the auditory.[3] Those charms may be staved off, Marcellus says, by another sound, a kind of countercharm. At Christmas the cock crows all night; "The nights

137

are wholesome, then no planets strike, / No fairy takes, nor witch hath power to charm, / So hallow'd and so gracious is that time" (ll. 167–69).

Horatio ratifies this hearsay about a sound: "So have I heard and do in part believe it" (l. 170). What is merely heard, even when seconded by another hearing, can only elicit partial or tentative belief, whereas the eye is sovereign over the domain of truth: "Foul deeds will rise, / Though all the earth o'erwhelm them, to men's eyes," Hamlet says at the end of the next scene (1.2.257–58). And the skeptical Horatio, when converted to belief, swears, "Before my God, I might not this believe / Without the sensible and true avouch / Of mine own eyes" (1.1.59–61). By the end of the opening act, eye and ear are polarized *within* a single character, a voiceless vision on the one hand and a disembodied voice (echoed by unsubstantiated hearsay) on the other. The opening scene prepares us for the further distancing of the two senses as a difference *between* two characters, brothers and rivals.

The glittering spectacle of Claudius's court in act 1, scene 2 again grants precedence to the eye, but in such a way as to make us suspicious not only of what we see before us but also of the very instruments by which we see. The King and Queen, I have already noted, both employ visual metaphors in this scene. Laertes' acknowledgment that he "came to Denmark / To show my duty in your coronation" (l. 53), before Hamlet gets in his lines about "shows"; Hamlet's cryptic rejoinder to his stepfather, "Not so, my lord, I am too much in the sun" (l. 67), meaning in part, "you shine on me or favor me too much"; the Queen's urging Hamlet, "let thine eye look like a friend on Denmark" (l. 69); Hamlet's contemptuous cataloging of the external and visible trappings of showy mourning (ll. 77–86); Claudius's request that Hamlet "remain / Here in the cheer and comfort of our eye" (l. 115–16); and his subsequent "This gentle and unforc'd accord of Hamlet / Sits smiling to my heart" (ll. 123–24) after his wish has been honored: all suggest associations of the eye with misleading appearances and with the treacherous exercise of power. No longer the confident ratifier of truth that it was in the opening scene, sight seems the most errant and uncertain of senses in this, the second scene of the play.

Toward the end of the scene, after its visual impact has lessened considerably with the departure of the King and Queen and their retinue, ocular terms still persist, indicating that the eye's sovereignty is independent of the staging, the directly visual interest of the present scene. Following the memorable associations forged by Claudius between the eye and the royal presence, the references to the visual return to a much more homely register. Horatio's and Hamlet's pleasantries "I am glad to see you well" and "I am very glad to see you" (1.2.160,167)

138

are followed by a playfully sardonic exchange: "My lord, I came to see your father's funeral," "I think it was to see my mother's wedding" (176,178). Hamlet's woeful "Would I had met my dearest foe in heaven / Or ever I had seen that day, Horatio" (182–83) is prelude to his arresting assertion, "methinks I see my father," together with the clarifying, "In my mind's eye, Horatio" (184–85). Horatio's puzzling assertion, "I saw him once" (186); Hamlet's asseveration, "I shall not look upon his like again" (188); and the subsequent echoing of "saw" twice in quick succession ("My lord, I think I saw him yesternight," "Saw? Who?"): all these rapid eye movements culminate in the resounding drumbeat of Hamlet's heavily accentual line, "For God's love let me hear!" (195). Not only the explicit reference to the nearly forgotten ear (uncannily like the nearly forgotten king of so recent memory), but also the reveille call to the auditor's ear with the unusual series of heavily accented syllables in Hamlet's line prefigures the inflated importance the ear will have toward the end of the first act. It will be cast in a central role in the plot of *Hamlet,* serving as scene and vehicle of a murder. The auditor's ear will also be restored to prominence, since the closing scene of the play, like the opening one, engages the sense of sight so much less than the showy scene 2. Rhetorically, the ear will become closely associated with the murdered king, beginning with the Ghost's urging Hamlet to "lend thy serious hearing" (1.5.5). It is the organ of the past but also of the future. The ear's era is to come, once the "eye" of Denmark is dispatched.

In act 1, scene 4 the play continues to be inhospitable to a convergence of seeing and hearing. The appearance of the Ghost, still speechless, is preceded by the offstage noise of the King's carousing and a backward reference to the first of many offstage and invisible noises in the play, the striking of the witching hour, which Marcellus has heard but Horatio has not.[4] Scene 5 takes us deepest into the ear's cavities of any scene in the play. Rather than staging a convergence of the seen and the heard in the figure of the ghostly apparition that now speaks, this final scene of the first act, propelling the ear into prominence with such solemn phrases as "Speak, I am bound to hear" (1.5.6), balances the opening scene, with its emphasis on the difficulty and importance of seeing. Even though the setting and atmosphere of scene 1 and scene 5 are nearly identical, between the two we have traveled the full distance from the ocular to the auricular.

The Ghost's speech grants precedence to the ear by suggesting how easy it is for an auditory overload to short-circuit the organ of seeing: "I could a tale unfold whose lightest word / Would harrow up thy soul, freeze thy young blood, / Make thy two eyes like stars start from their spheres" (1.5.15–17). His scenario reverses the customary procedure of messengers in Shakespeare. Rather than reenacting in the ear a *scene* of violence or translating a violent scene into a report that will in turn inflict violence on the ear, the Ghost will tell a tale that will incapacitate the eyes and do them violence. The ear in this scene is cast as the organ of privacy and secrecy,[5] in contrast to the eye, which thus far rules the public sphere. There are no "private eyes" in *Hamlet,* only private ears. When Polonius conceals himself in the fateful Closet Scene, he stations himself within "the ear" of Gertrude and Hamlet's "conference." As in the opening act of *Othello,* when Desdemona makes an appeal to the ear of the Duke to grant her refuge from the controlling gaze of her father, the ear in *Hamlet* similarly seems a refuge and court of appeal, as well as a potentially subversive space of representation eluding the control of the sovereign's gaze.

It is not surprising, therefore, that the Ghost chooses to characterize his old kingdom not as an eye—as did his brother when contracting Denmark's body politic into a "brow of woe"—but as an ear, and an abused one not unlike his own:

> 'Tis given out that, sleeping in my orchard,
> A serpent stung me—so the whole ear of Denmark
> Is by a forged process of my death
> Rankly abus'd—
>
> (1.5.35–38)

Soon we learn what all this symbolic attention to the "attent ear" is leading up to: the discovery that the dark and secret cavern of the ear was the site and channel of a murder. "In the porches of my ears [Claudius] did pour / The leperous distilment" (1.5.63–64). It is a violence that is symbolically reenacted in the Ghost's speech, with Hamlet's ears this time the victim.

Curiously, now that Hamlet and Denmark and we have become "all ears," and the Ghost, subsequent to moving beneath the platform stage in the area referred to as the "Hell," has become a purely auditory phenomenon, the Ghost's departure is occasioned not by a sound but by a visual sign. "The glow-worm shows the matin to be near / And gins to pale his uneffectual fire" (ll. 89–90). In the opening scene, conditions were reversed: the departure of the Ghost, then a purely visual phenomenon, was cued by an auditory signal, an offstage noise from an invisible source, the crowing of a cock. It is almost as if, in both scenes and in both manifestations, as dumb picture and imageless voice, the Ghost is being recalled by the occluded or forgotten sense, eye or ear. It is worth noting that in scene 5, the general visibility that comes with dawn is represented by a negative, the increasing *invisibility* of the glow-worm. That the eye's reclamation of its kingdom with the coming of dawn should be heralded by a reverse signal, of something visible fading into invisibility, might very well suggest that the eye's sovereignty is specious, or at least far from absolute. This seems consistent with the general argument of an act designed to put its spectators/auditors on guard against both the eye and the King who describes himself as one.

"The Very Faculties of Eyes and Ears"

The eye is nor ordeined nor apted to any other worke, than to make use of the light by seeing; and to every singled part there is assigned some more peculier operation or administration. . . . To the like confusion it tendeth if the parts be prodigiously dislocated or transferred from their proper to other unfitting places, whereof oftentimes the whole bodie getteth the name of a monster mishapen and distorted. The sences must hold to their station like to sentinels.

—Edward Forset[6]

And therefore Salomon, speaking of the two principal senses of inquisition, the eye and the ear, affirmeth that "the eye is never satisfied with seeing, nor the ear with hearing."

—Francis Bacon[7]

In his account of the effects of the Player's declamation on both actor and audience, Hamlet stresses the partnership of eye and ear. When the Player in the midst of his declamation falters in describing Hecuba's passion, "all his visage wann'd, / Tears in his eyes, distraction in his aspect, / A broken voice, and his whole function suiting / With forms to his conceit" (2.2.548–51). The agents of the audible and visible, eye (now blinded by tears) and voice, stumble simultaneously, as they do in the audience members that Hamlet imagines for the Player, had he Hamlet's "cue for passion."

> He would drown the stage with tears,
> And cleave the general ear with horrid speech,
> Make mad the guilty and appal the free,
> Confound the ignorant, and amaze indeed
> The very faculties of eyes and ears.
> (2.2.556–60)

141

Presenting the visible and audible in partnership, the Player's Speech functions as a refuge from the rivalry between eye and ear that characterizes the play as a whole.

Its bloody beginning, spoken by Hamlet and intended no doubt to be eye-opening, culminates in a reference to Pyrrhus's "eyes like carbuncles" (2.2.459). When the First Player takes over, an increase in the number of alliterative sound effects culminates in the explicit domination of Pyrrhus' ear: "a hideous crash / Takes prisoner Pyrrhus' ear" (2.2.472–73). A captive audience, his instrument of hearing taken prisoner, Pyrrhus now paradoxically becomes a "painted tyrant" (l. 476). At just the moment Pyrrhus becomes all ears, we become (metaphorically, of course, since we do not literally see him) all eyes: transfixed by a sound, Pyrrhus becomes a silent picture. At the moment the Trojan citadel collapses, our ears are silenced as if by fiat. The scene, together with the rhetoric charged with creating it, becomes auditory for us again only after Pyrrhus's ears have been released.

> But as we often see against some storm
> A silence in the heavens, the rack stand still,
> The bold winds speechless, and the orb below
> As hush as death, anon the dreadful thunder
> Doth rend the region.
>
> (2.2.479–83)

A parallel moment occurs in the Hecuba portion of the speech, which becomes predominantly visual (ll. 501–5) at precisely the moment she becomes blinded by tears ("bisson rheum"). It is as if a system of benevolent surrogacy is in place, whereby the audience's sense (whether visual or auditory) takes over when one of Pyrrhus's or Hecuba's senses falters.[8] We see when Pyrrhus hears. We see Hecuba most vividly when she has become blinded by her own tears. (Similarly the gods see Hecuba at the moment she becomes an overwhelmingly auditory phenomenon.) The pathos of the speech, the sense of its characters' isolation, is reinforced by the auditor's senses always being out of phase with those of the speech's characters.

But all the dissociative effects in the speech are merely apparent, since all is suggested through almost exclusively auditory means, an actor's declamation (embellished, of course, with gestures). The Player's Speech is a melodrama of eye and ear, both in the extremity of the auditory and visual effects that it evokes and insofar as there is no real danger in that speech of the eye's estrangement from the ear. Just as the often immoderate, hungry, and erring eye in *Romeo and*

142

Juliet is supervised by the ear, appointed master of the revels by the Prologue—"if you with patient ears attend" (1 Prologue, 13)—so are all dissociations between the visual and the auditory in the Player's Speech superintended by the ear.

A reunion of sorts between the two senses takes place in the final section of the speech, following Polonius's interruption. Of the vision of Hecuba he has just conveyed, the Player predicts,

> Who this had seen, with tongue in venom steep'd,
> 'Gainst Fortune's state would treason have pronounc'd,
> But if the gods themselves did see her then,
> When she saw Pyrrhus make malicious sport
> In mincing with his sword her husband's limbs,
> The instant burst of clamour that she made,
> Unless things mortal move them not at all,
> Would have made milch the burning eyes of heaven
> And passion in the gods.
>
> (ll. 506–14)

The sight of Hecuba would produce in a human bystander an instantaneous declamation "with tongue in venom steep'd," the violence witnessed by the eye calling forth a reciprocal and responsive auditory violence. The situation is reminiscent of Shakespeare's earlier plays, in which the verbal translation or effect is nearly always commensurate with the visual scene.

Out of phase throughout most of the Player's Speech, the auditory and visual are synchronized most perfectly in the gods' response to Hecuba. For the human bystanders, who witness a sight and then produce a verbal clamor to match it, visual and auditory events remain successive; for the gods they are simultaneous. In a startling conflation of the visual and auditory, the gods, who presumably could not declaim " 'Gainst Fortune's state" owing to the obvious conflict of interests, "see" (l. 508) her as an auditory phenomenon, "the instant burst of clamour that she made." Unlike human bystanders, they do not see a sight that would in turn evoke a noisy declamation. Presumably they bypass the semiotic relays involved in the human response. For the gods hearing and seeing do not seem alternative modes of apprehension, practiced successively. The human bystander sees Hecuba, then responds with an outburst of passionate speech. Similarly, we hear Pyrrhus only after we cease to see him, and we see him only after he has been stilled, like the painting of a tyrant. But for the gods, the two sensory functions seem simultaneous and indistinguishable. That they see Hecuba and her instant burst of clamor may even be taken to suggest an ideal interweaving of the visible and the audible that is also the condition to which Shakespeare's theater seems to have aspired. Placed back to back, the human and divine responses to Hecuba seem symmetrical. We see her, and respond by verbalizing, proclaiming Fortune a traitor, a visual cause producing a verbal effect. Conversely, the gods' burning eyes (the stars), responding to Hecuba's clamor, would put forth milky tears: an auditory cause producing a visible effect on (figurative) eyes.

The latter portion of the Player's Speech echoes and anticipates the complicated sight lines of the play-within-the-play. There, we watch Hamlet and Horatio watch the King, who watches the play. Here, the gods and human bystanders watch Hecuba watch Pyrrhus, who in turn confronts Priam. But whereas in *Gonzago* the complex series of sight lines serves the purposes of overseeing, discovery, and censure, in the Player's Speech the intersecting sight lines bind the various levels of spectatorship in a community of sympathy. Hecuba is herself a spectator in this scenario, making the sense of community with the onlooking gods and mortals all the more compelling. In other words, the Player's Speech is an oasis in which the eye and its gaze have something other than the prevailing function they have in the remainder of the play: "to threaten and command," as Hamlet says of not his uncle's but his father's "eye like Mars" (3.4.57). It is as if the entirety of *Hamlet* is a commentary upon Shakespeare's earlier premises about the relations between eye and ear, which are in many ways exemplified and recapitulated in the Player's Speech.

Show and Tell

"The play suffers from too much telling rather than showing," a critic remarks of *Timon of Athens*,[9] though the complaint could just as easily be made of King James: his preference for discourse, particularly texts, rather than Elizabethan displays of the monarch's body before the public gaze, for asserting and maintaining his power. A pattern of competition between showing and telling is, however, powerfully established in *Hamlet,* at least two years before the beginning of Jacobean rule. It may be that the transition between Elizabethan showing and Jacobean telling, rather than simply marking the personal preferences and idiosyncracies of two monarchs, participates in a larger historical trend that might be characterized as the divergence of showing and telling.

Hamlet's advice to the Players before the play is put on—"Suit the action to the word, the word to the action" (3.2.17–18)—might well be adopted as a slogan by the school holding that eye and ear should be equally engaged during a theatrical performance, that the theater should avoid the extremes of the overly visual or poetic. But in the performance that Hamlet helps stage, a far different relation between word and action, the visual and verbal, obtains. The puzzling relation of the dumb-show to the inner play signals the failure of showing and telling to converge, as they arguably did in the Player's Speech. It is appropriate that *Gonzago,* a play that may finally be about nothing so much as the nonconvergence of showing and telling, should have as its central action a poisoning through the ear, followed by what may be described as an apotheosis of the eye. On the heels of his success catching the conscience of the King, Hamlet in a dramatic reversal realigns his interests and his father's with the eye, casting his uncle as a "mildew'd ear" (3.4.64). This reversal doesn't resolve but only accentuates the rivalry between showing and telling, the visual and verbal, that marked the first two acts of the play.

Ordinarily the dumb-show "presented things that could not be conveniently given in dialogue, or alternatively, if it foreshadowed things which *would* be given in dialogue later, it did so emblematically."[10] Both of these established functions of the dumb-show suggest a more integral relation with the play of which it is a part than the relation of dumb-show to play in *Gonzago,* which lacks any emblematic relation to what will be given later in dialogue. As Harold Jenkins notes, "What is peculiar in *Hamlet* is that the dumb-show exactly rehearses without dialogue what is then repeated with it."[11] What is most striking about this repetition is not its redundancy, which has a justifiable extratheatrical function: to provide Hamlet with not one but two opportunities to catch the conscience of the king. Rather, it is the altogether different effects the two enactments have on Claudius. One of the infamous cruxes of *Hamlet* criticism has to do with why the King doesn't betray himself during the dumb-show, which faithfully duplicates the action of *Gonzago,* including the image of the crime he has committed. The two most popular theories are that he did not see the dumb-show (being distracted, for example, by conversation with another member of the onstage audience), and that "he was strong enough to stand the sight of the crime once but not twice."[12] But if we see the dumb-show as part of a more general pattern, then the uncertainty it calls forth as to why showing and telling have such divergent effects may be consistent with the play's larger argument about the incommensurability of the visual and verbal. One might also speculate that there is a poetic justice entailed by Claudius, the King who figures himself as an eye, being most vulnerable not when he sees but when he hears the image of his crime. It is almost as if the crime he committed, poisoning the ear of the king his brother, must be repaid by violence done *his* ears.

The dumb show is followed by some elaborate banter between Hamlet and Ophelia on the subject of showing and telling, banter that tries to make light of, not shed light on, one of the central difficulties of the play. It begins with Ophelia's question, "What means this, my lord?" Hamlet answers in a line that sports exaggerated sound effects, as if trying to answer or redress the imbalance of eye and ear produced by the purely visual dumb-show: "Marry, this is miching malicho. It means mischief" (3.2.134–35). The subsequent play on "show" and "tell" upon the entrance of the Prologue suggests a confidence on Hamlet's part, also to be found in his advice to the Players, in the commensurability of the verbal and visual, a confidence that is not warranted by the play as a whole:

> Ham. We shall know by this fellow. The players cannot keep counsel: They'll tell all.
> Oph. Will a tell us what this show meant?
> Ham. Ay, or any show that you will show him. Be not you ashamed to show, he'll not shame to tell you what it means.
> (3.2.137–42)

Hamlet's faith in the ease of passing from showing to telling is comically betrayed by the Prologue, who fails to do as the audience would have expected, to act as "presenter" to explain the meaning of the dumb-show. Hamlet's aggressive quips to Ophelia are further betrayed by the radical isolation of the visible and audible in the staging of *Gonzago*. The inner play exhibits a division between showing and telling not only in the theatrically redundant inclusion of the dumb-show (which has the effect of isolating the visual interest of the play from the verbal) but also in its highly rhetorical and periphrastic style. The colorless rhetoric of *Gonzago* doesn't import the visible into the verbal to nearly the degree that the Player's Speech does; it provides nothing like the vivid pictures of Pyrrhus and Hecuba. The general isolation of the visible and verbal in *Gonzago* is fairly indicative of conditions in the rest of the play.

Following Claudius's rising and calling for "lights" (an inappropriate response, surely, since he has been undone by the eye), Hamlet exhibits a renewed faith in shows and showing, utterly unlike his denigration of showy mourning in the Council Scene, where he claimed to have "that within which passes show" (1.2.85). In an elaborate chiasmus, not only does he realign his interests with those of the eye, but in the Closet Scene he re-describes his father as an eye—"An eye like

Mars to threaten and command" (3.4.57)—reserving the other organ for a description of Claudius, now a "mildew'd ear" (3.4.64). "Didst perceive?" Hamlet exults in conversation with Horatio immediately following the scalding of Claudius's eyes. The eye, traditionally the most reliable purveyor of truth, has now regained its sovereignty, having unmasked the usurper. So much is implied by Hamlet's little rhyme— or rather nonrhyme—to Horatio: "For thou dost know, O Damon dear, / This realm dismantled was / Of Jove himself, and now reigns here / A very, very—pajock" (3.2.275–78). "You might have rhymed," Horatio offers, indicating that he expected Hamlet to supply the word "ass." The refusal of rhyme illustrates in miniature the demotion of the ear, now a mere messenger and lackey in the eye's pursuit of truth. "Didst perceive?" (l. 281).

Two scenes later ocular terms guide him in his assault upon his mother's conscience. The old counselor opens the scene with one of his favorite phrases, "Look you," an appropriate summary of Hamlet's activity with his mother, to whom he is busily giving a lesson in seeing better, and also a signal of how Polonius's death might be prevented, if he would not divorce his own and Hamlet's eyes and ears by concealing himself. Polonius's speech ends, "I'll silence me even here. / Pray you be round" (3.4.4–5). Besides a forewarning of the permanent silencing of this particularly noisy character, the lines may suggest a more general suppression of the auditory as the standing of the visible rises. The decision to "silence me even here" may even bear a homonymic warning to the ear ("here"/"hear") about its own suppression, especially since he describes his position to the King as "in the ear / Of all their conference" (3.1.186–87). As happens so frequently in Shakespeare's middle and later tragedies, this divorce between eye and ear has disastrous consequences. Polonius silences himself so that he may become a better auditor, but only an auditor. Stationing himself in the "ear" of their conference, he cannot see them. Hearing the word "murder" without being able to see that there is no likelihood of such an event taking place, he gives himself away. Symbolically, he capsizes in the auditory canal. Two other references early in the scene suggest an isolation of the ear from the other senses and from "sovran reason" that is supposed to govern them all: Gertrude's challenge, "What have I done, that thou dar'st wag thy tongue / In noise so rude against me?" (3.4.39–40); and Hamlet's retort, which implies that it is she, not he, who has isolated the auditory until it becomes mere noise, through her deed making of "sweet religion" "a rhapsody of words" (3.4.47–48).

While Polonius hears, Gertrude will be made to see with a vengeance: "You go not till I set you up a glass / Where you may see the inmost part of you" (3.4.18–19). It is the eye that must intervene, establish its sovereignty over the other senses, and help restore the sovereignty of reason. At the end of his accusatory speech, Hamlet declaims, "Heaven's face does glow / O'er this solidity and compound mass / With tristful visage, as against the doom, / Is thought-sick at the act" (3.4.48–51). The lines imputing a face and a gaze to heaven suggest a heavenly role for eyes in general,[13] distant indeed from any role in which they are cast in the first two acts.

Hamlet tries to give his mother a lesson in seeing better, which she will follow up, Hamlet hopes, with an equally ocular vigilance toward the King and toward her own meaner impulses. "Look here upon this picture, and on this, / The counterfeit presentment of two brothers" (3.4.53–54). Hamlet is confident that these two miniature portraits of her present and former husband are self-interpreting. They are pictures that call forth their own unmistakable glosses, Hamlet imagines. So long as one has a good pair of eyes, the pictures supply their own commentary. "Have you eyes? . . . Ha, have you eyes?" runs the refrain of Hamlet's assault on Gertrude's ears (3.4.65,67).

But our own eyes and ears have supplied us with a quite different interpretation of Old Hamlet. The difference between Hamlet's extravagant, idealizing praise of his father and the military and purgatorial image of his father that haunts us from act 1 suggests a more slippery relation between the visual and verbal than the one Hamlet wishes for, as susceptible to capricious turns of interpretation as Hamlet's playful-sardonic identification of cloud-shapes with Polonius. Hamlet's lines imagining his mother's sensory disunity (leading to her union with the "eye" of Denmark) summarizes better than Hamlet would wish the condition in all of Elsinore: "Eyes without feeling, feeling without sight, / Ears without hands or eyes, smelling sans all" (3.4.78–79).

"Pictures or Mere Beasts"

The play's most extreme form of verbal/visual dissociations is madness, which is closely tied to the sphere of the visible. In a reference to Ophelia, Claudius calls the mad "pictures, or mere beasts" (4.5.86). It is a reference that acts to erode the difference between the two men that Hamlet so arduously sought to establish in the closet scene, a difference Hamlet claimed was summarized by their pictures. In retrospect, we may imagine those portraits as each containing a hint of the madman's leer.

The King's direction to Horatio to "give [Ophelia] good watch" has an even more sinister implication. For if the mad are pictures, the close watch seems to take an active part in *reducing* Ophelia to a picture: a crime, by the way, that has been repeated countless times outside the play, for she has been a favorite subject for painters, especially during the nineteenth century.[14] Claudius also sets "watch" over Hamlet: "Madness in great ones must not unwatch'd go" (3.1.190), suggesting that "watching" is an exercise in domination and control. The word "watch" in connection with both lovers sets off many echoes of earlier "watches," including the sentinels' in act 1, the King's spies' watches, the "watch" or insomnia into which Hamlet descends in his apparent madness (2.2.148), and the watch that we, the members of the audience have undertaken, one that doubles and participates in all the others.

In the mad Ophelia, the divorce between the visual and verbal is rehearsed in its most succinct and shocking form. In the scene describing her death, lovingly painted by Gertrude and overladen with visual details, Ophelia far more than Hamlet becomes a "picture," a phenomenon of pure visibility. Ophelia may very well forecast a new, ocular positioning of madness that departs from the more traditional Renaissance concept of madness embodied by her lover.

Foucault attributes a new, ocularist form of madness arising in the classical era (roughly 1650–1800) to the disintegration of the close association of words and things, which no longer constitute a "uniform layer" at the end of the Renaissance.

> In the Renaissance, madness was present everywhere and mingled with every experience by its images or its dangers. During the classical period, madness was shown, but on the other side of bars; if present, it was at a distance, under the eyes of a reason that no longer felt any relation to it and that would not compromise itself with too close a resemblance. Madness had become a thing to look at: no longer a monster inside oneself, but an animal with strange mechanisms, a bestiality from which man had long since been suppressed.[15]

To be sure, most features of madness in *Hamlet, King Lear, The Winter's Tale,* and other Shakespearean drama—including the ubiquity of madness, the intertwining of the themes of madness and of death, and the haziness of the boundary between reason and unreason—confirm what Foucault has to say about madness not in the classical period but in the Renaissance, before what he terms "the great confinement" of the poor beginning in France with the creation of the Hôpital Générale. But in the characters of Hamlet and Ophelia, Shakespeare plays two divergent conceptions off one another, conceptions that roughly correspond to what Foucault characterizes as Renaissance and classical ideas of madness.

"Water and madness have long been linked in the dreams of European men," Foucault writes, a remark that calls to mind both Ophelia's drowning and Hamlet's embarkation for England.[16] The "old union of water and madness"[17] eventually gave rise to the popular image of the ship of fools. The treatment of madmen as "ritual exiles" replacing the disappearing leper[18], and the old practice of handing madmen over to boatmen,[19] certainly invite comparison with the ship on which Hamlet is exiled, arguably a backward glance at the Ship of Fools, which according to Foucault navigated its way into literature and iconography rather suddenly at the end of the fifteenth century. Foucault argues that madness, besides displacing leprosy as the preferred form of social otherness, replaces death in the second half of the fifteenth century as western culture's sovereign theme. As the Middle Ages give way to the Renaissance,

> The mockery of madness replaces death and its solemnity. From the discovery of that necessity which invariably reduces man to nothing, we have shifted to the scornful contemplation of that nothing which is existence itself. Fear in the face of the absolute limit of death turns inward in a continuous irony; man disarms it in advance, making it an object of derision by giving it an everyday, tamed form, by constantly renewing it in the spectacle of life, by scattering it throughout the vices, the difficulties, and the absurdities of all men. Death's annihilation is no longer anything because it was already everything, because life itself was only futility, vain words, a squabble of cap and bells. The head that will become a skull is already empty. Madness is the *déjà-la* of death. . . . What death unmasks was never more than a mask; to discover the grin of the skeleton, one need only lift off something that was neither beauty nor truth, but only a plaster and tinsel face. From the vain mask to the corpse, the same smile persists. But when the madman laughs, he already laughs with the laugh of death; the lunatic, anticipating the macabre, has disarmed it.[20]

This somber passage through which nonetheless can be heard a very audible squabble of cap and bells would do exceedingly well as a gloss on the Graveyard Scene. Better than any other theatrical icon, Yorick's skull may mark the historical transition from "death and its solemnity" to "the mockery of madness." The peculiar fascination of Yorick's skull, its appearance simultaneously as a powerful agent of unmasking (of life) and as the ultimate mask, the mask of madness that, as Foucault argues, anticipates and prevents death from accomplishing its unmasking, together with Hamlet's grotesque superimposed image of the skull "painted o'er" with cosmetics even though the skull itself seems no less a mask than the lady's face he takes it to mock: these apparent contradictions begin to make perfect sense within the horizon of a general infiltration of the theme of madness into that of death, thereby disarming the latter. Madness, Hamlet discovers, is a defense against not only discovery (by Claudius) but also death. It is vastly therapeutic for him as well as for Lear. Hence the generally becalmed nature of the Graveyard scene, in which Hamlet dresses up all those tossed skulls with faces only to unmask them, to show that the faces were already only masks. It is not so much life but death that is unmasked and defeated in a kind of symbolic fencing, Yorick's blunt skull serving as Hamlet's rapier.

Though Hamlet's madness conforms quite closely to Foucault's account of madness in the Renaissance, Ophelia's seems more consistent with madness as the classical period conceived it: externalized, ocularist, a "thing to look at" rather than "a monster inside oneself." The priest's denial of music in the "broken rites" of Ophelia's burial seems oddly to conspire with other attempts to silence her, and symbolically consistent with her ocularist version of madness, the view of the madperson as a mere picture. She becomes the personal equivalent of the dumb-show whose meaning she seemed so eager to know, moving us to consider that in retrospect *The Murder of Gonzago,* with its polarization of visual and verbal effects, was perhaps more significant as herald of her madness than as instrument for confirming Hamlet's uncle's guilt.

To See, or Not to See

Hearing Adonis speak after a long silence, an effusive Venus responds, "Had I no eyes but ears, my ears would love / That inward beauty and invisible" ("Venus and Adonis," ll. 433–34). The association of the ear with the immaterial and essential has a less rapturous spokesperson in George Hakewill, whose *Vanitie of the Eye* (1615), like much of the iconoclastic thought of the time, implied that it was only hearing that had access to "universalls, immaterials, and the inward parts of things."

Frequently Hamlet is driven by a craving for visibility, allying him with members of the audience who must actively try to visualize much of what is only evoked through rhetoric, and who no less than the son Gertrude presumes to be mad frequently "bend [our eyes] on vacancy" (3.4.117): "Who calls me villain, breaks my pate across, / Plucks off my beard and blows it in my face, / Tweaks me by the nose, gives me the lie i'th'throat / As deep as to the lungs—who does me this?" (2.2.567–70). The reverse passage, from the visible to the invisible, marks Fortinbras's quick passage over the stage in act 4, described by Hamlet in soliloquy.

Examples gross as earth exhort me,
Witness this army of such mass and charge,
Led by a delicate and tender prince,
Whose spirit, with divine ambition puff'd,
Makes mouths at the invisible event,
Exposing what is mortal and unsure
To all that fortune, death, and danger dare,
Even for an eggshell.

(4.4.46–53)

"The invisible event" refers to the future event, invisible because not yet realized. Fortinbras's grimacing at the invisible future is a striking image, especially as Hamlet has just used an ocular metaphor to describe both our reasoning powers ["Sure he that made us with such large discourse, / Looking before and after, gave us not / That capability and godlike reason / To fust in us unus'd" (4.4.36–39)] and the exemplary militancy of Fortinbras ["*Witness* this army"]. It is hard to conceive how "looking before and after" can help to guide the human actor, can be other than theatrical posturing, the striking of an attitude, if what we "see" there is invisible.

The sentence beginning with an exhortation to look ("Witness") exhibits a progressive attenuation of the visual sense. The first thing we see would be hard to miss, "an army of such mass," even the slender version of that army that could have been represented on the stage of the Globe. Vision becomes gradually weakened with "delicate and tender prince," fading out almost entirely with his invisible "spirit, with divine ambition puff'd," which gazes upon and makes faces at invisible events. The speech's imagery becomes even less visual in the next line with a series of abstract terms: "mortal and unsure"; "fortune, death, and danger." The alliterative "death and danger dare" may even encourage the foolish ear to rush in where angelic eyes fear to tread. Finally, the sentence ends with a metaphor that has the potential to be visualized but that seems incongruous if construed too concretely. To try to *see* a massive army closing in on an eggshell tempts a misapplication of the visual sense, like an actor mistaking his cue and entering at the wrong moment. "Eggshell" probably should remain a word and hence invisible rather than hatch into a visual image. A similar question famously applies to the idea of taking arms against a sea of troubles. Several critics have tried to turn that phrase into a concrete image by imagining Celts storming the waves with their swords.[21] To see, or not to see, that is the question. Whether 'tis nobler in the mind only to *hear* that "sea of troubles," and thereby drown in acoustical wave upon wave. In trying

152

to judge our responsibility toward the play's imagery, we share Hamlet's difficulty of negotiating between the visible and the invisible.[22]

The attenuation of the sense of sight in this speech is made to suggest Fortinbras's putative spirituality. It is curious that so many instances of invisibility hover around Fortinbras, who is usually cast by critics as the bold, earthy, spirited but unspiritual man of action, the necessary counterpart to the airily contemplative Hamlet. But in a speech before the Captain just prior to his soliloquy, Hamlet applies the category of the invisible to Fortinbras in a less complimentary context, this time to describe not the future but the past, the cause of Fortinbras's military adventurism: "This is th'impostume of much wealth and peace, / That inward breaks, and shows no cause without / Why the man dies" (4.4.27–29). Most diseases in this play work unseen. Not only the military bug caught by Fortinbras but also whatever disease afflicts Gertrude's soul works subterraneously. Hamlet urges his mother not to lay the "flattering unction to [her] soul" that her son is mad, for "It will but skin and film the ulcerous place, / Whiles rank corruption, mining all within, / Infects unseen" (3.4.149–51). Hamlet's description evokes the far from ideal instance of the Danish court, a world of invisible motives, where the nexus of visible and invisible is beyond everyone's grasp, and where the relations between the visible and the invisible are strained to the breaking point. Claudius's power seems to derive not from the "privileged visibility" of an Elizabeth but rather from his sole knowledge and governance of a world of invisible motives. His moral failings are tied to his breaking the rules of Renaissance power, which issues from the visible spectacle of monarchy, a spectacle whose signs are legible, translatable into a reliable speech. In addition to functioning as a central spectacle, an actor "set upon stages in the sight and view of all the world," as Elizabeth said in 1586, the body of the Renaissance monarch also functions as a privileged text, a legible representation of the body politic endowed with all the signs of power.

In that twilight of the English monarchy that was the late eighteenth century, the monarch was no longer conceivable in theatrical terms, as an actor set upon the stage of the world, and monarchical power would no longer be tied to its privileged visibility. If, as Foucault has suggested, the whole relation between the seen and the heard, the visible and invisible, has been redefined in the intervening years, one would expect the relation of the monarchy to visibility and spectacle to have shifted as well. Indeed, the image of the monarch conjured by William Godwin in his influential antimonarchist *Enquiry Concerning Political Justice* (1793) is not the potent center, or even the vulnerable center as in Elizabeth's formulation, of a world of theatrical spectacle. Instead the king is beset by an invisible world of secrets and secret motivations. What remains visible in the monarch's world is mere distraction, "splendour and affairs," a false allure:

> Every thing is carefully kept out of sight, that may remind them they are men. . . . Exposed to a hundred fold more seductions than ordinary men, he has not, like them, the checks of a visible constitution of things, perpetually, through the medium of the senses, making their way to the mind. . . . Every thing is trusted to the motives of an invisible world; which, whatever may be the estimate to which they are entitled in the view of philosophy, mankind are not now immerged in splendour or affairs, and have little chance of success, in contending with the impressions of sense, and the allurements of visible objects.[23]

The king, in Godwin's view, has less access to the visible world and "the checks . . . a visible constitution of things" affords, than any of his subjects. The world he describes is not that of the theater but that of the novel, devoted in some sense to uncovering "the motives of an invisible world." *Hamlet's* world is not yet Godwin's, of course. Claudius, unlike Godwin's monarch, has exceptional access to invisible motives, and his penetrating gaze is certainly not obstructed by the flattery of courtiers and advisors and the false allure of the visible. Invisible motives may yet be made visible by theatrical means, the staging of *Gonzago*. But to the extent that motives remain beyond theatrical means of their discovery— and that is certainly a fair description of more than one character's motives in the play—*Hamlet* is powerful antitheater, an inverted image of the Elizabethan association of power with a privileged visibility, and the Renaissance play that most forcefully suggests the inadequacy of the stage as an Elizabethan model for governance and power.

Hamlet's description of Fortinbras's action as invisible abscess suggests that Fortinbras shares Hamlet's dilemma, even without sharing his taste for speculation and for the specularity of theater: a vexed relation between the visible and the invisible, which is also the problem of action itself. If to act is to make visible a prior hidden and invisible idea, then the attenuation of the visible in Hamlet's account of Fortinbras may very well be the expression of Hamlet's iconoclastic side. His puzzling delay in carrying out his revenge seems a corollary of his iconoclasm, the iconoclasm of the Protestant Reformation whose roots are in Wittenberg, the university home of Martin Luther, Hamlet, and Horatio.

If action makes visible a preexisting intent, then not to act is a perfectly natural direction for an iconoclast to take. In a speech to Ophelia, Hamlet casts the imagination as a kind of mediator linking invisible thoughts to visible deeds: "I am very proud, revengeful, ambitious, with more offences at my beck than I have thoughts to put them in, imagination to give them shape, or time to act them in" (3.1.124–27). Given the play's brooding over the difficulty of linking "thoughts" and "acts," it is unlikely that the "imagination" is serving as a reliable emissary between the realms of the visible and the invisible. Fortinbras's action is no more the simple translation into the visible of an invisible plan or idea than are any of Hamlet's. As prelude to the mere "picture" that Ophelia will have become in the next scene, the nearly silent Fortinbras (almost a dumb-show unto himself, who delivers exactly seven lines, and only at the very beginning of this scene), with his slightly mad adventurism, may even be implicated in the theme of madness as a speechless picture, and as the ultimate form of the dissociation of the visual from the verbal. Given the shrunken empire of the eye in the scene with Fortinbras, Hamlet's blustering "Have you eyes. . . . Ha, have you eyes?" in the Closet Scene would appear to grant too much importance and power to the sovereign gaze: a conclusion that is confirmed by the final spectacle of the play, where what we "see," though it may instill "woe or wonder," will not help us to comprehend.

An Unsightly End

Though both of Hamlet's survivors, Horatio and Fortinbras, will do their best to make them converge, the visual and verbal are as much out of phase at the end as at any previous time. After saying farewell to Horatio and the Queen, Hamlet addresses those onstage spectators without speaking parts as "You that look pale and tremble at this chance, / That are but mutes or audience to this act" (5.2.339–40). "Mutes," as Jenkins informs us, refers to "actors without speaking parts." The line serves to remind us that we in the audience as well as all onstage characters, living and dead, are fast becoming part of a dumb-show. Much in the play resembles a dumb-show: Hamlet in his madness, Ophelia in hers, a Ghost that refuses to speak, a soldier who says little, and the "mutes or audience" of the closing scene, to name a few. Unlike in Shakespeare's earlier plays, where pictures or pictorial elements "speak," often most eloquently—for instance, the mute and mutilated Lavinia in *Titus Andronicus,* or Juliet on her balcony before she begins to speak—in *Hamlet* and most tragedies subsequent to it, the emphasis tends to be not on the speaking picture but on the speechless picture and on the difficulty of translating images into words.

155

In the final scene of the play, the word "sight" is used repeatedly as if to underscore the sense of an overpowering but meaningless ocular experience. To Fortinbras's query, "Where is this sight?" Horatio responds, "What is it you would see? / If aught of woe or wonder, cease your search" (5.2.367–68). The First Ambassador remarks, "The sight is dismal; / And our affairs from England come too late. / The ears are senseless that should give us hearing" (5.2.372–74). And glancing at the grisly scene one last time, Fortinbras observes, "Such a sight as this / Becomes the field, but here shows much amiss" (5.2.406–7). All these uses of the word suggest that Horatio's report promising to explain all that has transpired will be a strenuous act of translation. His difficulty is also intimated in his instructing the ambassadors and Fortinbras to "give orders that these bodies / High on a stage be placed to the view" (5.2.382–83). The elevation of the bodies to a high platform resembling a theatrical stage accentuates the muteness and untranslatability of this spectacle. That Horatio's report takes place after the culmination of the play—unlike, say, Friar Lawrence's recapitulation of events at the end of *Romeo and Juliet*—further suggests the difficulty he will have in suiting the word to the action.

Fortinbras doubles Horatio's role as interpreter of the sight:

> Let four captains
> Bear Hamlet like a soldier to the stage,
> For he was likely, had he been put on,
> To have prov'd most royal; and for his passage,
> The soldier's music and the rite of war
> Speak loudly for him.
> Take up the bodies. Such a sight as this
> Becomes the field, but here shows much amiss.
> Go, bid the soldiers shoot.
> (5.2.400–408)

The overpowering sight needs sound—the peal of cannons, "the soldier's music"—not only as an interpretive caption, so to speak, but also as a way of balancing a sense that has gotten out of control, exceeded its domain like Fortinbras, and therefore become senseless.[24] But Fortinbras's attempt to translate the sight into sound is as vain and desperate as Horatio's. The soldier's music may "speak loudly" for Hamlet, but in the sense of bombastic and largely meaningless noise, not in the sense that Fortinbras intends. This meaning is likely since the firing of shot echoes the "pieces" going off in the background of act 1, scene 4, when the King and his court, saturated with wassail, are reveling as Hamlet, Horatio, and the sentinels dryly and soberly watch. We therefore do not experience that promised accord between sight and sound suggested by Fortinbras's twin orders: to make a more dignified spectacle of the corpses and to provide a sound commensurate with the sight. Also, because the shots are heard only after the bodies are removed from the stage, the play's closing moment demonstrates in miniature the asynchronism of eye and ear that characterizes the play's whole development.

The slightly earlier tragedy *Julius Caesar* also seems fascinated with the issue of the translatability of sight or spectacle into words. The two famous speeches by Brutus and Antony over the corpse of Caesar indicate something of a slippery relation between word and image. But the earlier play doesn't take its inquiry nearly as far as *Hamlet* does. Having been asked by Mark Antony for "reasons / Why, and wherein, Caesar was dangerous," Brutus concurs, "Or else were this a savage spectacle. / Our reasons are so full of good regard, / That were you, Antony, the son of Caesar, / You should be satisfied" (3.1.221–26). "Regard" keeps Brutus's intent within the realm of the visual. His phrase suggests that his explanation will produce a picture far more handsome than the savage spectacle of a corpse or text without explanation. The potentially brutal sight of Caesar's mangled corpse is immediately dressed up by Brutus's words as by a mortician's hands. Subsequent to Brutus's self-justifying speech, Antony in his rousing eulogy provides an alternate gloss on the sight, displacing Brutus's. Caesar's corpse— "piteous spectacle," "a most bloody sight," as the plebeians interject during Antony's oration (3.2.200,204)—seems typical of "sights" or images in the Renaissance, whose natural condition seems to be a power to generate interpretation or commentary. *Hamlet* suggests that any text (like Horatio's) that tries to couple itself with its spectacle will be a usurping text.

It is telling that what Fortinbras proposes to do is not, like Mark Antony, to tamper with a text (already presumed by onstage and offstage audiences to be adequate to the sight) but to tamper with the spectacle: "Take up the bodies." It is a gesture that powerfully shows how challenging and ultimately futile the proposal to marry word and image has become. Whereas Mark Antony dissolves by suspect means and for private reasons the kinship of spectacle and rhetorical elaboration in the localized instance of Caesar's corpse, neither Fortinbras nor anyone else onstage can decipher the hieroglyph that is the spectacle of *Hamlet's* final scene. All that remains is to alter the resistant spectacle.

At the beginning of *The Order of Things,* in an analysis of Velàzquez's painting *Las Meninas,* which he takes to be a representation of the very conditions of representation in the classical period, Foucault writes,

"The relation of language to painting is an infinite relation. It is not that words are imperfect, or that, when confronted by the visible, they prove insuperably inadequate. Neither can be reduced to the other's terms: it is in vain that we say what we see; what we see never resides in what we say. And it is in vain that we attempt to show, by the use of images, metaphors, or similes, what we are saying; the space where they achieve their splendour is not that deployed by our eyes but that defined by the sequential elements of syntax."[25] *Hamlet* and many of Shakespeare's tragedies subsequent to it already exhibit a considerable strain between what we see and what we say. Part of the vigor of Shakespeare's so-called mature tragedies derives from their willingness to question the presumed continuity in the Renaissance between "what is seen and what is read, between observation and relation,"[26] even though the very existence of the poetic drama of the Renaissance, including *Hamlet,* was premised on such continuity. Given the different orders occupied by the verbal and the visible in the classical period, it is no wonder that the age of poetic drama following the Restoration would seem so remote and out of reach.

6

THE EAR'S SUPERVISION OF THE EYE
IN EARLY SHAKESPEAREAN DRAMA

Not working with the eye without the ear,
And but in purged judgment trusting neither.
                        —*Henry V,* 2.2.135–36

S till the most widely held view of the relation between the visual and
   the verbal in Shakespeare is "that the dichotomy between what is
said and what is shown on stage in a Shakespeare play is an unreal one;
and that verbal and visual unity is a characteristic of Shakespearian
drama."[1] Shakespeare is widely held to have regarded eye and ear as
equal partners. Ben Jonson, by contrast, echoed the antiscenic and
iconoclastic strain of Elizabethan thinking. The "Prologue for the Stage"
to *The Staple of News* wishes, "Would you were come to hear, not see
a play," adding that the actors must provide "shows" to satisfy the
audience's tastes, although the poet would "have you wise, / Much
rather by your ears, than by your eyes."[2]

But the assumption that in Shakespeare eye and ear enjoy the most
amicable of relationships, a variation on the organicist metaphors of
which his plays have so often been the victims, not only deprives them
of an important source of their drama and tension but also causes
to be overlooked the considerable differences separating Shakespeare's
earlier treatment of verbal/scenic relations from his later.[3] Far from
being a non-issue, the shifting relations between image and word,
spectacle and rhetorical elaboration, are one of the most persistent of
Shakespearean characteristics. His drama plays for increasingly high

stakes since the rhetorical theater of the Renaissance, relatively sparse in scenery, depended for its very life on the assumption of translatability between the verbal and visual. In Shakespeare's middle and later tragedies, relations between the seen and the heard—relations crucial to the audience's reception of the plays, to changing notions of the subject and of subjectivity,[4] and to the Elizabethan association of power with a "privileged visibility"[5]—increasingly become openly contested.

A great deal of significant work in the last two decades of Shakespeare studies focuses on the subject of vision and visibility. Most such work has been either Foucauldian in orientation, stressing vision and visibility as forms of power, or Lacanian (or Lacanian-Sartrean), investigating the gaze as both constitutive of and posing a threat to subjectivity.[6] Prior to both sets of questions is that of translation between the visual and verbal. It is this issue that I think most clearly exposes the connection between metatheatrical questions in Shakespearean tragedy and Foucauldian questions of power as it relates to vision and visibility: for instance, the transition from the theater of *supplice,* of public and spectacular torture and execution, to discipline and surveillance, from "the Shakespearean age when sovereignty confronted abomination in a single figure" to "the everyday melodrama of police power and the complicities that crime establishes with power."[7] The development of Shakespearean tragedy, I will contend, foretells what Foucault in his earlier work, *The Order of Things,* characterizes as the dissociation of words and things and of the functions of eye and ear in the period roughly from 1650 to 1800, as well as the general dominance of vision in nearly all areas of cultural activity during that period.[8] Foucault's work suggests ways of locating Shakespearean drama within the history of the relations of eye and ear in the seventeenth century. It is a history to which Shakespearean drama, it may be said, delivers the prologue.

Because of Foucault's notorious tendency to lean predominantly on French sources, it is necessary to compensate for the biases that result.[9] For instance, he overstates the harmony of the relations between eye and ear in the Renaissance. He overlooks a long tradition that privileges the sense of sight above all others, a tradition with classical sources that still had a great deal of currency in Elizabethan England.[10] And in England, where Reformation iconoclasm had taken strong hold, relations between the visual and verbal were already subject to considerable strain, even during the period Shakespeare was writing.[11] In some places in Shakespearean tragedy, that strain seems paradoxically to grow out of the presumed fraternity of the visual and verbal. What made the rhetorical drama of the Renaissance work so well in the first place was the Renaissance belief in the mutual translatability of the visual and the verbal. Because of that translatability, visual aspects of the Renaissance theater were often emblematic; configurations of characters and props could wordlessly communicate a rather definite textual message.[12] Conversely, the eye could delegate much of its authority to the ear; words could take on most of the responsibility for evoking a "scene." Such delegation, analogous to Prospero's delegation of responsibility to his younger brother Antonio, results not infrequently in usurpation of the eye's sovereignty by the ear, a subplot of more than one of Shakespeare's mature tragedies, though not, I would contend, of the earlier plays. *King Lear* features not one abdication but two. No less than the sovereign whose gaze receives so much attention in the play, the eye abdicates, relinquishing sovereignty to the ear. "Look with thine ear," the inspired mad king counsels the eyeless Earl of Gloucester.

But in spite of differences between French and English contexts, Foucault's "archaeology" of the human sciences provides useful coordinates for charting the changing relations between the audible and visible as Shakespeare's career develops. Of equal importance, his work is useful for situating such changes within a larger historical shift: the coming into dominance of the sense of sight in the later seventeenth and eighteenth centuries, a development that seems equally true for England and Locke as it does for France and Descartes.[13]

The Renaissance episteme, as Foucault characterizes it, is distinguished by a belief in "the profound kinship of language with the world." For the Renaissance words and things constituted a "uniform layer in which the *seen* and the *read,* the visible and expressible, were endlessly interwoven." After the Renaissance, "The primacy of the written word went into abeyance. . . . Things and words were to be separated from one another. The eye was thenceforth destined to see and only to see, the ear to hear and only to hear." Because signs were no longer regarded as "parts of things themselves," language was demoted in the classical period, becoming only "a particular case of representation."[14] Sight, "the sense by which we perceive extent and establish proof," acquired "an almost exclusive privilege": a privilege that caused anatomy, for instance, to lose the status it enjoyed in the Renaissance, and botany to advance well beyond zoology in the classical period.[15]

In a general way English Renaissance drama supports Foucault's premise that in the Renaissance the seen and the heard were "endlessly interwoven." Stephen Orgel writes in *The Illusion of Power,* in the Renaissance "few symbols went unexplained by language. In this respect the drama resembled the other visual arts in the Renaissance: every painting—even a portrait—had its moral or allegorical meaning; every emblem had its motto; the architectural orders had their significances; even nature, God's great artifact, could be conceived as a book. . . . The verbal was inseparable from the visual."[16] One manifestation of this inseparability is that in Elizabethan drama, it is common (as it is not in the later illusionistic theater) for characters, "even in the heat of action," to "pause to describe in words the actions we see taking place. . . . In the Elizabethan public theater, nothing spoke for itself; every action implied a rhetoric."[17] Conversely, just as few symbols went unexplained by language in the Renaissance, language could make visible what was not immediately present, through the trope variously called *enargeia* or *evidentia* on which the Renaissance theater was so dependent. In *A Treatise of Schemes and Tropes* (1550), Richard Sherry defines *enargeia* as "when a thynge is so described that it semeth to the reader or hearer that he beholdeth it as it were doyng."[18] Language could make visible what was not present because it was already a messenger from the realm of the visual, a translation from a mental "image." According to John Hoskyns' popular *Directions for Speech and Style* (1599), every act of speech entails an act of translation from a prior image: "The conceits of the mind are pictures of things and the tongue is interpreter of those pictures. The order of God's creatures in themselves is not only admirable and glorious but eloquent."[19] The practice of Shakespeare's earlier tragedies seems consistent with the notion that the tireless interpreter the tongue continually translates from the visual— "conceits of the mind," which are "pictures of things"—to the verbal, a notion that will be subjected repeatedly to skeptical treatment in Shakespeare's mature tragedies, where the tongue has lost much of its ability to interpret "those pictures," whether the mind's or the eye's.

As the sense of sight is increasingly isolated from and incommensurable with the sense of hearing in the middle and later tragedies, there arises an uncertainty and uneasiness about the value of being seen. In *Measure for Measure* Duke Vincentio's dislike of public appearances echoes that of Shakespeare's patron, King James; the exhausted tyrant in *Macbeth* is destined to become the "show and gaze o'th'time"; the antitheatrical hero of *Coriolanus* has a horror of becoming a theatrical spectacle for the Roman plebeians whom he despises; Cleopatra trembles at the prospect of being transformed into Octavius' trophy; and in *Hamlet,* the courtier's privilege and delight of being, in Ophelia's words, "the observed of all observers" is transfigured by the end of the play into the madman's and the corpse's reduction under the power of the gaze to a nightmare of pure visibility.

In addition, power shifts from the privileged visibility of a body to the eye that sees. In an account of the theatrical nature of Elizabethan politics, Stephen Greenblatt writes, "Elizabethan power . . . depends upon its privileged visibility. As in a theater, the audience must be powerfully engaged by this visible presence and at the same time held at a respectful distance from it."[20] By contrast with Elizabethan power, Jacobean power seems redefined to accommodate its sovereign's relative discomfort with public appearances. It is associated less with the sovereign's body than with his sequestered and sheltered gaze, spying into the secrets of his realm from offstage. James counseled his son in his advice-book *Basilikon Doron,* "Delight to haunt your Sessions [of law], and spie carefully their proceedings."[21] In the same work he warned him that kings are placed on a stage "where all the beholders' eyes are attentively bent to look and pry into the least circumstances of their secretest drifts."[22] The general reconfiguring of power from spectacle to beholder is closely related to the dissociation of verbal-scenic relations, for the power of spectacle is predicated on its interpretability, on its acting in ways akin to a text. As power becomes dissociated from theatrical spectacle in plays like *Measure for Measure, King Lear, Antony and Cleopatra,* and *Coriolanus,* it becomes an increasing strain for characters and theatergoers alike to double parts as spectators and auditors, to unite "the very faculties of eyes and ears" (Hamlet, 2.2.560). In what follows, I want to briefly rehearse several plots that Shakespeare spins out of the simple premise of the amity or enmity of eye and ear.[23]

"I See a Voice!": The Wedding of Eye and Ear as Dreamed on a Midsummer's Eve

They mounted high, sit on a loftie hill:
(For they the Prince's best intelligence,
And quickly warn of future good, or ill)
Here stands the palace of the noblest sense:
      Here Visus keeps, whose Court then crystall smoother,
      And clearer seems: he, though a younger brother,
Yet farre more noble is, farre fairer than the other.

Auditus, second of the *Pemptarchie,*
Is next, not all so noble as his brother;
Yet of more need, and more commoditie:
His seat is plac'd somewhat below the other:
      Of each side of the mount a double cave;
      Both which a goodly portall doth embrave,
And winding entrance, like Maeanders erring wave.
              —Phineas Fletcher[24]

Sometimes in Shakespeare the relations between eye and ear resemble a romance plot of loss and restoration, a separation of two family members—younger and elder brothers, as Phineas Fletcher would have it in my epigraph—that is finally overcome in a scene of recognition. We can imagine those two senses that play leading roles in *The Tempest* (given the prevalence of both music and of scenes provoking wonder) as each wandering about that island in a state of forlornness, like the separate groups of castaways, before they are reunited in Prospero's masque. With its fusion of music, dance, text, and spectacle, the masque promises to harmonize the dissociated forms of auditory and visual experience that are so prominent in *The Tempest,* enchantment and wonder, which repeatedly threaten to paralyze thought and action.

In *A Midsummer Night's Dream,* the eye, sovereign among the senses according to a tradition dating back at least to Aristotle's *De Anima,* is easily mastered by a simple device: the juice of the flower love-in-idleness. Bottom's speech following his awakening in act 4 suggests that the story of eye and ear in that play doubles the comic plot of inversion and anarchic confusion: "The eye of man hath not heard, the ear of man hath not seen, man's hand is not able to taste, his tongue to conceive, nor his heart to report, what my dream was" (4.1.209–12). Given the chaotic realignment of faculties and their functions in Bottom's speech, it is unlikely that the visual medium of the dream will be successfully translated into an auditory one, a ballad, though that is Bottom's hope: "I will get Peter Quince to write a ballad of this dream: it shall be call'd 'Bottom's Dream,' because it hath no bottom; and I will sing it in the latter end of a play, before the Duke" (4.1.212–16).

Among the many confusions and inversions carried back from country to court at the end of the play (and not simply redressed, as it might appear), the confusion of the audible and visible will persist in the artisans' play before the Duke and Duchess. The marriage of spectacle and rhetoric, which in some sense is the aspiration of the play and Shakespeare's dramaturgy as a whole, is caricatured not only in Bottom's dream but also in Pyramus-Bottom's line, "I see a voice; now will I to the chink, / To spy and I can hear my Thisbe's face" (5.1.190–91), and Bottom's postmortem invitation, "Will it please you to see the epilogue, or to hear a Bergomask dance between two of our company?" (5.1.338–40).

But such a confusion is not confined to the working men of the comedy. When the Master of the Revels Philostrate presents a list of entertainments to the Duke, he enjoins, "Make choice of which your Highness will see first" (5.1.43). The first entertainment on the list, however, is a song, as if to suggest that the confusion of the visual and the auditory is not solely an ass's error: "The battle of the Centaurs, to be sung / By an Athenian eunuch to the harp" (5.1.44–45). Conversely, Theseus's choice of "Pyramus and Thisbe" is accompanied by a chorus of "hears" and "heards," even though this play, like much courtly entertainment of the time, will prove to be relentlessly visual.[25]

The six lovers presume to know just the right balance of auditory and visual elements required in a play. They denigrate the visual, whose exaggeration by the artisans, their interjections during the performance suggest, produces the crudest kind of theater. In scoffing at the crudely literal and visual staging by the artisans, the aristocratic lovers rather dubiously imply they have the power to command their own eyes, by translating words to images, rhetoric into scene. Such a claim seems hubristic, to say the least, given the recent emancipation of their eyes. (Demetrius's eyes, of course, remain charmed, as in a figurative sense are all the rest.) Both darkness ("Dark night, that from the eye his function takes" [3.2.177–8]) and the juice of a flower, having thoroughly overruled the lovers' eyes, are fairly representative of the ways *our* eyes are overruled by the rhetorical drama of the public theaters. And in a speech by Oberon, flowers, the instrument by which eyes are mastered in this play, themselves seem to possess eyes ("Stood now within the pretty flowerets' eyes," 4.1.54), thereby usurping the lovers' privilege of gazing. Given the mastery of their eyes by darkness and flower, it is comically appropriate that they be granted so many visual aids by the artisans to help them interpret the play of "Pyramus and Thisby."

Eyes and ears come close to acquiring class associations in *A Midsummer Night's Dream,* as if to echo the tradition that characterizes sight as the "noblest sense," as Phineas Fletcher calls it. Whereas the molestations of the aristocratic lovers always seem to involve their eyes, the disfigurement of the workingman involves his ears. Not only in Bottom's ass's ears but also in Theseus's hounds, magnified ears are associated with animality. Theseus's hounds have "ears that sweep away the morning dew" (4.1.120), and their barking, producing "the musical confusion / Of hounds and echo in conjunction" (4.1.109–10), seems destined similarly to pique and enlarge the ears of their human auditors. Both ass and hounds, whatever else they may echo, function as figures, or disfigurations, of Shakespeare's large-eared spectator. Ears must have been stretched a bit in the Elizabethan theaters, a circumstance that would seem to enlarge most auditors' sympathy with Bottom.

Conversely, our sympathy with the lovers may stem from our sharing the deprivation of their eyes. Shakespeare's theaters, no less than the darkness of the woods and the flower love-in-idleness, may be said to take "from the eye his function." But unlike the lovers, who are too fully creatures of the eyes, Elizabethan auditors, because of their kinship with long-eared Bottom, were not necessarily reduced to helpless victims when the eyes' functioning was denied.

A Midsummer Night's Dream repeatedly investigates the confusion of the visual and auditory, as well as the exaggeration of the one sense at the expense of the other. Nowhere do such investigations approach the middle and later tragedies' crisis of faith in the commensurability of the visual and verbal. In fact, the comic confusions of eye and ear often suggest something like a marriage plot. "So doth the woodbine the sweet honeysuckle / Gently entwist; the female ivy so / Enrings the barky fingers of the elm" (4.1.41–43); so do Titania's arms entwine her hairy lover; and so do the senses of eye and ear gently entwist and embrace in this play. The companionability of eye and ear is compactly illustrated in Titania's lines,

> I pray thee, gentle mortal, sing again:
> Mine ear is much enamour'd of thy note;
> So is mine eye enthralled to thy shape;
> And thy fair virtue's force perforce doth move me
> On the first view to say, to swear, I love thee.
>
> (3.1.132–36)

Eye and ear are fellow prisoners. The immediate effect of vision, "the first view," is an act of speech, suggesting that the two are not prisoners incommunicado: one sense understands and is able to communicate the other's travails.

If Titania makes eye and ear friends or sisters enthralled to the same creature, like Helena and Hermia or Lysander and Demetrius, Bottom makes them mutual lovers, in a way prefiguring the end of the play. Unlike Bottom, his fairy lover keeps eye and ear decorously aligned with "shape" and "note" respectively. But it is the artisanal entwisting of the audible and visible that is, at bottom, the play's device. This play and Renaissance theater as a whole may try to foster just the sort of synaesthesia Bottom unwittingly evokes in his speeches. After all, "To hear with eyes belongs to love's fine wit" (sonnet 23, l. 14). And to see with ears was so habitual in Renaissance theaters that Bottom might not have been far off the mark when proceeding to the chink "To spy and I can hear my Thisby's face."

"Tiber Trembled"

A translation from spectacle to report seems more controlled at the conclusion of Shakespeare's middle tragedy *Julius Caesar* than it promises to be in the ballad Bottom plans to commission from Peter Quince. Following Cassius's death, Messala seems less than eager to impart the news:

> Seek him, Titinius, whilst I go to meet
> The noble Brutus, thrusting this report
> Into his ears. I may say thrusting it;
> For piercing steel and darts envenomed
> Shall be as welcome to the ears of Brutus
> As tidings of this sight.
>
> (5.3.73–78)

Messala's lines suggest that spectacle and report, visual and aural signs, are stages in a uniform process of semiosis. The ear serves as relay for the eye. There is no difficulty of translation here, no incommensurability between verbal and visual evidence. The ear is simply the stage on which the violence of the original scene is to be reenacted. Messala's metaphor of words as swords and poisoned darts proves apt. Not long after his ear is brutalized by the report, Brutus seeks a piece of "piercing steel" to put an end to himself. Anticipating his own death, he imagines eye and ear, like two noble Romans and devoted friends, expiring simultaneously: "Brutus' tongue / Hath almost ended his life's history. / Night hangs upon mine eyes" (5.5.39–41).

The generally companionable relation of eye and ear in *Julius Caesar* is established early on, in the tribune Marullus's chastisement of the people for shifting their devotion so swiftly and effortlessly from Pompey to Caesar. Marullus's speech holds captive the mind's eye as well as the ear, echoing the effects of both Pompey's procession and the populace's deafening response to it. Like most characters in Renaissance plays, Marullus gives his audience an earful.

> Many a time and oft
> Have you climb'd up to walls and battlements,
> To towers and windows, yea, to chimney-tops,
> Your infants in your arms, and there have sat
> The livelong day, with patient expectation,
> To see great Pompey pass the streets of Rome:
> And when you saw his chariot but appear,
> Have you not made an universal shout,
> That Tiber trembled underneath her banks
> To hear the replication of your sounds
> Made in her concave shores?
>
> (1.1.37–47)

167

"Tiber trembled" is a microcosm of the entire speech and episode, reenacting in miniature the trembling of the waters occasioned by the people's roar. The verb is a trembling replication of the noun, all but one of the sounds of "Tiber" reverberating in "trembled." Furthermore, those sounds reverberate in a different order, giving the impression of a disorder produced by trembling, like that of a turgid river. Besides being a trembling version of "Tiber," "trembled" is also a swollen or dilated one, echoing the description of the Tiber crashing against its concave banks in response to the people's roar.

Further echo-effects in this speech about echoes are concentrated in the word "replication." Not only does it designate the echoing roars of the people against the banks of the Tiber, it also bears echoes of the reverberation of nature to the human as well as the reverberation of the auditory to the visual: the instantaneous translation of the eagerly awaited sight of Pompey into a tremendous sound equal to the sight. It is this reverberation of the auditory to the visual, the representation to the represented, that is crucial to the success of Marullus's rhetorical tour de force and that is reenacted in the movement of Marullus's speech as a whole. In other words, the original replication of the visual in the auditory within the space of the represented—the spectacle of Pompey's triumphal procession being met by the popular shout—is in turn "replicated" by the movement of Marullus's speech. That speech begins by delivering a vivid picture, though not of the Pompeyan spectacle but rather of its answering spectators. (This concentration of the visual interest of the speech on the vocal populace itself bodes the many replications between the visual and auditory in this speech.) Those images soon give way to a wash of consonance, to wave upon wave of replicated sounds as the speech becomes markedly less visual toward its close. Within the space of Marullus's representation, and in the space between represented and representation, therefore, the original replication of the visual in the auditory is twice reenacted.

The mutual animation of the auditory and the visual in Marullus's speech illustrates the achieved virtuosity of a playwright working from the Renaissance premise of the commensurability of the seen and the heard. Shakespeare's theater, more than any other English theater since, depended on the mutual animation of words and images, relying as it did largely on rhetoric to create "a swelling scene." In his next tragedy after *Julius Caesar*, he would "question more in particular," as Hamlet says to Rosencrantz and Guildenstern, this important premise of his own theatrical practices. In so doing, he would challenge not only the theatrical dependency on "words, words, words" to reproduce nearly the whole realm of the visible but also, and conversely, the power of the visible, particularly the spectacle of monarchy, to signify, including its power to re-present the whole political body of the realm.

Talking Heads

Magni dominator poli,
Tam lentus audis scelera, tam lentus vides?
                                    (*Titus Andronicus,* 4.1.81–82)

Titus Andronicus features many dissociative effects where either the visual or the auditory sense temporarily gains the upper hand. In the early tragedy, such dissociations always meet with disaster or are themselves the consequence of a disastrous event, unlike, say, *Hamlet* or *King Lear,* where similar dissociations are used to curative or restorative ends. Occasions in *Titus* where either the visual or the auditory becomes predominant include Aaron's spying through "the crevice of a wall" upon the grotesque exchange of Titus's hands for the heads of his sons; Bassanius's gaze when compared by Tamora to Actaeon's; the babbling noise of the hunt that Aaron and Tamora, shaded by the forest, can hear but not see, the same forest that sanctions Chiron and Demetrius's crime; Lavinia's pitiful reduction to a dumb picture; and the power of that "dear sight," according to Marcus, to reduce her beholders to a "stony image cold and numb," echoing the many gestures of enforced silencing that occur in this play. The unrelievedly visual experience of a disfigured Lavinia belongs to the middle of the tragedy, where the temporary divorce of sight from sound, of eye and ear, may be redressed in what follows. The middle and later tragedies are more prone than the early ones to end on a note of exile of the visual from the auditory without time or hope for reprieve.

Consistent with the coordination of the visual and verbal in the Shakespearean theater, sights are more often cast in the roles of oppressors, and the eyes as victims, in Shakespeare than in the period that succeeds him, during which, as Foucault's work has demonstrated, those roles are customarily reversed. That is certainly the case in Lavinia's transformation into "this sight" (3.1.247), "this dear sight" (3.1.257). Even in this most extreme instance of dissociation, seeing and hearing do not remain long estranged. Like pictures in Renaissance emblem books, this one learns to "speak." Her father swears, "I can interpret all her martyred signs" (3.2.36), and vows to her, "Thou shalt not sigh, nor hold thy stumps to heaven, / Nor wink, nor nod, nor kneel, nor make a sign, / But I of these will wrest an alphabet, / And by still practice

169

learn to know thy meaning" (3.2.42–45). Similarly, the severed heads of Titus's falsely accused sons Quintus and Martius: "For these two heads do seem to speak to me" (3.1.272). The play's practice is to regard the seen and the heard as warp and woof of a single text. "These words, these looks, infuse new life in me," Titus addresses Tamora toward the end of the opening scene (1.1.466). An enraged Marcus conjectures,

> O, had the monster seen those lily hands
> Tremble like aspen leaves upon a lute
> And make the silken strings delight to kiss them,
> He would not then have touched them for his life.
> Or had he heard the heavenly harmony
> Which that sweet tongue hath made,
> He would have dropped his knife and fell asleep,
> As Cerberus at the Thracian poet's feet.
>
> (2.3.44–51)

The symmetry of the speech, proceeding first from a visual/auditory event (seeing her hands make music) described in mostly visual terms, yielding to the auditory (her singing voice), in turn leading to a visual, emblemlike description, itself forecasts the eventual repair of the tearing of the visual from the auditory through Lavinia's mutilation.

For all the references to blindness in this play—for instance, Marcus's next lines, "Come, let us go and make thy father blind, / For such a sight will blind a father's eye" (2.3.52–53)—*Titus Andronicus* does not take those references in the direction of *King Lear.* The earlier play stops short of making eye and ear competitors, rival and often mutually uncomprehending modes of apprehension.

The Ear's Supervision of the Eye in *Romeo and Juliet*

When Lady Capulet is exposed to the sight of her dead daughter and son-in-law, she immediately transforms them into an auditory emblem of mortality, a tolling bell: "O me! This sight of death is as a bell / That warns my old age to a sepulchre" (5.3.205–6). Her response, though expressive of her iciness, resembles those of more sympathetic characters in its insistence on textualizing and moralizing the sight. "Pitiful sight!" is the simple and, by comparison with Lady Capulet's egoistical response, moving exclamation of the Chief Watchman gazing upon the corpses of Paris and Juliet. Caesar's corpse is referred to in a similar phrase, as are the bodies in the fifth acts of *Hamlet* and *King Lear.* The corpses in the earlier tragedies, *Romeo and Juliet* and *Julius*

Caesar, are embalmed by the rhetoric of Friar Lawrence and Brutus (though Caesar's corpse springs to life again in Antony's oration before the people). No one is able to successfully serve that function with regard to the more spirited corpse of Hamlet.[26]

What constitutes reasonable faith and interest in vision? Romeo and Friar Lawrence represent two sides of the question. "When the devout religion of mine eye / Maintains such falsehood, then turn tears to fire" (1.2.90–91), Romeo responds to Benvolio's proposal that he attend the feast of the Capulets "with unattainted eye" (l. 87), willing to compare Rosaline's face with others. Friar Lawrence characteristically remarks, "Young men's love then lies / Not truly in their hearts but in their eyes" (2.3.63–64). The opposition comes into sharpest focus when the Friar responds to Romeo's injunction "Talk no more," "O, then I see that mad men have no ears" (3.3.61), to which Romeo parries, "How should they when that wise men have no eyes?" (l. 62). Lovers' exaggerated faith in their eyes reflects a similarly misplaced confidence in the play in eyes as agents (and representations) of political control. An ineffectual "watch" is raised following Romeo's banishment, and Prince Escalus attributes the tragic consequences to a temporary lapse of vigilance on his part, an error of the eyes: "And I, for winking at your discords too, / Have lost a brace of kinsmen" (5.3.293–94). Following the Prince's chastisement, the patriarchs of the two houses repeat the error of enthroning the visual by proposing to erect gold statues to the dead lovers. The play compensates for all these overestimations of sight by placing vision under the supervision of the auditory. We are enjoined by the Prologue not to see but to hear the play: "if you with patient ears attend" (Prol. 13).

Pictures regularly speak in *Romeo and Juliet,* so that the visual is not accorded an independent status. Juliet on her balcony overlooking her father's orchard speaks to Romeo before she starts to speak: "She speaks, yet she says nothing. What of that?" (2.2.12). Not only does the eye speak—"Her eye discourses, I will answer it" (2.2.13)—but it is also, in Lady Capulet's conceit, the margin of the book that is the face, a page margin that will gloss and help to explain whatever Juliet finds uncertain or obscure about the County Paris: "And what obscur'd in this fair volume lies, / Find written in the margent of his eyes" (1.3.85–86). Construed as marginal commentary on a text, the very instrument of seeing is decisively prevented from asserting an independence from language and interpretation and becoming anything like an omniscient instrument of surveillance. When the eye is most empowered in *Romeo and Juliet*—for instance, in the masque scene when Romeo's disguise allows him secretly to survey the scene before him, to see but not to be

171

seen—it is also the most frustrated, for the concealed eye finds it harder to recognize others, who are similarly protected by masks. Capulet's speech toward the beginning of the scene associates the donning of masks not with empowerment of the eye by which Romeo devoutly worships but rather with entry into the kingdom of the ear: "I have seen the day / That I have worn a visor and could tell / A whispering tale in a fair lady's ear" (1.5.21–23). And it is by the ear rather than the eye that Romeo is discovered by Tybalt at the feast: "This by his voice should be a Montague" (1.5.53). Voice and ear betray this rapturous disciple of the devout religion of the eye, an enthusiast who immediately before Tybalt's line of discovery has been busily instructing his eye and ignoring the sense that will undo him: "Did my heart love till now? Forswear it, sight. / For I ne'er saw true beauty till this night" (ll. 51–52). The many references to the blindfolded Cupid (1.1.169; 1.4.4; 2.1.33; 3.2.9–10) also figure in the play's delicate system of checks and balances between eye and ear, suggesting as they do that the lover's religion of the eye is futile and self-canceling, a form of blindness.

"Hear all, all see," Capulet enjoins Paris, inviting the suitor to feast both his senses upon all the elegant young women of Verona at his house (1.2.30). Mercutio mocks, "Alas poor Romeo, he is already dead, stabbed with a white wench's black eye, run through the ear with a love song" (2.4.13–15).[27] In Romeo and Juliet Shakespeare casts eye and ear as companions; later in his career he begins to construe them as rivals. The growing rivalry between the visual and verbal components of his theater does not simply register his growing virtuosity as a playwright, his ability to make theatrical capital by casting in antagonistic roles the two senses of the spectator/auditor that the theater primarily engages. The shift in Shakespeare's handling of the relations between seeing and hearing may very well participate in a larger drama of the dissociation of the seen and the heard, which will produce such developments as the rise of modern science and the construction of the bourgeois subject.

"All eyes!": The Growing Independence of Vision in Shakespeare's Jacobean Plays

Differences in the ways that Othello and Romeo and Juliet pun on "eye" and "I" are a good measure of the relative independence of sight in the later tragedies. Punning on "eye," "ay," and "I" occurs frequently enough in Romeo and Juliet to constitute a pattern. In general, "eye" and "I" play the parts of sparring partners, even enemies. Toward the beginning of the scene in which Mercutio and Tybalt are slain, Benvolio protests, "Here all eyes gaze on us," which Mercutio answers with the pronouncement, "Men's eyes were made to look, and let them gaze. / I will not budge for no man's pleasure, I" (3.1.52–54). Mercutio calls on the homonym to assert the staunchness of his "I," which will answer to and be the equal of the "eye" of the other.

In the next scene, the chain of antagonistic effects between "eye" and "I" continues. Juliet, hearing from her nurse ambiguous news linking Romeo to death, launches into a salvo of "Ay," that syllable of affirmation and confirmation; "eye," frequently the means or instrument of confirmation; and "I," the subject who in this instance will be not confirmed but annihilated by the very vowel with which she uses to designate herself:

> Hath Romeo slain himself? Say thou but "Ay"
> And that bare vowel "I" shall poison more
> Than the death-darting eye of cockatrice.
> I am not I if there be such an "I,"
> Or those eyes shut that makes thee answer "Ay.' "
> If he be slain say "Ay," or if not, "No."
> Brief sounds determine of my weal or woe.
>
> (3.2.45–51)

For Juliet "Ay" will have the effect of the basilisk's "eye": namely, of slaying her "I." The nurse's reply echoes Juliet's echo effects, though in a much less elaborate way: "I saw the wound, I saw it with mine eyes— . . . I swounded at the sight" (3.2.52,56).

And in the next scene, when Friar Lawrence enjoins Romeo to hide when they hear a knock at the door, Romeo stubbornly resists, "Not I; unless the breath of heartsick groans / Mist-like infold me from the search of eyes" (3.3.72–73). A multiple pun lends emphasis to the phrase of refusal. "Not I" expresses both "not ay," a periphrasis for "no"; "not eye," the desire especially of Friar Lawrence that Romeo escape the watch; and Romeo's resignation to being discovered and negated by the searching "eye" of the watch. Throughout these middle scenes from the play, "eye" and "I" are mutually antagonistic. In this early tragedy we are far indeed from a Foucauldian "eye of power," where the subject's authority is asserted and defined in terms of the gaze.[28] Unlike in the later tragedies *Hamlet, Othello,* and *King Lear,* there is no recourse in these scenes to the ear as a friendly alternative to the eye, for it is by the ear that Romeo expects to be betrayed, even if he hides in the Friar's cell. His "heartsick groans" will reveal him, just as his voice betrayed him to the ear of Tybalt when a masquer at Capulet's feast. The distance between all these eyes and the "eye of power" Foucault locates in the

classical episteme is absolute and profound. In *Romeo and Juliet* the
eye is a vulnerable as well as an aggressive organ: it is more frequently
the site and means of the subject's cancellation than of the subject's
apotheosis, commonly playing the part of the I's antagonist rather than
its henchman.

In later plays like *Hamlet, Othello,* and *King Lear,* ear and eye are
regularly pitted against one another and used as a means of designating,
by a kind of shorthand, political alternatives. *Hamlet* first sketches
the difference between the old king and the new king in terms of
the difference between ear and eye. Both *Othello* and *King Lear* cast
the ear as a court of appeal, a potential check and balance on the
commanding eye. The play that is perhaps more critical of Renaissance
sovereignty than any other Shakespeare wrote, *King Lear* tells the story
of the dethronement of what Phineas Fletcher in one of my epigraphs
calls "the noblest sense." Lear expostulates in his madness, "A man may
see how this world goes with no eyes. Look with thine ears: see how
yond justice rails upon yond simple thief. Hark, in thine ear: change
places, and, handy-dandy, which is the justice, which is the thief?"
(4.6.148–52). *King Lear* is equally a story that instructs the eye to take
on a new function, the conveyance of recognition and sympathy rather
than authority and control.[29] Because like Shakespeare's other Jacobean
plays it helps to dissociate the senses of seeing and hearing, this story of
the eye's abdication may also prepare for its eventual return in triumph,
like that of the banished Bolingbroke, in the romances.

In *Othello* the eye has politically realigned itself, so to speak, now
identifying its own interests with those of the "I." After the Duke of
Venice requests that Desdemona be housed the night of her betrothal
with her father, Brabantio is the first to respond: "I will not have it so."
Othello immediately seconds, "Nor I." And Desdemona not only echoes
her husband's phrase but also transforms (paradoxically, for the rival ear
but not for the eye) those marks of subjectivity into the commanding
"eye" of her father, an "eye" no less imposing than its owner's "I":

> Nor I, I would not there reside,
> To put my father in impatient thoughts
> By being in his eye: most gracious duke,
> To my unfolding lend a gracious ear
> And let me find a charter in your voice.
> (1.3.240–45)

Desdemona associates the eye with personal identity, authority, and
control. The ear she paints as the organ of compassion, as elsewhere

the dark and secret spaces of the ear come across as the conduit for passion: for instance, in the scenes between Iago and the two characters, Roderigo and Othello, whose ears are most afflicted with the poison he deposits there, and in Desdemona's description of how Othello won her love.[30] Brabantio clearly underestimates the importance of both these roles: "I never yet did hear / That the bruis'd heart was pierced through the ear" (1.3.218–19).

In Othello's insistence to Iago on "ocular proof" as in speeches on the ruse of the Turkish fleet, the eye is associated with reason and control. The First Senator comments, "This cannot be / By no assay of reason . . .'tis a pageant, / To keep us in false gaze" (1.3.17–19). Othello's mistake in judgment with regard to Iago is, in our terms, to confuse the distinct offices of eye and ear, to associate Iago's constant buzzing in his ear with reason rather than passion. Such confusion could hardly take place in *Romeo and Juliet* because there the offices of eye and ear are not construed as distinct.

By the end of the seventeenth century, the modern, perspectival-ist, Cartesian subject—constructed largely by means of metaphors of vision—would be essential for constituting the field of the visual as a *unified* field.[31] In the Renaissance, by contrast, the subject's gaze is not essential for this purpose: such unity is already implicit in the conception of the visible as part of a larger text. Things, already imbued with meanings that need only to be discovered, do not require the subject's gaze to stabilize the flux of phenomena or to constitute them as a whole. Consequently, the dissociation of the seen and the heard is an essential part of the process by means of which modern notions of the subject and subjectivity will be constituted. Steps in that process seem already to have been taken in the space between Shakespeare's earlier and middle plays. The "I"/"eye" puns in Desdemona's exchange with her father, far more than the profusion of similar puns in speeches by Mercutio, Juliet, and Romeo, situate the gaze close to the center of the constitution of the modern subject.

Shakespeare's developing practice of relating the visual to the verbal owes much to the particular sovereigns under whom he wrote, his iconoclasm growing ever stronger under the reign of a monarch who was far less comfortable than his predecessor in subjecting his person to the gaze of his people. Through her pageantry Elizabeth often capitalized on the ability of the monarch's body to function as "speaking picture," to convey by means of the carefully staged display of that body both the signs of royal power and the idea of the nation. That she embodied something like Henry V's principle in my epigraph, "Not working with the eye without the ear," is perhaps most vividly illustrated in her notorious Rainbow Portrait of 1602. The signs of her royal power emblazoned upon her garments include not only eyes to indicate her all-seeing power but ears as well. As Cesare Ripa described it in *Iconologia,* "She is represented in a garment . . . woven with eyes and ears to symbolise her jealous hold over her dominion, and her desire to have the eyes and ears of spies, the better to judge her own plans and those of others."[32] King James, by contrast, more commonly associated royal power with the gaze of a sequestered eye, as many of Shakespeare's Jacobean plays reflect.

To my mind Foucault's narrative of the unraveling of that tapestry whose warp and woof are words and images and of the enthronement of a newly independent eye after the Renaissance, does not compete with more local or topical reference points for the changing status of the gaze in Shakespearean tragedy. Rather, Foucault's is a suggestive way of understanding the more local developments, in both the theatrical and the political sphere, in the context of a larger historical transformation, thereby adding to rather than subtracting from the meanings associated with Shakespeare's topicality. To be sure, Foucault exaggerates the amicability of eye and ear in the Renaissance by ignoring at least two currents of thought: the tradition dating back at least as far as Aristotle that granted special privileges to the eye long before the classical period; and the important iconoclastic tradition issuing from the Reformation, which caused many a charge of idolatry to be hurled at the Renaissance stage.[33] Spenser and the humanist poetics of the English Renaissance in general registered a distrust of visual perception.[34]

Both parties, of the ear and of the eye, associated the less valued sense with the passions. For Jonson, for instance, the channel of the ear provided the most direct route to the mind; appeals to the ear were less crudely emotional than appeals to the eye. Those in the Renaissance who privileged the eye generally did so on the same grounds: "the minde is like the eye," Sir John Davies writes in *Nosce Teipsum* (l. 105),[35] whereas it is in the dark and secret spaces of the ears that the passions are most apt to run riot. Attention to the countertradition of iconoclasm would demonstrate certain tensions between the visual and the verbal to be already well established in the Renaissance and challenge Foucault's notion of a swift, clean epistemological break that separates the Renaissance from the classical episteme. Nevertheless, the notion of a general shift toward ocularcentrism in all disciplines at the end of the Renaissance seems richly suggestive for understanding the second half of Shakespeare's career.

The ocularcentrism of the succeeding age will be manifested in a variety of ways: in the birth of a new ocular concept of madness, which according to Foucault persists, albeit in modified form, even in Freud;[36] a new disciplinary power derived from an elaborate system of surveillance;[37] the rise of modern science, with its stress on observation; the continuance and eventual triumph in the eighteenth century of the Gutenberg revolution; Descartes's emphasis on clear and distinct ideas; Locke's pictorial view of language;[38] Rousseau's dream of a transparent society, in which each individual might see the whole without obstruction, in which the hearts of all would be visible to all;[39] the Panopticon of Jeremy Bentham and his predecessors, which transformed visibility into an isolating phenomenon,[40] and in which power has shifted decisively from a privileged visibility reaching its apogee in the monarch to the vision of an unseen spectator; in eighteenth-century English poetry, in John Barrell's words, "the ideal of the universal observer who 'superior to the little Fray' of competing interests, understands the relations among them all";[41] the rise of the proscenium-arch theater, a theater that implicitly privileges vision in a way that the Renaissance public theaters did not, and the increasing dependence on theatrical scenery; and the resolutely visual *ut pictura poesis* tradition that dominated English literary neoclassicism,[42] to name just a few.

One of the most celebrated literary enterprises of eighteenth-century England, Joseph Addison's *The Spectator*, was similarly based on the ocularist metaphor and on the premise of both a definite hierarchy and an incommensurability of the seen and the heard. In the first number of *The Spectator*, Addison describes his extreme sullenness as a youth: "I had not been long at the University before I distinguished myself by a most profound silence; for during the space of eight years, excepting in the public exercises of the college, I scarce uttered the quantity of a hundred words; and, indeed, do not remember that I ever spoke three sentences together in my whole life."[43] It is as if he himself, even in youth, exemplified the dissociation of word and image, the visible and the audible, that would help define the period.

He then describes his existence as a secret agent of culture, building to a justification of his fundamental metaphor:

> My face is likewise very well known at the Grecian, the Cocoa-Tree, and in the theatres, both of Drury Lane and the Haymarket. I have been taken for a merchant upon the Exchange for above these ten years, and sometimes pass for a Jew in the assembly of stock-jobbers at Jonathan's. In short, wherever I see a cluster of people I always mix with them, though I never open my lips but in my own club.
>
> Thus I live in the world rather as a spectator of mankind than as one of the species, by which means I have made myself a speculative

statesman, soldier, merchant, and artisan, without ever meddling with any practical part of life.[44]

The mention of the theaters immediately suggests to Addison the theatrical metaphor. At the Exchange and at Jonathan's Coffee-House in Change Alley, Addison is an actor simply by maintaining silence. He is a cast of characters to himself, merchant *and* Jew, and soldier, statesman, and artisan besides. Hence his lack of need for speech: he implies that in his own dual position both as spectacle and as transcendent spectator (he is "a spectator of mankind" but not "one of the species") he transcends conflicts like the one between Antonio and Shylock.

Addison's theatrical metaphor, with its division of theatricality from speech, marks a clear break from Shakespeare's. Unlike Shakespeare's characters, for whom theatricalizing is largely (though not exclusively) a matter of speech, it is only by maintaining a scrupulous silence that Addison allows himself to become theatricalized. Both understanding *and* its correlate misunderstanding—for Addison is mistaken for merchant and Jew because he does not speak—are within the empire of the gaze; they are not, as they ordinarily are in the earlier plays of Shakespeare, joint responsibilities of the eye and ear. Furthermore, the misunderstanding generated by Addison's silence is far from threatening: such misunderstanding appears to work in the service of truth under the transcendent gaze of the spectator. For Addison as spectacle, as passive impersonator of merchant and Jew, is not merely a source of error but also a peacemaker. As spectacle Addison does not experience a Sartrean reversal of power, as a subject is reduced to the status of object beneath the gaze of the Other. Rather, Addison as spectacle remains under the calm, confident supervision of Addison as spectator, even becoming an instrument of the spectator's pursuit of truth. The eye in Addison's project is not even attended let alone supervised by the ear. But the road to the dominance of vision evident in a project like *The Spectator* is already being laid in the (still overwhelmingly rhetorical) middle and later plays of Shakespeare.

Bardolatry has led us for too long to suppose that Shakespeare, like no other before or since, achieved a perfect mix of word and image, spectacle and speech. As a result, we have to some extent been blind to the larger implications (or deaf to the rumblings) of what may otherwise appear to be the isolated and local severance of what is seen from what is heard in the tragedies. Theater history may be charged with a similar parochialism. It is frequently maintained that Jacobean theater, following the golden age of Elizabethan drama, upset the balance of power between eye and ear. Through "the gradual adoption of movable scenery," the Jacobeans caused "the ultimate separation of poetry and drama."[45] But movable scenery, far from being the villain in this tragedy of the theater, may be little more than a lackey in "the court of [the] eye," as Boyet calls it in *Love's Labour's Lost* (2.1.235).

"All eyes!" commands Prospero as the entertainment he has devised for Ferdinand and Miranda is about to begin (4.1.59). Although Prospero's masque may amount to an attempt to keep rather extreme forms of the visual and auditory, namely wonder and enchantment, within one another's rather wide orbits, his command should alert us to the conflicting demands of being an auditor and a spectator of Shakespeare's later plays—keep us watchful, like the sentinels in the opening scene of *Hamlet,* for the forces that will enthrone the eye just about the time the monarchy is presumed to have been abolished.

Many of the ordering principles of Renaissance tragedy are intimately related to those of Elizabethan social and political life. So to claim that Shakespearean tragedy is preoccupied with the unmasking of some of its rhetorical principles and representational practices is not at all to suggest a narcissistic self-involvement on the part of that body of work. I hope this study has helped demonstrate that one of the most effective ways of uncovering the broader cultural and political investments of Shakespeare's tragedies is by following those plays' continuing renegotiations with the ordering principles of the genre that they so brilliantly represent.

In retrospect it seems my method has imitated the much noted "double-time" of Shakespeare's dramatic practice: his tendency to use two time schemes, a speeded up movement in the foreground often summing up the slower movement of time in the background. In the preceding chapters, particulars of the reigns of Elizabeth and James alternate with material of a larger historical scope: the shift in the meaning of "representation" in the seventeenth century, the gradual dominance of the sense of sight in later seventeenth- and eighteenth-century thought and culture, or the rise of party politics and Locke's reluctant embrace of the inevitability of human partiality. This dual time scheme is important, I think, for more thoroughly understanding one of the greatest dramas within Shakespearean drama: the tremors in the epistemological ground that would soon make tragedy in its Renaissance forms obsolete.

NOTES

Fast Foreword

1. I have consulted primarily three editions of the plays: the Oxford Shakespeare, the New Cambridge Shakespeare, and the New Arden Shakespeare. Most citations from the plays refer to the New Arden editions (3rd series, where available: *Titus Andronicus, Antony and Cleopatra,* and *King Henry V*). Exceptions are *Macbeth* and *Henry IV, Part 1,* for which I have used the Oxford Shakespeare editions.

2. On Elizabeth's struggle for control of her representations, see Susan Frye's stimulating recent account, *Elizabeth I: The Competition for Representation* (New York: Oxford, 1993); and Frances Yates, *Astraea: The Imperial Theme in the Sixteenth Century* (London: Routledge & Kegan Paul, 1975). On James I, see Jonathan Goldberg, *James I and the Politics of Literature: Jonson, Shakespeare, Donne, and Their Contemporaries* (Stanford: Stanford University Press, 1989). Other important recent studies on the political implications of theatrical representation in the Renaissance include Franco Moretti, "The Great Eclipse," in *Signs Taken for Wonders: Essays in the Sociology of Literary Forms,* rev. ed., trans. Susan Fischer, David Forgacs, and David Miller (London: Verso, 1988); David Scott Kastan, "Proud Majesty Made a Subject: Shakespeare and the Spectacle of Rule," *Shakespeare Quarterly* 37 (1986): 459–75; Leonard Tennenhouse, *Power on Display: The Politics of Shakespeare's Genres* (London: Methuen, 1986); and Christopher Pye, *The Regal Phantasm: Shakespeare and the Politics of Spectacle* (London: Methuen, 1990).

3. William Empson, *Some Versions of Pastoral* (1935; rpt., New York: New Directions, 1974), 197–98.

4. Ibid., 198.

5. The best sources for understanding conflicting and developing concepts of "representation" in seventeenth-century England are Hanna Fenichel Pitkin, *The Concept of Representation* (Berkeley and Los Angeles: University of California Press, 1967); Raymond Williams, *Keywords: A Vocabulary of Culture and Society* (New York: Oxford University Press, 1976); and Louise Fargo Brown, "Ideas of Representation from Elizabeth to Charles III," *Journal of Modern History* 11 (1939): 23–40.

6. Most work on Shakespearean representation places the accent on the what, not the whom: that is, representation in the sense of mimesis or the imitation of reality. See, for example, Howard Felperin, *Shakespearean Representation: Mimesis and Modernity in Elizabethan Tragedy* (Princeton: Princeton University Press, 1977); and A. D. Nuttall, *A New Mimesis: Shakespeare and the Representation of Reality* (London: Methuen, 1983). One of the most

effective ways of viewing Shakespearean drama culturally and historically, however, is by placing the accent in questions of representation on how and whom: the very questions, in other words, that govern discussions of political representation.

7. The unmasking of drama enacted repeatedly in Shakespeare's most complex plays is a process, not an end result: hence *The Unmasking of Drama,* not *Drama Unmasked,* which would have moved these speculations far from the spirit of Shakespeare's plays and toward Victorian melodrama. Shakespeare's unmasking of drama doesn't result in full exposure of a face behind the mask—perhaps a *Hamlet*-like ghost, the ghost of literary representation future, or a *Macbeth*-like apparition, the spirit of the novel—but only of further masks, other inquisitions, theaters, theories, acts, or ways of seeing.

8. Stephen Greenblatt, *Shakespearean Negotiations* (Berkeley and Los Angeles: University of California Press, 1988), 64.

9. Moretti, *Signs Taken for Wonders,* 54.

10. *The Political Works of James I,* ed. C. H. McIlwain (Cambridge, Mass.: Harvard University Press, 1918), 63.

11. Sir Thomas Elyot, *The Boke Named The Gouernour,* vol. 1, ed. Henry Herbert Stephen Croft (New York: Burt Franklin, 1967), 9.

12. *Shakespearean Negotiations,* 64.

13. Michel Foucault, *The Order of Things: An Archaeology of the Human Sciences* (New York: Vintage Books, 1973), 39, 43, 130f.

14. Even the new historicists tend for the most part to study Shakespeare synchronically, in relation to contemporary cultural and political issues but for the most part outside a line of succession that would help to situate Shakespeare in relation to later cultural developments.

Chapter 1

1. G. R. Elton, *The Tudor Constitution: Documents and Commentary* (Cambridge: Cambridge University Press, 1960), 230.

2. See J. E. Neale, *Elizabeth I and Her Parliaments: 1559–1581* (London: Cape, 1953); *Elizabeth I and Her Parliaments: 1584–1601* (London: Cape, 1957); and *The Elizabethan House of Commons* (London: Cape, 1949). Lawrence Stone, *The Causes of the English Revolution, 1529–1642* (New York: Harper and Row, 1972), argues that "the winning of the initiative by the House of Commons was a radical step achieved under the smokescreen of the conservative ideology of a return to the past" (93).

3. Wallace MacCaffrey, *Elizabeth I* (London: Edward Arnold, 1993), 374.

4. W. Gordon Zeeveld, "*Coriolanus* and Jacobean Politics," *Modern Language Review* 57 (1962): 326. Zeeveld's is an important essay for showing the importance of parliamentary history to the play. See also the superb discussion of parliamentary questions in *Coriolanus* by Richard Wilson, *Will Power: Essays on Shakespearean Authority* (Detroit: Wayne State University Press, 1993), 83–117; Shannon Miller, "Topicality and Subversion in William Shakespeare's *Coriolanus,*" *Studies in English Literature* 32 (1992): 287–310; Mark A. Kishlansky, *Parliamentary Selection: Social and Political Choice in Early Modern England* (Cambridge: Cambridge University Press, 1986), esp. 3–9 (Kishlansky introduces his subject by referring to *Coriolanus*); and Clifford Chalmers Huffman, *Coriolanus in Context* (Lewisburg: Bucknell University Press, 1971), esp. 137–55. Wilson draws on and develops Kishlansky's arguments, showing in detail that "representation is in flux in this play as it was in Shakespeare's Warwickshire" (99).

5. Kishlansky, *Parliamentary Selection,* 7–8.

6. Ibid., 8. See also Derek Hirst, *The Representative of the People?: Voters and Voting in England under the Early Stuarts* (Cambridge: Cambridge University Press, 1975).

7. Sir Thomas Smith, *De Republica Anglorum,* ed. L. Alston (Cambridge: Cambridge University Press, 1906), 48–49.

8. Recently historians tend to downplay the difference between Elizabeth's and James's relations with their parliaments, differences that were exaggerated by the old Whig historical tradition according to which "Elizabeth had been committed to her parliaments and had generally managed to achieve productive working accommodations with them, [whereas] James found his parliaments incomprehensible and annoying and soon resolved to dispense with them altogether." Christopher Durston, *James I,* Lancaster Pamphlets (London: Routledge, 1993), 34. Durston usefully summarizes revisionist and post-revisionist history on James and his parliaments (34–43). T. E. Hartley, *Elizabeth's Parliaments: Queen, Lords and Commons, 1559–1601* (Manchester: Manchester University Press, 1992), argues "that Parliament in Elizabeth's reign was characterized by much greater opposition than Neale imagined" (165), without going to the extremes of some of Neale's revisionist critics.

9. Sixty-two borough seats were added in Elizabeth's reign, continuing at a greatly accelerated rate the trend of her predecessors Henry, Edward, and Mary.

10. Durston, *James I,* 35.

11. Zeeveld, *"Coriolanus* and Jacobean Politics," 325. See also Margaret A. Judson, *The Crisis of the Constitution: An Essay in Constitutional and Political Thought in England, 1603–1645* (1949; rpt., New Brunswick: Rutgers University Press, 1988), 283; and Louise Fargo Brown, "Ideas of Representation from Elizabeth to Charles II," *Journal of Modern History* 11 (1939): 23–40. Brown writes that "two ideas—that the commons represented property and that they represented the people—are to be met with throughout this period [from Elizabeth to Charles II]. In the parliaments of Elizabeth there was a marked growth in the commons of a sense of dignity and importance and of a feeling of responsibility as trustees of the nation" (39). Judson writes mainly of the 1620s when she writes that "the idea of parliamentary responsibility to the nation developed so rapidly" (283).

12. *The Political Works of James I,* ed. C. H. McIlwain (Cambridge, Mass.: Harvard University Press, 1918), 19.

13. Hanna Fenichel Pitkin, *The Concept of Representation* (Berkeley and Los Angeles: University of California Press, 1967), 248–49.

14. *Leviathan,* ed. C. B. Macpherson (Harmondsworth: Penguin Books, 1968), 220.

15. John Guy, *Tudor England* (Oxford: Oxford University Press, 1988), 352.

16. Ibid.

17. The theory of the humors implied a condition of wholeness that could be disturbed but not wholly effaced or forgotten by an imbalance of the humors, the dominance of one humor at the expense of the other three and to the detriment of the individual.

18. Williams, *Keywords,* 223.

19. Matthew Arnold, "The French Play in London," *Nineteenth Century* 30 (August 1879): 238. Cited in Loren Kruger, *The National Stage: Theatre and Cultural Legitimation in England, France, and America* (Chicago: University of Chicago Press, 1992), 92.

20. Without a sovereign to re-present them, the people do not yet constitute a body politic for Hobbes, so the sovereign's function of re-presenting the people is not a making present again: in other words, no assumed whole condition precedes the sovereign's representation; rather, such "re" presentation is necessary for the people to become (originally, for the first time) present as a whole body or body politic. See Hobbes, *Leviathan,* 220f.; and also Hanna Fenichel Pitkin's important discussion of representation in Hobbes in *Concept of Representation,* 14–37. Pitkin has included an extremely useful appendix on the etymology of "representation" and its derivatives (241–52).

21. In addition to Pitkin, *Concept of Representation,* 241–52, see the entirety of Raymond Williams's article on "Representative" in *Keywords,* 222–25.

In the 1640s a group of Leveller army officers drew up an important manifesto that called attention to problems of representation within the kingdom that became apparent when the whole concept of representation came to be redefined, dissociated from the older, quasi-mystical sense of the monarch's re-presenting the whole of the body politic. The first article of the document reads, "That the People of England being at this day very unequally distributed by Counties, Cities, and Burroughs, for the election of their Deputies in Parliament, ought to be more [fairly] proportioned, according to the number of the Inhabitants: the circumstances whereof, for number, place, and manner, are to be set down before the end of this present Parliament" ("An Agreement of the People, for a Firme and Present Peace, upon Grounds of Common-Right," October 1647). Among other things, this article presumes, contrary to Elizabethan and early Stuart thinking, that MPs were representative of particular constituencies rather than the whole political body.

22. The older meaning of "representative," Pitkin notes, involved both a legal fiction, as it pertained to Parliament (the idea, deriving from Roman law, being that "parties who have legal rights at stake in a judicial action are entitled to be present or at least consulted in its decision"), and a quasi-mystical conception, as it pertained to the monarch: "the king is not merely the head of the national body, not merely the owner of the entire realm, but he is the crown, the realm, the nation. The idea goes beyond either representation or symbolization as we now conceive them, and involves a mystic unity" (*Concept of Representation,* 245–46).

23. Ibid., 249.

24. Williams, *Keywords,* 225.

25. For a brilliant analysis of the redefinition of representation in a French context, see Keith Michael Baker, *Inventing the French Revolution* (Cambridge: Cambridge University Press, 1990), 224–51. I am indebted to my colleague Jean Pedersen for this reference.

26. Rymer's *The Tragedies of the Last Age* (1677) and *A Short View of Tragedy* (1692) are his most important works. The latter is a condemnation of all modern drama in the name of the ancients. In his defense of English drama against all rivals, ancient and modern, "Essay of Dramatic Poesy" (1668; rev., 1684), Dryden claims that the ancient tragedy and comedy "contained only the general characters of men and manners; as old men, lovers, serving-men, courtesans, parasites, and such other persons . . . ; all which they made alike; that is, one old man or father, one lover, one courtesan, so like another, as if the first of them had begot the rest of every sort." What distinguishes the English humor character is his or her particularity: "the person represented is fantastic or bizarre" and "immediately distinguished from the rest of men" (in Allan H. Gilbert, ed., *Literary Criticism: Plato to Dryden* [1940; rpt., Detroit: Wayne State University Press, 1962], 641).

27. It seems counterproductive to me, for the purposes of understanding literary history, simply to adopt an anti-Rymerian stance, privileging the Shakespearean mode of re-presentation at the expense of subsequent forms of representation. For instance, simply to celebrate the Shakespearean, or more broadly the Renaissance, conception of character for the element of comprehensiveness lacking in its literary successors is to miss an essential historical point about the relatedness of literary and political forms of representation. Most of us probably prefer for literary purposes the Shakespearean microcosm to the Restoration type. Nevertheless, we would most likely balk at the prospect of a form of political representation akin to the representation informing the Shakespearean hero (what I am calling re-presentation), preferring for our own political destinies the more modern senses and forms of representation that began to emerge in the middle and later seventeenth century and that had their literary analogues in the representative or typical characters of the Restoration stages. For example, the conclusion of Leonard Barkan's valuable study, *Nature's Work of Art: The Human Body as Image of the World* (New Haven: Yale University Press, 1975), seems from one angle (the angle provided by Shakespeare's *Coriolanus*) a misplaced nostalgia for absolutist governments: "The concerns of more recent times, the self-doubting creator, nature and the world viewed for their own sakes, the belief in chaos and ineffability, are innately different from the feelings which produced the microcosmic image of the body. The loss of certainties about poet, cosmos, and proportion has not been consistent or total since 1650, but the poetry of the Renaissance is the last which celebrated all these certainties. All the rest is modern literature" (282), Barkan concludes, adapting Verlaine.

28. See Williams, *Keywords*, 223.

29. *Coriolanus* shows signs of the shift in the representation of the human body that Francis Barker traces in his Foucauldian study *The Tremulous Private Body: Essays on Subjection* (London: Methuen, 1984). Barker sees in a diary entry by Samuel Pepys "the very derealization of the body which subsequent historiography has been heir to" (12). No longer spectacular and corporeal, a new, sexually embarrassing, privatized body is defined, not directly in discourses but furtively behind the text. It appears to me that *Coriolanus's* part in this movement lies more in the dismantling of the public, corporeal, spectacular body of the Renaissance and less in the construction of a new privatized body.

30. In an alternative reading, Page duBois links Coriolanus's wounds not to the subject of privatizing the public and textual body but to images of bleeding and their relation to feeding in the play. Specifically, Coriolanus's wounds link him with the menstruating and lactating mother. These two readings of Coriolanus's wounds may be mutually consistent rather than competing, insofar as the maternal would have been associated with the private as opposed to the public sphere. It is also important to recognize the extent of the images relating wounds to rhetoric and to a public, speaking body in Shakespeare and the ways in which Coriolanus's wounds differ, say, from Julius Caesar's. See duBois, "A Disturbance of Syntax at the Gates of Rome," *Stanford Literature Review* 2 (1985): 185–208. Her reading is related to that of Janet Adelman, " 'Anger's My Meat': Feeding, Dependency, and Aggression in *Coriolanus*," in *Representing Shakespeare: New Psychoanalytic Essays*, ed. Murray Schwartz and Coppélia Kahn (Baltimore: Johns Hopkins University Press, 1980), 129–49.

31. Cf. Menenius's earlier line, "Every gash was an enemy's grave" (2.1.155).

32. The gloss is that of Philip Brockbank in the New Arden edition of the play, p. 187.

33. Earlier, Menenius implores Coriolanus to address the citizens "In wholesome manner" (2.3.62).

34. See Zvi Jagendorf's valuable paper, "*Coriolanus*: Body Politic and Private Parts," *Shakespeare Quarterly* 41 (1990): 455–69, esp. 462f. for a discussion of wholeness as an aristocratic and royal fantasy.

35. For an account of this speech in the context of the whole history of the metaphor of the body politic from classical and early Christian sources to the seventeenth century, see David G. Hale, *The Body Politic: A Political Metaphor in English Renaissance Literature* (The Hague: Mouton, 1971), esp. 96–107. See also two essays on *Coriolanus* in Jean Howard and Marion O'Connor, eds., *Shakespeare Reproduced: The Text in History and Ideology* (London: Methuen, 1987): Michael Bristol, "Lenten Butchery: Legitimation Crisis in *Coriolanus*," 207–24; and Thomas Sorge, "The Failure of Orthodoxy in *Coriolanus*," 225–41. The argument of Sorge's interesting paper is that the organicist rhetoric of the body politic is redirected from manipulative to communal ends: "While the body analogy as a means of manipulation in favour of the ruling classes loses influence, its hidden ritualistic history of communal harmony . . . comes to the fore and provides a basis on which a competing body . . . with its own 'mouths' and 'hands' is being formed" (237).

36. See Andrew Gurr, " '*Coriolanus*' and the Body Politic," *Shakespeare Survey* 28 (1975): 63–69, for a demonstration of ways in which the concept of the body politic became problematic under Elizabeth's successor. The treatment of the body politic concept in *Coriolanus*, according to Gurr, mirrors a sense of "the unfitness of the body politic concept" clarified by James's "challenge to sovereignty" (65).

37. On King James's relation to spectacle, see Goldberg, *James I*, esp. 29–32; and Pye, *Regal Phantasm*. *Measure for Measure* especially has been taken as making fairly explicit reference to King James's uneasiness at being on public and theatrical display, through the figure of Duke Vincentio.

38. An exception is Menenius's early threat to the citizens—which uses an image of incorporation to threaten the Roman people—before that image of incorporation turns comical in the fable of the belly. He paints the Roman state as one incorporate warrior-body

that it would be useless to challenge: "you may as well / Strike at the heaven with your staves, as lift them / Against the Roman state, whose course will on / The way it takes, cracking ten thousand curbs / Of more strong link asunder than can ever / Appear in your impediment" (1.1.66–71).

For Michael Bristol, "Lenton Butchery," the language of the body in *Coriolanus* is an important vehicle for expressing a popular political culture, an alternative to the aristocratic or patrician one. It strikes me, however, that the language and figure of the body is in some ways used more conservatively by the people than it is by Coriolanus. I would agree with Bristol that the language of the body in the play does serve to point up the failure of an aristocratic political model in the play, but I would stress that the language of the body belongs to that model and ironizes it from within rather than serving as an independent alternative to it.

39. In addition to its more general meaning, "fragments" has the specific meaning of "table scraps," thereby glancing at the particular quarrel over the hoarding of corn.

40. Kenneth Burke would call those voices "negative synecdoches," having a dissociative rather than integrative effect. See *The Philosophy of Literary Form: Studies in Symbolic Action,* 3rd ed. (Berkeley and Los Angeles: University of California Press, 1973), 60.

41. Philip Brockbank, ed., *Coriolanus* (London: Methuen, 1976), 93.

42. See Ibid., 23.

43. The classic study of names in *Coriolanus* remains that of D. J. Gordon, "Name and Fame: Shakespeare's *Coriolanus,*" in *The Renaissance Imagination: Essays and Lectures by D. J. Gordon,* ed. Stephen Orgel (Berkeley and Los Angeles: University of California Press, 1975), 203–19.

44. See Brockbank, *Coriolanus,* 23, 41, 147. Brockbank concludes, "It follows that we must assume that Shakespeare wrote *Martius Caius Coriolanus* wherever all three occur together, and reasons for emending must be other than textual."

45. See the excellent collection *Public Duty and Private Conscience in Seventeenth-Century England: Essays Presented to G. E. Aylmer,* ed. John Morrill, Paul Slack and Daniel Woolf (Oxford: Clarendon Press, 1993), esp. the essay by Kevin Sharpe, "Private Conscience and Public Duty in the Writings of James VI and I," 77–100. Sharpe notes the recurrent tension between private conscience and public duty in Shakespeare's plays and the Renaissance theater generally, as well as that between the pubic and private James: "The king who thundered against the vices of intemperance, drunkenness, and especially sodomy (a crime he exempted from pardon and which, he told Henry, 'ye are bound in conscience never to forgive') was a drunkard and homosexual" (100). In Sharpe's view, James "tried to heal the divisions in the commonwealth, by resolving the disjunctures in himself—between his natural and mystical body, his person and office—ruling his own conscience and his kingdom, as he claimed, according to Scripture," failing in this endeavor at least "in the public sphere" (99). In the respect that both Coriolanus and his Rome polarize the spheres of public and private, both reflect Jacobean England, though of course, unlike James, Coriolanus is no peacemaker between public and private.

46. Human learning, Fulke Greville writes in *A Treatie of Humane Learning,* should attend the Church, "That priuate hearts may unto publike ends / Still gouern'd be, by Orders easie raines" (st. 93) (*Poems and Dramas of Fulke Greville,* ed. Geoffrey Bullough [Edinburgh and London: Oliver and Boyd, 1938], 177). A split between the orders of public and private that would have been apparent in the acts of enclosure would have conflicted with the rhetoric of King James that stressed the continuity between the public and private spheres. James continually made reference to the analogy between king and father. He did much to foster the patriarchalism that was on the rise in seventeenth-century political thought. See Gordon Schochet, *Patriarchalism in Political Thought: The Authoritarian Family and Political Speculation and Attitudes Especially in Seventeenth Century England* (Oxford: Basil Blackwell, 1975). For a rich and stimulating discussion of ways in which public and private life gradually came to

be differentiated in the Renaissance—unlike the Middle Ages, when public and private life were virtually indistinguishable from one another—see *A History of Private Life III: Passions of the Renaissance,* ed. Roger Chartier, trans. Arthur Goldhammer (Cambridge, Mass.: Harvard University Press, 1989).

47. See E. C. Pettet, "*Coriolanus* and the Midlands Insurrection of 1607," *Shakespeare Survey* 3 (1950): 34–42; and Gurr, " 'Coriolanus' and the Body Politic."

48. Pettet, "*Coriolanus* and the Midlands Insurrection," 34.

49. After writing this, I came across the recent and splendid essay by Arthur Riss, "The Belly Politic: *Coriolanus* and the Revolt of Language," *ELH* 59 (1992): 53–75. Riss also makes the connection between acts of enclosure and *Coriolanus's* dramatization of the "conflict between communal and private notions of the body" (55). Riss's essay is especially valuable for its relating the conflict over private and public to the struggle between literal and figurative levels of figures of speech. My own reading, in some ways parallel to Riss's, tries to situate the conflict between the authorities of private and public in relation to the many ways in which the play challenges an older Renaissance concept of representation built on the sovereign trope of synecdoche.

See Lawrence Danson, *Tragic Alphabet: Shakespeare's Drama of Language* (New Haven: Yale University Press, 1974), 142–62, for a discussion of synecdoche as the dominant trope in *Coriolanus.* A more recent discussion of the play's synecdochic rhetoric of wholeness and fragmentation may be found in Jagendorf, "*Coriolanus.*"

50. William W. E. Slights, "Bodies of Text and Textualized Bodies in *Sejanus* and *Coriolanus,*" *Medieval and Renaissance Drama in England* 5 (1991): 191.

51. The malfunctioning of Coriolanus's name as an index of his "incorporation" into the Roman body politic is echoed by other failed acts of incorporation in—and of—the play. Among these would have to be included the faction *Coriolanus* promotes among its critics, indicative of our inability to incorporate all aspects of the play, particularly the political or public with the psychological or private, into an adequately comprehensive reading of the play. The play invites us to read it from either a psychological or political vantage point—and there have been many persuasive instances of both kinds of readings—but makes very elusive a reading that would be equally attentive to the claims of both rival interpretive approaches. Readings of the play tend to focus either on political issues it explicitly raises and on its possible topical references or else on the psychology of Coriolanus, particularly his relation to the overbearing mother Volumnia, but seldom on both. The faction that is referred to so often in *Coriolanus* spills beyond the borders of the play to structure possible critical responses to it.

The difficulty incorporating the public with the private, the political with the psychological material in a reading of the play may be an essential rather than accidental feature of the play, since such difficulty reflects the many failed acts of incorporation that are so evident in its torturing of the established rhetoric of the body politic. Recent important readings of the play have been relatively successful in incorporating the political and the psychological. Exceptional among these are Janet Adelman's " 'Anger's My Meat' "; and Stanley Cavell, in *Disowning Knowledge in Six Plays of Shakespeare* (Cambridge: Cambridge University Press, 1987), 143–77.

For the use of "body language"—"translating the physical body into text"—as a means of "incorporating political opponents into a trivializing or fatal narrative," see Slights, "Bodies of Text," 181–93. Such acts of "incorporation," however, usually misfire in this play, and I believe most of Shakespeare's contemporaries would have seen the primary political threat as issuing from this failure rather than from the attempted acts of "incorporation" themselves.

52. Aufidius urges Coriolanius to "take / Th'one half of my commission" (4.5.138–39). Aufidius's servingmen regret that he is sharing honor with Coriolanus: "But the bottom of the news is, our general is cut i'th'middle, and but one half of what he was yesterday; for the other has half, by the entreaty and grant of the whole table" (4.5.202–5). Brutus says that "Half all Cominius' honours are to Martius" (1.1.272).

53. See Tim Harris, *Politics under the Later Stuarts: Party Conflict in a Divided Society, 1660–1715* (London: Longmans, 1993). See also J. R. Jones, *Country and Court: England, 1658–1714* (Cambridge, Mass.: Harvard University Press, 1978), 33: "Parties and their domination of elections were abnormal and suspect, and were officially and effectively discouraged in the 1685 election." According to Jones, the Triennial Act of 1694, requiring regular and frequent elections, "produced a permanent 'rage of party' in the constituencies." Even John Locke held them to be a necessary evil. Locke used the word "party" extensively to designate dissenting religious sects. For Locke party zeal thwarts the human understanding, though he advocated toleration for parties and sects, setting him apart from political thinkers of the Renaissance. Locke wrote extensively on the relation of the individual's mind to the ideologies produced by sectarian groups. For a discussion of "party" in Locke, see Neal Wood, *The Politics of Locke's Philosophy: A Social Study of "An Essay Concerning Human Understanding"* (Berkeley and Los Angeles: University of California Press, 1983), 101–9. For a recent discussion of the "rage of party" in the 1690s, see Steven N. Zwicker's essay in Kevin Sharpe and Steven N. Zwicker, eds., *The Politics of Discourse: The Literature and History of Seventeenth-Century England* (Berkeley and Los Angeles: University of California Press, 1987), 6–10, 230–34. One of the earliest discussions of the rise of party in late seventeenth-century England is that of J. H. Plumb, *The Growth of Political Stability in England, 1675–1725* (London: Macmillan, 1967).

54. See Menenius's jab at the tribunes' ineptness at patching up a quarrel: "When you are hearing a matter between party and party . . . All the peace you make in their cause is calling both the parties knaves" (2.1.72–73,77–79).

55. The language of faction attaches to Coriolanus at other moments as well, especially toward the end of the play when his allegiances at some level are divided between the Volscians and Romans. Menenius, for example, describes himself to a Volscian guard as "always factionary on the party of your general" (5.2.29).

56. D. J. Gordon has some excellent things to say on this issue in his justly famous essay, "Name and Fame," esp. 214f. See also the excellent essay by Zvi Jagendorf, who writes of Coriolanus's "horror of playing a part" in relation to the play's rhetoric of fragmentation. Coriolanus fears the "self-fragmentation of acting" ("*Coriolanus*," 466–67).

57. Coriolanus's references to the fragmentariness of the plebs seem ratified in a strange way by a Messenger's report to the tribunes, "I have seen the dumb men throng to him, and / The blind to hear him speak" (2.1.260–61), though the fragmentation implicit in those lines is checked by Junius Brutus's subsequent lines to fellow tribune Sicinius Velutus, "Let's to the Capitol, / And carry with us ears and eyes for th'time, / But hearts for the event" (2.1.266–68).

58. James Holstun, "Tragic Superfluity in *Coriolanus*," *ELH* 50 (1983): 485–507, is especially valuable on incongruities between the political order of the play and of Renaissance England.

59. See Bernard McElroy, *Shakespeare's Mature Tragedies* (Princeton: Princeton University Press, 1973), for a discussion of the tendency to generalize and universalize as a salient characteristic of the protagonists of Shakespeare's great quartet.

60. North's Plutarch grants Coriolanus a generality that the play contests: "Nowe in those dayes, valliantnes was honoured in ROME above all other vertues: which they called *Virtus,* by the name of vertue selfe, as including in that generall name, all other speciall vertues besides" (New Arden Edition, 314). *Coriolanus* makes the generality, universality, or representativeness of its protagonist a contested issue, thereby opening up the whole quarrel over political representation between patricians and plebs.

61. Historically, the tribunate was created in 494 B.C. in response to usury riots; the corn riots took place three years later.

62. Microcosm and macrocosm were powerfully ordering synecdoches for Shakespeare's audiences. For a full treatment of the plays' structure in terms of microcosm and macrocosm, see Thomas Stroup, *Microcosmos: The Shape of the Elizabethan Play* (Lexington: University of Kentucky Press, 1965).

63. The "worlds elsewhere" in Shakespeare's other plays—e.g., the green worlds of his comedies, the convent, prison, and moated grange in *Measure for Measure,* the tavern in *1 Henry IV*—are ordinarily incorporated into the main world and do not exceed the synecdochic and representational reach of the play.

64. See Holstun, "Tragic Superfluity," 500.

65. That the figure was becoming superannuated in the political rhetoric of Jacobean England has been well established. See Gurr, "Coriolanus and the Body Politic"; Hale, *Body Politic*; and Barkan, *Nature's Work of Art,* 1–116. For a discussion of English Machiavellianism and the decline of the figure of the body politic, see J. G. A. Pocock, *The Machiavellian Moment: Florentine Political Thought and the Atlantic Republican Tradition* (Princeton: Princeton University Press, 1975), 333–400. Leonard Tennenhouse, in his important essay "*Coriolanus*: History and the Crisis of Semantic Order," *Comparative Drama* 10 (1976): 328–46, argues that the play marks the passage of an old patrician order based on the body and action to a new one based on words and associated with the tribunes.

Chapter 2

1. For the shift in the nature and meaning of "representation," discussed more fully in chapter 1, see Williams, *Keywords,* 222–25; and Pitkin, *Concept of Representation,* esp. 241–52. Keith Michael Baker discusses the shift toward a postabsolutist concept of representation in a French context in chapter 10 of *Inventing the French Revolution,* 224–51.

On the importance of the category of wholeness to the organization of knowledge in the Renaissance, see Foucault's section on the Renaissance episteme in *Order of Things.* The later rise of natural history, in Foucault's account, made the relation between parts and wholes highly problematic. The need to name and classify meant that certain parts of what one observed had to be excluded from consideration. On the vogue for "anatomies" aiming "to portray a unified order" and their significance as a way for organizing knowledge in the Renaissance, see Devon L. Hodges, *Renaissance Fictions of Anatomy* (Amherst: University of Massachusetts Press, 1985).

2. Georg Lukács, "The Sociology of Modern Drama," trans. Lee Baxandall, *Tulane Drama Review* 9 (1965): 157.

3. For a discussion of ways in which Elizabethan plays were structured according to the microcosm/macrocosm analogy (which Kenneth Burke has called the "perfect synecdoche" because the microcosm both resembles and is part of the macrocosm to which it belongs), see Stroup, *Microcosmos.*

4. *Leviathan,* 223.

5. Samuel T. Coleridge, *Coleridge's Shakespearean Criticism,* vol. 1, ed. Thomas M. Raysor (London, 1930), 89.

6. See the classic account of Ernst Kantorowicz, *The King's Two Bodies: A Study in Medieval Political Theology* (Princeton: Princeton University Press, 1957).

7. *Political Works of James I,* 297.

8. Ibid., 298.

9. Ibid., 309.

10. Ibid., 297.

11. Ibid., 297–98.

12. As Hobbes would articulate the logic of absolutism later in the century, "A multitude of men, are made *one* person, when they are by one man, or one person, represented. . . . For it is the *unity* of the representer, not the *unity* of the represented, that maketh the person *one.* And it is the representer that beareth the person, and but one person: and *unity,* cannot otherwise be understood in multitude" (*Leviathan,* 220).

13. Locke, *Of the Conduct of the Understanding,* ed. Thomas Fowler (New York: Burt Franklin, 1971), 7.

14. Locke, *Two Tracts on Government,* ed. Philip Abrams (Cambridge: Cambridge University Press, 1967), 96.

15. Locke, *Conduct,* 7.

16. Ibid.

17. Locke, *Two Treatises of Government,* rev. ed., ed. Peter Laslett (1953; rpt., New York: New American Library, 1965), 396.

18. A similar but more general challenge to the aristocratic assumption of the superiority of men of parts is discernible in Bacon's *Advancement of Learning,* bk. 6, chap. 3. One of the rhetorical sophisms Bacon singles out in order to expose its fallacy reads as follows: "That which consists of many divisible parts is greater than that which consists of few parts and is more one." The detection or exposure of this sophism involves recognizing that a plurality of parts only *seems* greater, especially when they are disordered so as to resist comprehension: "for all things when viewed part by part appear greater; whence likewise plurality of parts makes a show of magnitude" (*The Works of Francis Bacon,* ed. James Spedding et al. [Boston: Taggard and Thompson, 1860–64], vol. 9, p. 152).

19. Locke, *Conduct,* 11.

20. Ibid., 13–14.

21. Locke, *Tracts,* 96.

22. Ibid., 97.

23. Ibid., 98.

24. Locke, *Conduct,* 7.

25. Locke, *Treatises,* 382.

26. Ibid., 370.

27. Ibid.

28. Cited in Corinne Comstock Weston and Janelle Renfrow Greenberg, *Subjects and Sovereigns: The Grand Controversy over Legal Sovereignty in Stuart England* (Cambridge: Cambridge University Press, 1981), 8.

29. Locke's epistemology, no less than his political reflections, shows clear signs of strain within what Kenneth Burke characterizes as the the the trope of representation, synecdoche. Such strain is evident in his development of the notion of a "nominal essence" to replace the earlier and received notion of immaterial essence. The nominal essence is a rhetorical construction based on the trope of synecdoche. For when we categorize and name something, according to Locke, we select a few primary and secondary qualities from a larger number of such qualities, bundle them together, and give that bundle a name. The name therefore refers directly to a grouping of selected sensations rather than to an object. Locke's nominal essence is a synecdoche but one unanchored in any relations of resemblance of an object's perceptible qualities to a "real essence." As Gabriele Bernhard Jackson explains in the course of a stimulating essay on eighteenth-century poetic diction, for Locke "a name is a synecdoche that the mind can never complete. Unable to predict what additional secondary qualities an unknown real essence may have power to produce ("the Properties of any sort of Bodies . . . being therefore at least so many, that no Man can know the precise and definite number" [III.9.13]), we can never understand a whole object even in the sense of knowing all its possible impressions on us" ("From Essence to Accident: Locke and the Language of Poetry in the Eighteenth Century," *Criticism* 29 [1987]: 40).

One wouldn't expect synecdoche to malfunction as widely or consistently in the writings of an absolutist like Hobbes as it does in the writings of the founder of English liberalism. But signs of strain there are: for instance, in the discrepancy between Hobbes's declared method and his actual practice in analyzing how commonwealths function. Tom Sorrell has written recently of Hobbes's method, usually thought of as deriving from a belief in the parallelism of natural and civic philosophy, "It is sometimes claimed [on the basis of Hobbes' 'Preface to the Reader' in *De Cive*] that the causal inquiry into the properties of bodies politic is a special case of a type of inquiry Hobbes thinks can be carried out with respect to bodies generally.

One starts with a conception of a 'whole' body, either a natural body or an artificial body like a commonwealth; one then takes notice of its 'parts' or 'properties'; and from the causes of the properties one reconstructs or 'composes' in reasoning the 'whole' one began with, the whole therefore becoming more intelligible than it was before resolution takes place." But this standard view of Hobbes's working method is mistaken, Sorrell argues. Hobbes "is only incidentally concerned to explain how bodies politic are functionally organized, i.e., to explain how the functioning of the whole commonwealth depends on the functioning of a lot of working parts. He is only incidentally concerned, that is, with the sort of explanatory task that would exploit the general method for decomposing wholes into parts" (*Hobbes* [London: Routledge and Kegan Paul, 1986], 17–18).

Though it lies well beyond the scope of this chapter to make the argument, the part-for-whole and whole-for-part forms of synecdoche become far more marginal for what Foucault calls the classical episteme than they were for the Renaissance. For the classical period, it is general-for-particular and particular-for-general forms of synecdoche that become dominant for analysis of all kinds. The implications of this rhetorical shift seem to me to offer rich possibilities for literary investigation.

30. Enid Welsford, *The Fool: His Social and Literary History* (New York: Doubleday and Company, 1961), 258.

31. Paul Goodman makes this argument in *The Structure of Literature* (Chicago: University of Chicago Press, 1954), 153f. See also David Marshall's recent *The Surprising Effects of Sympathy: Marivaux, Diderot, Rousseau, and Mary Shelley* (Chicago: University of Chicago Press, 1988).

32. William Godwin, *Enquiry Concerning Political Justice and Its Influence on Morals and Happiness,* vol. 2, ed. F. E. L. Priestley, University of Toronto Department of English Studies and Texts, no. 2 (Toronto: University of Toronto Press, 1946), 71–72.

33. Freud's definition of the uncanny makes reference to severed, metonymic body parts, related in Freud's reading to the castration-complex: "Dismembered limbs, a severed head, a hand cut off at the wrist, feet which dance by themselves—all these have something peculiarly uncanny about them. . . . As we already know, this kind of uncanniness springs from its association with the castration complex" ("The Uncanny," in *Studies in Parapsychology,* ed. Philip Rieff, trans. A. Strachey [New York: Macmillan, 1963], 57). It would be interesting to read Freud by means of Renaissance politic rhetoric, almost an inversion of the widespread practice of reading Shakespeare through Freud. Freud's boldly synecdochic notions like the castration-complex might prove to have latent political analogues, especially for a Jew in late nineteenth-and early twentieth-century Vienna.

34. On fetishes as synecdoches, see Burke, *Philosophy of Literary Form,* 26–27.

35. The very word "health" that Shakespeare enlists so frequently as a metaphor of political well-being (occasioned by the Renaissance conception of the state as body) is linked etymologically to "whole." In Renaissance medical conceptions, "health" is a species of synecdoche. On hearing the news of Northumberland's sickness, the conspirator Worcester delivers a speech showing the degree to which "healthy" and "whole" are synonyms: "I would the state of time had first been whole [i.e., sound, healthy] / Ere he by sickness had been visited, / His health was never better worth than now" (*1 Henry IV,* 4.1.25–27).

36. Kenneth Burke identifies proper names as one important category of synecdoche in *Philosophy of Literary Form,* 27–28.

37. Antony's fantasy of the general and his soldiers, whole and parts, changing places, is a particularly interesting variation on this character trope, involving as it does two symmetrical synecdochic substitutions. He imagines himself being divided into the multitude that are his men, and his men being composed into the single body of their leader: "I wish I could be made so many men, / And all of you clapped up together in / An Antony, that I might do you service / So good as you have done" (4.2.16–19).

38. Goodman, *Structure of Literature,* 132.

39. Ibid., 162.

40. Ibid., 163.

41. Ibid., 129.

42. Ibid., 127.

43. Ibid., 130.

44. David Hume, *Selected Essays,* ed. Stephen Copley and Andrew Edgar (Oxford: Oxford University Press, 1993), 32–33.

45. Williams, *Keywords,* 223.

46. See Ann Thompson and John O. Thompson, *Shakespeare: Meaning and Metaphor* (Brighton: The Harvester Press, 1987), pp. 89–131; and John Hunt, "A Thing of Nothing: The Catastrophic Body in *Hamlet,*" *Shakespeare Quarterly* 39 (1988): 27–44.

47. Both the Elizabethan and Jacobean eras saw the integration of Britain (named for the legendary Brutus) as a re-integration of a kingdom that was once whole but has become sundered. Such a view, needless to say, provided much-needed justification for the attempted annexation of Ireland.

48. Presumably King James could have read such failure as tacitly supporting his project: i.e., what seems tragic about the Jacobean tragedies is the failure of political integration, which might serve as a warning to the recalcitrant English who suspected the plan to unite the kingdoms.

49. Nicholas Brooke makes this point in his recent Oxford edition of the play (Oxford: Oxford University Press, 1990), 211.

50. R. S. White, *Innocent Victims: Poetic Injustice in Shakespearean Tragedy,* rev. ed. (London: Athlone Press, 1986), 63. Such rhetoric participates in—perhaps unconsciously adopts—a widespread tradition in the Renaissance linking women to fragmentation, dispersal, and incompleteness. See Nancy Vickers, "Diana Described: Scattered Woman and Scattered Rhyme," *Critical Inquiry* 8 (1981–82): 265–79; and " 'The Blazon of Sweet Beauty's Best': Shakespeare's Lucrece," in *Shakespeare and the Question of Theory*, ed. Patricia Parker and Geoffrey Hartman (New York and London: Methuen, 1985), 95–115.

51. Thus, Mary Cowden Clarke authored a hefty three-volume study of *The Girlhood of Shakespeare's Heroines* (1851–52).

52. *Wilhelm Meister's Apprenticeship and Travels,* trans. Thomas Carlyle (Boston: Estes and Lauriat, 1883), 198; bk. 4, chap. 3.

53. A. C. Bradley, *Shakespearean Tragedy* (1904; rpt., Greenwich, Conn.: Fawcett Publications, n.d.), 94.

54. Ibid., 96, 98.

55. John Erskine Hankins, *The Character of Hamlet and Other Essays* (Chapel Hill: University of North Carolina Press, 1941), 11.

56. Alvin Kernan, "Politics and Theatre in *Hamlet,*" *Hamlet Studies* 1 (1979): 10.

57. Elaine Showalter, "Representing Ophelia: Women, Madness, and the Responsibilities of Feminist Criticism," in *Shakespeare and the Question of Theory,* ed. Patricia Parker and Geoffrey Hartman (London: Methuen, 1985), 78. See also Martha C. Ronk, "Representations of *Ophelia,*" *Criticism* 36 (1994): 21–43.

58. On the relation of Osric to Hamlet, see Russ McDonald, "Osric," *Hamlet Studies* 5 (1983): 59–65.

59. See Harold Jenkins's provocative discussion in his New Arden edition of the play (London: Methuen, 1982), 536.

60. Ibid., 536–42.

61. On the categories of resemblance in the Renaissance, see the opening section of Foucault's *Order of Things,* 17–45.

62. Ibid., 46–50.

63. A causal relation is itself a species of synecdoche, Burke suggests in *Philosophy of Literary Form,* 28: "If event 2, for instance, follows from event 1 and leads into event 3, each

of these events may synecdochically represent the other." It is this form of synecdoche that is converted to metaphorical sameness and repetition in the condensed figure of the dead men's fingers.

A couple of reflections occasioned by Burke's suggestive remark: it is the synecdoches so essential to the construction of drama that are threatened by Macbeth's "To-morrow, and to-morrow, and to-morrow," Shakespeare's most famous instance of a sequence collapsed into repetition and sameness. Among other things, Macbeth's speech challenges in a radical way the very rhetoric and logic of dramatic form. *Macbeth* may be, at least on its surface, the most synecdochic of Shakespeare's tragedies in that it allows us more powerfully than any other to see the end in the beginning, according to M. J. B. Allen, "Toys, Prologues, and the Great Amiss: Shakespeare's Tragic Openings," in D. Palmer and M. Bradbury, eds., *Shakespearean Tragedy* (London: Edward Arnold, 1984). According to Allen, "In certain imaginative contexts, and most notably in tragic drama, we are privileged as spectators to understand something of the end at the very beginning. . . . Endings are so important in tragedy, their force fields dominate their plays. . . . All radii lead towards them and they constantly suggest themselves, even . . . in their beginnings. Perhaps pre-eminently in their beginnings; for we keep wanting to read the play into the beginning, to outwit or outdistance the dramatic events by anticipating or overanticipating them in the beginning, even when we lack sufficient knowledge to do so, when, that is, the dramatist consciously thwarts our attempts and compels us to wait upon his delaying of revelation. . . . It is the felt connection between the beginning and the end that, I believe, is the hallmark of tragedy" (4, 28–29). The powerfully synecdochic form of *Macbeth,* where the entire sequence of events seems coiled and ready to be sprung in the beginning of the play is threatened by Macbeth's speech, which, by collapsing synecdochic figures into a view of history as unrelieved repetition, indirectly issues challenges to the synecdochic rhetoric of tragic form as well as of Renaissance kingship.

64. Geoffrey Leech, *A Linguistic Guide to English Poetry* (London: Longmans, 1969), 150.

65. *Philosophy of Literary Form,* 26. In a very different vein, the French rhetoricians known as Group μ have put forward another argument for the basic nature of synecdoche, by advancing a conception of metaphor as constructed from "two complementary synecdoches that function in a precisely inverse way" (Group μ, *A General Rhetoric,* trans. Paul B. Burrell and Edgar M. Slotkin (Baltimore: Johns Hopkins University Press, 1981), 109. See also 102f. and 114f. See Ann and John O. Thompson for an investigation of body parts in *Hamlet* that builds on the theoretical work of Group μ.

66. *Philosophy of Literary Form,* 26–30.

67. On the demise of one of the most potent Renaissance synecdoches in the seventeenth century, see David G. Hale's fine study, *Body Politic.* See also Barkan, *Nature's Work of Art;* Gurr, "Coriolanus and the Body Politic," *Shakespeare Survey* 28 (1975): 63–69; and Pocock, *Machiavellian Moment,* 333–400.

Chapter 3

1. *Political Works of James I,* 19.

2. Lawrence Stone, *The Family, Sex and Marriage in England, 1500–1800* (New York: Harper and Row, 1979), 74.

3. Ibid., 73.

4. Ibid., 73.

5. Ibid., 73.

6. Ibid., 74.

7. *The Poetry and Prose of William Blake,* ed. David V. Erdman (New York: Doubleday, 1965), 630. There are countless similar remarks to be found in Blake, both in the Reynolds annotations and elsewhere. A small sampling from the notes on Reynolds: "Singular & Particular Detail is the Foundation of the Sublime" (637); "What is General Nature is there

Such a Thing / what is General Knowledge is there such a Thing [*Strictly Speaking*] / All Knowledge is Particular" (637); "Generalizing in Every thing the Man would soon be a Fool but a Cunning Fool" (638); "A History Painter Paints The Hero, & not Man in General. but most minutely in Particular" (641); "Rembrandt was a Generalizer Poussin was a Particularizer / Poussin knew better than to make all his Pictures have the same light & shadow any fool may concentrate a light in the Middle" (650). Blake's favoring general terms like "particularizer" and "generalizer" to stage his confrontations with Reynolds, Rembrandt, and others—terms that embrace such particulars as handling of light and shadow—show how he is betrayed by the paradoxes of his own (needless to say, general) principles of particularity.

One of the many ironies of Blake's pronouncement on the idiocy of generalizing is that, were it considered in the context of the French Revolution, the political event around which so many of Blake's writings revolve, it might appear reactionary. It was the archreactionary Joseph de Maistre who wrote, "I see Man nowhere. I see Germans, Frenchmen, Italians, but never Man." Resisting the Enlightenment-inspired generalizing pronouncements of the revolutionaries concerning "Man," this spokesman for a presumably universalist institution, the Catholic Church, was forced to have recourse to a countergeneralizing rhetoric to get across his counterrevolutionary purposes. By contrast, the word "générale" played a central (and heroic) role in French Revolutionary pamphlets.

8. I am, of course, simplifying the range and number of critical rhetorics on Shakespeare. Like humanist criticism of Shakespeare, other critical approaches favor a generalizing rhetoric: notably, myth criticism and structuralism. Poststructuralism seems to me a special case, and difficult to categorize as either predominantly particularizing or generalizing. It shares a resistance to generalizing with the recent new historicism, though it exercises that resistance in very different ways: not through an insistence on historical specificity and "local" readings but through a dismantling of the stability and self-consistency necessary for so-called concepts to lay claim to a generality that allows them to function as concepts.

9. John Guy, *Tudor England* (Oxford: Oxford University Press, 1988), 352–78, provides a useful summary of the shaping of England as a modern state.

10. For an important discussion of the politics of universalizing Elizabeth, see Frances A. Yates, *Astraea: The Imperial Theme in the Sixteenth Century* (London: Routledge & Kegan Paul, 1975).

11. Cleanth Brooks, "Implications of an Organic Theory of Poetry," in *Literature and Belief: English Institute Essays, 1957,* ed. M. H. Abrams (New York: Columbia University Press, 1958), 63.

12. Cleanth Brooks, "Irony as a Principle of Structure," in Morton Dauwen Zabel, ed., *Literary Opinion in America: Essays Illustrating the Status, Methods, and Problems of Criticism in the U.S. in the Twentieth Century,* 3rd ed., vol. 2 (Gloucester, Mass.: Peter Smith, 1968), 731. Kenneth Burke has a far more flexible way of conceiving generalizing epigrams that occur within literary texts. See his *Counter-Statement* (1931; rpt., Berkeley and Los Angeles: University of California Press, 1968), 33.

13. M. H. Abrams, *The Correspondent Breeze: Essays on English Romanticism* (New York: Norton, 1984), 40–41.

14. Ibid., 46. Abrams, I believe, is never very loyal to his antigeneralizing rhetoric. A passage like the following on the "correspondent breeze" image is perhaps sufficient to initiate a whisper of treason and betrayal: "There is no precedent for the way in which the symbolic wind was called upon by poet after poet, in poem after poem, all within the first decades of the nineteenth century." It is true that here he is concerned to establish the singularity of *romantic* breezes, but "by poet after poet, in poem after poem" is a telling phrase, and a rather good characterization of Abrams's own method, which rarely settles on the densities and particularities of a text, poetic or otherwise. There are also many passages in Abrams that suggest a kinship with the archetypal critics he condemns.

15. Greenblatt, *Shakespearean Negotiations,* 65. In the chapter on "Shakespeare and

the Exorcists," Greenblatt writes, "For me the study of literature is the study of contingent, particular, intended, and historically embedded works." "Particular" and related words are sprinkled throughout Greenblatt's writings and that of other new historicists. Leah Marcus favors the word "local" in her impressive series of topical readings, *Puzzling Shakespeare* (Berkeley and Los Angeles: University of California Press, 1988). "Local" or topical reading has been "closed off in favor of more general, less 'parochial' systems for organizing meaning" (216). In her epilogue she confesses to a "bias built into the project for localization—that is, quite obviously a bias toward the local as opposed to the more general." This "bias" is not necessarily distorting, however, since the Renaissance also exhibited a "preference for 'local' place and local meaning" that "tended to correlate with resistance to various forms of political and cultural totalization" (217). I think it can be demonstrated that within the plays themselves, countergeneralizing rhetorics are often challenges to "political totalization," but it is also important to recognize the massive scale on which the construction of Renaissance political discourses and in many ways Renaissance plays relied on generalizing rhetorics. Marcus herself makes this point when she writes of Shakespeare's possible complicity with the universalizing "humanist enterprise": "We simply need to acknowledge the Renaissance drive to regularize and generalize meaning as one of the local conditions that we have to take into account" (41). But Marcus often overlooks that dependency when it comes to Renaissance plays. Thus, when she cites Hamlet's line about the players, "Abstracts and breefe Chronicles of the time," she writes, "Then, it was the particular that made plays most meaningful, most memorable, most dangerously attractive. . . . When contemporaries attended and talked about plays it was the currency of the stage, its ability to 'Abstract' personalities and 'Chronicle' events in the very unfolding that was the primary object of fascination. Local meaning was at the center. . . . More generalized meaning was more peripheral" (26–27). But another set of assumptions entirely, one focusing on the importance of generalizing to the production of meaning, is equally available in Hamlet's line about the players.

Renaissance quarrels with generalizing are quite different from the ones that go on in many of our recent critical discourses, whose assumptions about "general" and "particular" often seem those that have issued from the romantic period. For a brilliant account of the "romanticism of detail" in recent cultural criticism, see Alan Liu, "Local Transcendence: Cultural Criticism, Postmodernism, and the Romanticism of the Detail," *Representations,* no. 32 (Fall 1990): 75–113.

16. Jean Howard, "The New Historicism in Renaissance Studies," *English Literary Renaissance* 16 (1986): 39.

17. Edward Said, "Michel Foucault, 1926–1984," in *After Foucault: Humanistic Knowledge, Postmodern Challenges,* ed. Jonathan Arac (New Brunswick, N.J.: Rutgers University Press, 1988), 6.

18. Ibid., 6.

19. Ibid., 2–3.

20. McElroy, *Shakespeare's Mature Tragedies,* 20. McElroy, of course, is here applying Sidney's view of poetry to Shakespearean tragedy.

21. Ibid., 20. A similar rhetoric painting Shakespeare as supreme harmonizer of the particular and the general informs much of Shakespearean criticism. Another example: "The idea that the individual embodies the universal is widely manifest in the culture of Renaissance England. Men of letters embraced Neo-Platonic philosophy, with its system of correspondences, its belief that the physical things of this world partake of ideal forms. . . . It is my contention that the Tudor and Stuart playwrights also routinely fuse individual character with Platonic essence, thereby satisfying both the tendency to individualize and particularize and the tendency to personify and typify" (Huston Diehl, "Iconography and Characterization in English Tragedy 1585–1642," in *Drama in the Renaissance: Comparative and Critical Essays,* ed. Clifford Davidson, C. J. Gianakaris, and John H. Stroupe [New York: AMS Press, 1986], 12–13). At least one variation on this view has a historical orientation:

James Siemon writes that the interest of Renaissance drama derives in part from its historical moment, in which "attention to the particulars of the self and its actions—social, historical, and psychological elements—begins seriously to challenge the predominant tendency of medieval thought, which made these dimensions of reality subservient to timeless, universal principles" (*Shakespearean Iconoclasm* [Berkeley and Los Angeles: University of California Press, 1985], 66). A critic who has recently written about "general" and "particular" as a problem rather than a nonproblem and who identifies them as an important rhetorical issue in Shakespeare is Patricia Parker, "Transfigurations: Shakespeare and Rhetoric," in *Literary Fat Ladies: Rhetoric, Gender, Property* (London: Methuen, 1987), 67–96. See esp. 85–89.

22. Georg Lukács, *The Historical Novel,* trans. Hannah and Stanley Mitchell (Lincoln: University of Nebraska Press, 1983), 94.

23. A critic who seems to me far more vulnerable to such a charge is M. M. Bakhtin, whose references to the drama as "homophonic" (in contrast to the polyphonic novel) suggest that it is a genre of less complexity and interest than the novel. Many readers of Bakhtin, from his scattered references to drama, have expected a fuller treatment by him of the genre of drama, but in the materials so far published Bakhtin has nowhere provided such a treatment. For comments on Shakespearean drama's homophony, see *Problems of Dostoevsky's Poetics,* trans. R. W. Rotsel (Ann Arbor: Ardis, 1973), 27–28.

24. Lukács, *Historical Novel,* 99.

25. Ibid., 140.

26. Ibid., 140.

27. We are especially prone to making that assumption because our culture has embraced the idea that literature has a particularizing mission, a duty to provide alternatives to the generalizing discourses of science. Even Shakespearean criticism tends for the most part to make that assumption, an anachronistic one, to be sure, since in Shakespeare's time, especially in the writings of Francis Bacon, it is science that is regularly credited with serving a particularizing mission, rescuing us from our false idols, the inherited and unexamined theories and commonplaces handed down by tradition. See especially Bacon's *Novum Organum* (or New Method); in the section "The Doctrine of the Idols" he writes that man must be "so firm of mind and purpose as resolutely to compel himself to sweep away all theories and common notions, and to apply the understanding, thus made fair and even, to a fresh examination of particulars" (1:97; see also 1:19; 1:36; and 1:51, to cite a few of the many of Bacon's aphorisms on this theme). A similar association of science with fresh attention to particulars can be found somewhat later in Thomas Sprat's landmark *History of the Royal Society* (1667), ed. Jackson I. Cope and Harold Whitmore Jones (St. Louis: Washington University Studies, 1958), 31: "The True Philosophy must be first of all begun, on a scrupulous, and severe examination of particulars: from them, there may be some general Rules, with great caution drawn." Sprat, a clergyman rather than a scientist, understood and assimilated the basic principles of Bacon's program for the reformation of science.

28. Hiram Haydn, *The Counter-Renaissance* (New York: Charles Scribner's Sons, 1950), xvii. For a poetic treatment of this idea, see Fulke Greville, "A Treatie of Humane Learning" (ca. 1620–22), esp. stanzas 22–24.

29. Ibid., 143.

30. *The Essays of Montaigne,* trans. John Florio, III, (New York: AMS Press, 1967), 21.

31. Haydn, *Counter-Renaissance,* 152, 159.

32. Moretti, *Signs Taken for Wonders,* 54.

33. See James R. Siemon's excellent study, *Shakespearean Iconoclasm.*

34. Bernard Beckerman, *Shakespeare at the Globe, 1599–1609* (New York: Macmillan, 1962), 66. See also Alan Dessen, *Elizabethan Stage Conventions and Modern Interpreters* (Cambridge: Cambridge University Press, 1984), 84–104. George F. Reynolds, in "Some Principles of Elizabethan Staging, Part I," *Modern Philology* 2 (1904–5): 581–614, and *Modern Philology* 3 (1905–6): 69–97, long ago showed how certain generalizing aspects of Renaissance

stagecraft are inherited from the medieval stages: e.g., unlocated scenes, the use of a few paces to represent great distances in journeying scenes, and the retention on stage of a prop like a throne chair in scenes where it would not be called for and in which it would have only a general symbolic value.

35. Beckerman, *Shakespeare at the Globe,* 66.

36. Two landmarks of that tradition, whose origin was the Athenian philosopher Theophrastus, were Joseph Hall's *Characters of Virtues and Vices* (1608) and Sir Thomas Overbury's *Characters* (1614).

37. Burke, *Counter-Statement,* 192–94.

38. Ibid., 196.

39. Ibid., 197.

40. See Joel Fineman, *Shakespeare's Perjured Eye* (Berkeley and Los Angeles: University of California Press, 1986).

41. Not so the Romans, outside their representation in the play: as the *O.E.D.* notes, "The sense 'belonging to a good family' common to the Romance tongues is not found in Latin."

42. The general and climactic word "man" appears a few lines earlier, bereft of the dignity that Antony restores to it. Upon the noisy entrance of Antony, Octavius, and their army, it is in a more particular sense that Octavius asks Brutus's friend Messala, "What man is that?" indicating Strato, one of Brutus's servants. "My master's man," Messala replies (5.5.52–53). Not only is "Man" here employed in a question asking for a particular identification (rather than in a statement elevating the particular man to the status of most high general), but it also indicates a particular social standing, that of servant. The use of "man" to designate a servant indicates a different and competing sense of generality: the servant is general in the sense of common, not universal. The juxtaposition of such disparate uses of the general term "man" may be read as a subversive gesture. That is, we might be tempted to hear beneath Antony's exclamation, "This was a man!" Octavius's "What man is that?" so that the climactic function of Antony's praise by means of the general term would be severely undercut: This was (or would have been) a first-rate servant! It is perhaps more likely that the first and more particular use of "man" is either an inoculation against the likelihood of a jocular reading of Antony's line or a warning lest we construe "man" too exclusively rather than more generally, forgetting to include the Stratos of the world.

43. Jackson, "From Essence to Accident," 63, n. 53.

44. Furthermore, Locke will reverse the priority of general and particular implied by the microcosm/macrocosm pair. Unlike the empiricist tradition, the Renaissance microcosm/macrocosm analogy suggests that the particular is modeled after, and therefore succeeds rather than antecedes, the general.

45. Only a summary of the address was delivered to the whole House of Commons via its Speaker. The House of Commons at this point in Elizabeth's reign was vociferous in its challenge to Elizabeth's prerogative to make grants of monopolies.

46. *The Public Speaking of Queen Elizabeth: Selections from Her Official Addresses,* ed. George P. Rice (New York: Columbia University Press, 1951), 107.

47. *Political Works of James I,* 297.

48. Ibid., 288.

49. See Marcus, *Puzzling Shakespeare,* for a series of brilliant topical readings of Shakespeare's plays and the argument that the First Folio of 1623 inaugurated a long tradition of suppressing the topicality of Shakespeare's plays by universalizing them and their author.

50. Julius Caesar only dissembles the ability of a Brutus to subordinate private and personal interest to "the general good" (1.2.84). He is a Cassius, whose most characteristic line perhaps is "but for my single self" (1.2.93), dressed up for public or general consumption as a Brutus.

51. That Hamlet is far more comprehensive than Fortinbras's image of him is implied

by Ophelia's line about her lover, "The courtier's, soldier's, scholar's eye, tongue, sword." In other words, Hamlet is a composite of Laertes, Horatio, and Fortinbras, but more general and universal than each.

52. Booth, *King Lear, Macbeth, Indefinition, and Tragedy* (New Haven: Yale University Press, 1983), 9.

53. Ibid., 6.

54. Ibid., 7–8.

55. *The Characters of Shakespear's Plays,* in *The Collected Works of William Hazlitt,* vol. 1, ed. A. R. Waller and Arnold Glover (London: J. M. Dent, 1902), 233.

56. Coleridge, *Shakespearean Criticism,* 23.

57. Harry Levin, *The Question of Hamlet* (Oxford: Oxford University Press, 1959), 11.

58. Bradley, *Shakespearean Tragedy,* 99.

59. William Empson, *The Structure of Complex Words* (Ann Arbor: University of Michigan Press, 1967), 321.

60. Stone, *Family, Sex and Marriage,* 73.

61. J. L. Austin, *How to Do Things with Words* (Cambridge, Mass.: Harvard University Press, 1962).

62. See James Calderwood, *To Be and Not to Be: Negation and Metadrama in Hamlet* (New York: Columbia University Press, 1983), esp. 133–43, for a dazzling discussion of forms of symbolic suicide in the play.

63. Inga-Stina Ewbank writes of the rhetoric of this scene, "Hamlet and Ophelia no longer speak the same language. . . . Though he does not know it, and would hate to be told so, his language has moved away from Ophelia's and toward Polonius's. It is a language based on the general idea of 'woman' rather than a specific awareness of Ophelia" (" 'Hamlet' and the Power of Words," *Shakespeare Survey* 30 [1977]: 101).

64. Levin, *Question of Hamlet,* 132–33.

65. *Hamlet,* 210.

66. Levin, *Question of Hamlet,* 133.

67. *Hamlet,* 210.

68. Coleridge, *Shakespearean Criticism,* 23.

69. Two related and highly interesting readings of the play both cast Hamlet in a predominantly particularizing role. According to Richard Fly, "Accommodating Death: The Ending of *Hamlet,*" *Studies in English Literature* 24 (1984): 257–74, Hamlet heroically resists the generalizing pressures, including those of the grave, that work to blunt the individual response.

James Calderwood has subtly and elegantly argued in *To Be and Not to Be* that both Hamlet and *Hamlet* are particularized by Hamlet's not performing the act of revenge. Such an act, Calderwood argues, would "genre-alize" the play and its hero, and also cause Hamlet to absorb "something of the generic character of action" (19) and the generic aspects of genetic relationships (10). Throughout his book Calderwood stresses the balance between the particular and universal aspects of Hamlet: "In universalizing his problem Hamlet particularizes himself" (25); "In both modes [as truant and revenger, person and role] he advances from the particular toward the universal, passing (as person) from self toward son, from individual toward society, and (as role) from structural irrelevance toward contextual integration" (35). Such an argument, though subtle and always deftly turned, seems to me to echo and appropriate a whole tradition of praise of Shakespeare for particularizing his heroes and their motives and for an achieved equilibrium between the universal and the particular. It is the tradition of Shakespeare as adept of the "concrete universal" (26f.).

By contrast, I want to stress the tension and disequilibrium between these two tropological poles of "Hamlet," a disequilibrium that seems characteristic of many of the most interesting aspects and moments of Shakespeare's Jacobean tragedies as well. Also, Calderwood appears to assume a putatively universal aesthetic norm, that of the "concrete universal," as the basis of his argument. It would seem to me worth investigating how the much heralded balance of the particular and general in Shakespearean drama is contingent upon or at least parallel to the ideology of the newly emergent national state out of the universality of late medieval feudalism.

70. *The Political Works of James I*, 19.

71. Cf. Bridget Gellert Lyons's excellent discussion of melancholy in *Hamlet*, chap. 4 of *Voices of Melancholy: Studies in Literary Treatments of Melancholy in Renaissance England* (New York: Barnes and Noble, 1971), 78: "Melancholy is the source . . . of [Hamlet's] awareness of the corroding effects of time or change that make specific actions appear meaningless."

72. See G. R. Hibbard's recent edition of the play in the Oxford Shakespeare series (Oxford: Oxford University Press, 1987), 67–130, for the argument that the differences between the Second Quarto and the Folio versions are owing in large part to the author's cuts and revisions.

73. Sister Miriam Joseph, *Shakespeare's Use of the Arts of Language* (New York: Columbia University Press, 1947), 101.

74. Ibid., 101.

75. Katherine Lever, "Proverbs and *Sententiae* in the Plays of Shakspere," *Shakespeare Association Bulletin* 13 (July and October 1938): 173–83, 224–39.

Chapter 4

1. Karl Marx and Frederick Engels, *The German Ideology*, ed. C. J. Arthur (New York: International Publishers, 1970), 102. Marx seems to have been attracted to *Timon of Athens* because of its concern with the enmity between general and particular and the role of money as instrument of generalizing in the sense of confounding. He objects to the way that money in a capitalist system stubbornly asserts itself as a god-term, refusing to yield up its generality to the particularity of that for which it may be exchanged. In "The Power of Money in Bourgeois Society," a sort of gloss on *Timon of Athens*, he writes, "He who can buy bravery is brave, though he is a coward. As money is not exchanged for any one specific quality, for any one specific thing, or for any particular human essential power, but for the entire objective world of man and nature, from the standpoint of its possessor it therefore serves to exchange every property for every other, even contradictory, property and object: it is the fraternization of impossibilities. It makes contradictories embrace" (*The Economic and Philosophic Manuscripts of 1844*, ed. Dirk J. Struik, trans. Martin Milligan [New York: International Publishers, 1964], 169). Money in Marx's Shakespearean characterization is tied not to the division of property but to the erasure of the "proper" and of distinct "properties." Marx cites Timon's address to his gold approvingly:

> Thou visible god,
> That sold'rest close impossibilities,
> And mak'st them kiss; that speak'st with every tongue,
> To every purpose! O thou touch of hearts,
> Think thy slave Man rebels, and by thy virtue
> Set them into confounding odds, that beasts
> May have the world in empire! (4.3.389–95)

Marx's protest against the generalizing (in the sense of confounding) effects of money resembles many another protest in the romantic tradition on behalf of particulars. A hard-headed version of such a protest takes place in this remarkable passage from *The German Ideology*, where he picks a quarrel with the sentimental preachiness of the work of the young Hegelian Max Stirner: "*Communism* is simply incomprehensible to our saint [Stirner] because the communists do not put egoism against self-sacrifice or self-sacrifice against egoism, nor do they express this contradiction theoretically either in its sentimental or in its highflown ideological form. . . . The communists . . . do not put to people the moral demand: love one another, do not be egoists, etc.; on the contrary, they are well aware that egoism, just as much as self-sacrifice, *is* in definite circumstances a necessary form of the self-assertion of individuals. Hence, the communists by no means want . . . to do away with the 'private individual' for the sake of the 'general,' self-sacrificing man. . . . Theoretical communists, the only ones who have time to devote to the study of history, are distinguished precisely because they alone have *discovered* that throughout history the 'general interest' is created by individuals who are defined as 'private persons.' They know that this contradiction is only a *seeming* one because one side of it, the so-called 'general,' is constantly being produced by the other side, private interest, and by no means opposes the latter as an independent force with an independent history" (102). What might be termed the economic nominalism of this passage, its insistence that so-called general interest is a creation and projection of private interest, places it at a considerable distance from the ideology of Shakespeare's plays, including this one, which he admired so much for its analysis of money.

2. Thomas Starkey, *A Dialogue between Reginald Pole and Thomas Lupset,* ed. Kathleen M. Burton (London: Chatto & Windus, 1948), 107.

3. Nigel Smith, *Perfection Proclaimed: Language and Literature in English Radical Religion, 1640–1660* (Oxford: Clarendon Press, 1989), 55.

4. Abiezer Coppe, *A Fiery Flying Roll* (London, 1649).

5. Smith, *Perfection Proclaimed,* 55.

6. On the connections of the Ranters to the Levellers, see Christopher Hill, *A Nation of Change and Novelty: Radical Politics, Religion and Literature in Seventeenth-Century England* (London: Routledge, 1990); and A. L. Morton, *The World of the Levellers: Religious Radicalism in the English Revolution* (London: Lawrence & Wishart, 1970).

7. The date of *Timon* is more conjectural than it is for Shakespeare's other plays, since no performance of it was recorded during Shakespeare's lifetime and no text of the play prior to the posthumous First Folio exists. Nevertheless, primarily on the basis of "internal" evidence, most critics date the play at about 1605–8, roughly contemporary with *Coriolanus.*

8. David Bevington refers to the play as "schematic" in Hardin Craig and David Bevington, eds., *Shakespeare: The Complete Works,* rev. ed. (Glenview, Ill.: Scott, Foresman and Co., 1973), 1018; Frank Kermode writes that *Timon* is "a tragedy of ideas, much more schematic than *Hamlet,*" in *The Riverside Shakespeare* (Boston: Houghton Mifflin, 1974), 1443–44. Many descriptions of the play use similar if not identical language. More recently, Ninian Mellamphy, "Wormwood in the Wood Outside Athens: *Timon* and the Problem for the Audience," in the collection entitled *"Bad" Shakespeare: Revaluations of the Shakespeare Canon,* ed. Maurice Charney (London and Toronto: Associated University Presses, 1988), 166–75, has written of Timon himself as an "abstraction" (173). For Mellamphy, the play is also marked by thematic abstraction and by a monotonous tone of opprobrium directed "at the too generalized target of ungrateful man" (173). For Lesley Brill, *Timon's* plot and characterization are "markedly spare" ("Truth and *Timon of Athens,*" *Modern Language Quarterly* 40 [1979]: 21). I do not mean to suggest that responses to Timon and to the play as a whole have been largely unanimous. On divergent opinions toward characters and the play, see the useful summary in Brill, 17f.

9. On *Timon* as a morality play, see Lewis Walker, "*Timon of Athens* and the Morality Tradition," *Shakespeare Studies* 12 (1979): 159–77; Anne Lancashire, "*Timon of Athens:* Shakespeare's *Dr. Faustus,*" *Shakespeare Quarterly* 21 (1970): 35–44; A. S. Collins, "*Timon of Athens:* A Reconsideration," *Review of English Studies* 22 (1946): 96–108; and Michael Tinker, "Theme in *Timon of Athens,*" in *Shakespeare's Late Plays,* ed. Richard C. Tobias and Paul G. Zolbrod (Athens: Ohio University Press, 1974), 76–88.

10. See H. J. Oliver's Arden Shakespeare edition (London: Methuen, 1959), xxv–xxviii, for a summary of the evidence for incompleteness.

11. Howard B. White makes a similar claim in *Copp'd Hills Towards Heaven: Shakespeare and the Classical Polity* (The Hague: Martinus Nijhoff, 1970), 36: *Timon* is "quite possibly the most complete political tragedy in Shakespeare."

12. Sir Thomas Elyot, *The Boke Named The Gouernour,* vol. 1, ed. Henry Herbert Stephen Croft (1880; rpt., New York: Burt Franklin, 1967), 8–9. For the metaphor of the multitude as the many-headed monster, see chap. 8 of Christopher Hill, *Change and Continuity in Seventeenth-Century England* (Cambridge, Mass.: Harvard University Press, 1975), 181–204.

13. Coriolanus's lines are a faithful echo of North's Plutarch, in which Coriolanus similarly denounces the view that "corne should be gevern out to the common people *gratis,* as they used to doe in cities of Græce, where the people had more absolute power: dyd but only nourishe their disobedience, which would breake out in the ende, to the utter ruine and overthrowe of the whole state."

14. See the discussion in James Emerson Phillips, Jr., *The State in Shakespeare's Greek and Roman Plays* (New York: Columbia University Press, 1940), 172–73.

15. Leo Paul S. de Alvarez has suggested that the Athens of the end of the play, embodied in the figure of Alcibiades, is an imperial one, more Roman than Greek. See *"Timon of Athens,"* in *Shakespeare as Political Thinker,* ed. John Alvis and Thomas G. West (Durham, N.C.: Carolina Academic Press, 1981), esp. 178–79. Throughout most of the play, however, Athens, with all of the levelling rhetoric and Timon's failure to discriminate both in his philanthropic and misanthropic phases, seems a democratic one, roughly equivalent to the Rome of *Coriolanus,* which seems a similar "demonstration of the dangers of democratic government" (Phillips, *State,* 147).

16. There were, in fact, political alternatives between absolutism and a levelling democracy, though absolutist tracts like Elyot's had an interest in suggesting otherwise. See the discussion of David Norbrook in *"Macbeth* and the Politics of Historiography," in Sharpe and Zwicker, *Politics of Discourse,* 78–116. According to Norbrook, analysis of Shakespeare's plays, including the most sophisticated of recent political criticism holding that "subversion in fact subtly reinforced the very power structures that were being challenged," tends to "reduplicate the stark oppositions presented by absolutist propaganda: either monarchy or anarchy; 'take but degree away. . . .' Such a focus fails to do justice to the many Renaissance thinkers who had a conception of political order which involved neither hereditary monarchy nor total anarchy" (79). My analysis of *Timon of Athens* shows Shakespeare not exactly offering alternatives to the "stark oppositions of absolutist propaganda" but rather complicating and mutually enfolding those oppositions that absolutist thinking tries to polarize.

17. Elyot, *Boke,* 1–3.

18. Ibid., 3–4.

19. There are many other places in Shakespeare where a similarly orchestrated sequence of levelling and universalizing may be found: for instance, in Richard's prison speeches at the end of *Richard II* or in Macbeth's "tomorrow" speech taken together with Malcolm's closing lines.

20. That absolutist thinking tended to conceive disorder in terms of similarly abrupt and radical "theatrical" shifts of identity does not mean that Renaissance plays necessarily supported rather than criticized or challenged the ideology of absolutism. Many scenarios could be constructed from the confrontation of two orders of generality, not simply the absolutist one from degree to its sudden effacement and back again. Among alternative scenarios is the subversive one staged in *Timon of Athens,* where, as I shall argue in the next section, the two orders of generality, the confounding and the universalizing, are themselves confounded.

21. Cervantes, *Don Quixote,* trans. Samuel Putnam (New York: The Viking Press, 1949) part 2, chap. 12, pp. 579–80.

22. For extended discussions of the *paragone* in *Timon,* see John Dixon Hunt, "Shakespeare and the *Paragone:* A Reading of *Timon of Athens,*" in *Images of Shakespeare,* ed. Werner Habicht, D. J. Palmer, and Roger Pringle (London and Toronto: Associated University Presses, 1988), 47–63; and W. M. Merchant, "*Timon* and the Conceit of Art," *Shakespeare Quarterly* 6 (1955): 249–57. The connection between the dialogue of Painter and Poet and the Renaissance *paragone* was first pointed out by art historian Sir Anthony Blunt, "An Echo of the 'Paragone' in Shakespeare," *Journal of the Warburg Institute* 2 (1938–39): 260–62.

23. Owen Feltham, *Resolves,* 4th ed. (London, 1631), no. 38.

24. Recent Shakespeare scholarship has witnessed a renaissance of interest in topical readings, perhaps best represented by Marcus, *Puzzling Shakespeare.* Among earlier critics, G. B. Harrison is most closely associated with promoting a topical Shakespeare.

25. See Janet Adelman's celebrated essay, "'Anger's My Meat'" 129–49, esp. note 4, p. 145.

26. *Political Works of James I,* 288.

27. Among critics of the play, G. Wilson Knight, who has extensively performed the role of Timon as well as written about him, is remarkable for attempting to universalize Timon, making him the type of the romantic and solitary hero. To most critics, Timon has been as difficult to universalize as Coriolanus, seeming instead to be a general character of another sort: abstract, allegorical, or two-dimensional. Knight's works on the play include *The Wheel of Fire: Essays in Interpretation of Shakespeare's Sombre Tragedies* (London: Oxford University Press, 1930); *Shakespeare's Dramatic Challenges: On the Rise of Shakespeare's Tragic Heroes* (London: Croom Helm, 1977), 147–66; "*Timon of Athens* and Buddhism," *Essays in Criticism* 30 (1980): 105–23; and "*Timon of Athens* and Its Dramatic Descendants," *Review of English Literature* 2 (1961): 9–18.

28. See the gloss of H. J. Oliver, p. 9, following K. Deighton's gloss in the original Arden edition of the play (1905, 1929). A similar ambiguity is expressed by "levell'd," meaning "targeted at particular individuals" but also suggesting the levelling of degree repeatedly enacted and prophesied in the play.

29. Among others, E. A. J. Honigmann has suggested that *Timon of Athens,* like *Troilus and Cressida,* may have been written for performance at an Inn of Court. See "*Timon of Athens,*" *Shakespeare Quarterly* 12 (1961): 14.

30. See the stimulating article by Coppélia Kahn, "'Magic of Bounty': *Timon of Athens,* Jacobean Patronage, Maternal Power," in *Shakespeare Quarterly* 38 (1987): 34–57. As Kahn notes, David Bergeron made passing reference to *Timon of Athens* as providing a "literary analogue for James's prodigality," in *Shakespeare's Romances and the Royal Family* (Lawrence: University Press of Kansas, 1985), 45.

31. *Leviathan,* 224.

32. Sir Edward Coke, *The Fourth Part of the Institutes of the Laws of England* (London, 1809), chap. 1, p. 14. It was not until after midcentury that MPs were thought of as representing particular locales and constituencies.

33. Cited in Hill, *Change and Continuity,* 187.

34. *Certayne Sermons or Homilies* (1547), Homily X, Sig. K, i v.

35. The gloss is that of H. J. Oliver, p. 8.

36. See Lawrence Stone, *The Crisis of the Aristocracy, 1558–1641* (Oxford: Clarendon Press, 1965). Stone has been criticized for extrapolating from what seems to have been an urban or London phenomenon to all of England. Nevertheless, the main outlines of his argument still seem legitimate.

37. The best account of Winstanley and his influence is to be found in the works of Christopher Hill: for instance, *The World Turned Upside Down* (New York: Viking Press, 1972). See also Winstanley, *The Law of Freedom and Other Writings,* ed. Christopher Hill (1973; rpt., Cambridge: Cambridge University Press, 1983).

38. Morton, *World of the Levellers,* 18.

39. In his eulogy over the body of Brutus, Mark Antony affirms, "All the conspirators save only he / Did that they did in envy of great Caesar; / He only, in a general honest thought / And common good to all, made one of them" (5.5.69–72).

40. Richard Fly's discussion of Alcibiades strikes me as particularly useful, in "The Ending of 'Timon of Athens': A Reconsideration," *Criticism* 15 (1973): 242–52, esp. 249. See also Brill, "Truth and *Timon*," 19.

41. See Foucault, *Discipline and Punish: The Birth of the Prison,* trans. Alan Sheridan (New York: Pantheon Books, 1977); and the interview "The Eye of Power," in *Power/Knowledge: Selected Interviews and Other Writings, 1972–1977,* ed. Colin Gordon, trans. Colin Gordon et al. (New York: Pantheon Books, 1980), 146–65.

42. Shakespeare's middle and later tragedies, like his early ones, all supply such a voice, although the tendency becomes increasingly to ironize that voice, to make the act of summation seem inadequate to the action that preceded it. *Macbeth,* for instance, features its main character supplying a bewitching summation that is clearly specious as a generalization, since it is so intimately linked to his own condition. The acts of summation at the end of *King Lear,* to take another example, are so inadequate as to seem poignant, as Stephen Booth has detailed in *King Lear, Macbeth, Indefinition, and Tragedy* (New Haven: Yale University Press, 1983).

43. A very useful discussion of the particularizing or discriminating interest in *Timon* may be found in R. Swigg, "'Timon of Athens' and the Growth of Discrimination," *Modern Language Review* 62 (1967): 387–94.

44. In his important essay "*Coriolanus:* History and the Crisis of Semantic Order," Leonard Tennenhouse argues that the play marks the transition between an old patrician order based on the body and action, and a new one based on words, associated with the tribunes.

45. Hamlet seems a pivotal figure in this regard as in so many others. A potent theatrical generalist precisely because of his unprecedented ability to play any part (and therefore, at least symbolically, to serve as political head and representative of all the people, like Prince Hal), Hamlet also rests his claims to generality to an unprecedented degree on his generalizing rhetoric.

46. See Brill, "Truth and *Timon*," 24.

47. Haydn, *Counter-Renaissance.*

48. It is arguable that Apemantus is the most self-consciously theatrical element in the play. Specifically, he is a reflection of the critical spectator at his or her most daunting. "Let me stay at thine apperil, Timon. I come to observe; I give thee warning on't," he says in the banqueting hall of Timon's house (1.2.31–32).

49. See McElroy, *Shakespeare's Mature Tragedies,* 17–20, for commentary on the tendency to universalize as a prominent quality of mind shared by Hamlet, Othello, Lear, and Macbeth.

Chapter 5

1. Foucault, *Order of Things,* 43.

2. *Hamlet,* New Arden Edition, ed. Harold Jenkins (London: Methuen, 1982), 186.

3. See Northrop Frye's enormously suggestive essay "Charms and Riddles," in *Spiritus Mundi* (Bloomington: Indiana University Press, 1976). For Frye, charms and riddles are magical archetypes for the auditory and visual components of poetry respectively.

4. This seemingly slight circumstance is an auditory premonition of the Closet Scene, where Hamlet sees the apparition of his father but Gertrude does not.

5. Several times in Shakespeare the ear is referred to as a cave, a metaphor with a long history, figuring as it does, for example, in Wordsworth's "Ode: The Power of Sound."

6. Edward Forset, *A Comparative Discourse of the Bodies Natural and Politique* (1606),

rpt. in *The Frame of Order: An Outline of Elizabethan Belief Taken from Treatises of the Late Sixteenth Century,* ed. James Winny (New York: Macmillan, 1957), 103.

7. Bacon, *The Advancement of Learning and New Atlantis,* ed. Arthur Johnston (Oxford: Clarendon Press, 1974), 6.

8. Cf. Hermia's speech in *A Midsummer Night's Dream,*

Dark night, that from the eye his function takes,
The ear more quick of apprehension makes;
Wherein it doth impair the seeing sense,
It pays the hearing double recompense. (3.2.177–80)

9. David Margolies, *Monsters of the Deep: Social Dissolution in Shakespeare's Tragedies* (Manchester: Manchester University Press, 1992), 135.

10. Jenkins, *Hamlet,* 501.

11. Ibid., 501.

12. Ibid., 502.

13. Eyes signify divinity in a number of Renaissance sources. See Keir Elam, *Shakespeare's Universe of Discourse: Language Games in the Comedies* (Cambridge: Cambridge University Press, 1984), 157.

14. For a discussion of Ophelia in painting, see Showalter, "Representing Ophelia," 77–94.

15. Michel Foucault, *Madness and Civilization: A History of Insanity in the Age of Reason,* trans. Richard Howard (New York: Vintage Books, 1965), 70.

16. Ibid., 12.

17. Ibid., 13.

18. Ibid., 3–7.

19. Ibid., 8.

20. Ibid., 15–16.

21. Jenkins, *Hamlet,* 490.

22. On the question of seeing and not seeing, see Alan Dessen's excellent discussion in chap. 7 of *Elizabethan Stage Conventions and Modern Interpreters* (Cambridge: Cambridge University Press, 1984), 130–55.

23. Godwin, *Enquiry Concerning Political Justice,* 21–22.

24. The speech bears comparison with the tribune Marullus's speech at the beginning of *Julius Caesar,* 1.1.37f., examined in the next chapter. There Pompey's triumphal procession and the roar that accompanied it bespoke a perfect complementariness of the verbal to the visual. *Hamlet* seems to mark a new direction for Shakespeare in the exploration of verbal/scenic relations.

25. Foucault, *Order of Things,* 9.

26. Ibid., 39.

Chapter 6

1. Inga-Stina Ewbank, "'More Pregnantly Than Words': Some Uses of and Limitations of Visual Symbolism," *Shakespeare Survey* 24 (1971): 13. Ewbank usefully challenges this all too easy assumption in her essay.

2. *The Complete Plays of Ben Jonson,* vil. 4, ed. G. A. Wilkes (Oxford: Oxford University Press, 1982), 250.

3. For corroboration of this view with regard to specific plays, see Hunt, "Shakespeare and the *Paragone,*" 47–63, esp. 58: "But unlike other theatrical occasions when to see and to hear lead to judgments, this play recalls us constantly to the difficulties of matching word and image"; David Margolies, who complains that *Timon* "suffers from too much telling instead of

showing," *Monsters of the Deep,* 135; Huston Diehl, "Horrid Image, Sorry Sight, Fatal Vision: The Visual Rhetoric of *Macbeth,*" *Shakespeare Studies* 16 (1983): 191–203; Robert B. Pierce, "'Very Like a Whale': Scepticism and Seeing in 'The Tempest,'" *Shakespeare Survey* 38 (1985): 167–73; and Bernard Beckerman, "Shakespearean Playgoing Then and Now," in *Shakespeare's More Than Words Can Witness: Essays on Visual and Nonverbal Enactment in the Plays,* ed. Sidney Homan (Lewisburg, Pa.: Bucknell University Press, 1980), 142–59, esp. on *Henry VIII,* 153–54. Marjorie Garber's brilliant reading of Macbeth as "male Medusa" (*Shakespeare's Ghost Writers: Literature as Uncanny Causality* (New York: Methuen, 1987), 87–123) also supports my general argument.

4. See Fineman, *Shakespeare's Perjured Eye.* Fineman's argument is that Shakespeare's sonnets "remark themselves as something verbal, not visual, of the tongue and not the eye" and "recharacterize language as something duplicitously and equivocally verbal rather than as something truthfully and univocally visual." My argument is consistent with Fineman's, except that I want to stress the distance between the way that visual/verbal relations are worked out in the early plays and the way those relations become strained and complicated in his plays beginning with *Hamlet.* That transformation, it seems to me, may belong to the larger historical shift from what Foucault calls the Renaissance episteme to the classical. The summary of Fineman's work is his own, in "Shakespeare's Ear," *Representations* 28 (Fall, 1989): 6.

5. Stephen Greenblatt, *Shakespearean Negotiations,* 64.

6. Most new historicist work on the subject of the gaze issues from Foucault's work on the subject, especially his *Discipline and Punish.* Preeminent among works in this category is Greenblatt, *Shakespearean Negotiations.* In addition to the work by Joel Fineman already cited, Barbara Freedman's *Staging the Gaze: Postmodernism, Psychoanalysis, and Shakespearean Comedy* (Ithaca: Cornell University Press, 1991) is a brilliant Lacanian study of ways in which Shakespearean comedy challenges what she calls a "spectator consciousness." Christopher Pye's *Regal Phantasm* usefully and intelligently straddles the Foucauldian/Lacanian fence. Stephen Orgel's seminal *The Illusion of Power: Political Theater in the Renaissance* (Berkeley and Los Angeles: University of California Press, 1975) anticipates many of the issues of more recent work that takes off from Foucault. Other invaluable contributions to the subjects of vision, spectacle, and the gaze in Shakespeare include sections of Goldberg, *James I and the Politics of Literature;* Tennenhouse, *Power on Display;* and Siemon, *Shakespearean Iconoclasm.* For an older account, see the article by Cecil S. Emden, "Shakespeare and the Eye," *Shakespeare Survey* 26 (1973): 129–37. Outside the specific field of Shakespeare studies, work on vision and visuality has been of enormous consequence in feminist studies, film criticism, and art history. See, for example, the contributions of Luce Iragaray, "The Sex Which Is Not One," in *New French Feminisms,* ed. Elaine Marks and Isabelle de Courtirron (Amherst: University of Massachusetts Press, 1980); Evelyn Keller and Christine Grontowski, "The Mind's Eye," in Sandra Harding and Merrill B. Hintikka, eds., *Discovering Reality* (D. Reidel Publishing, 1983), 207–24; and Kaja Silverman, *The Acoustic Mirror: The Female Voice in Psychoanalysis and Cinema* (Bloomington: Indiana University Press, 1988). A seminal work on the gaze and the cinema is Christian Metz, *Psychoanalysis and Cinema: The Imaginary Signifier* (London: Macmillan, 1982). Equally important works in the area of art criticism are Michael Fried, *Absorption and Theatricality: Painting and Beholder in the Age of Diderot* (Baltimore: Johns Hopkins University Press, 1980); and Norman Bryson, *Vision and Painting: The Logic of the Gaze* (New Haven: Yale University Press, 1983). All the essays in Hal Foster, ed., *Vision and Visuality* (Seattle: Bay Press, 1988), are extremely helpful.

7. Foucault, *Discipline and Punish,* 283.

8. Foucault, *Order of Things,* 39, 43f.

9. For a broad survey placing Foucault in the context of what he takes to be an antivisual leaning in twentieth-century French thought, see Martin Jay, *Downcast Eyes: The Denigration of Vision in Twentieth-Century French Thought* (Berkeley and Los Angeles: University of California Press, 1993).

10. The tradition that accounted sight the "noblest sense" stretches back at least to Aristotle's *De Anima*. Following Aristotle, Aquinas, holding that the sense of sight contributed most to perception, ranked sight as the "noblest" and awarded second place to hearing, in his *Commentarium in De Anima Aristotelis*, II.xiv; sec. 417, and in his treatise on light, *De Natura Luminis*, in *Opuscula Omnia*. Following Aquinas, the Elizabethan Stephen Batman took the sensitivity of the eye to be evidence of its greater "nobility," in *Batman uppon Bartholome his Booke De Proprietatibus Rerum* (London: Thomas East, 1582), V.i. See also the essays in the recent collection *Modernity and the Hegemony of Vision,* ed. David Michael Levin (Berkeley and Los Angeles: University of California Press, 1993).

11. See Ernest B. Gilman, *Iconoclasm and Poetry in the English Reformation* (Chicago: University of Chicago Press, 1986); and Siemon, *Shakespearean Iconoclasm.* According to Gilman, the "aftershock of iconoclasm for literary criticism" persists into the eighteenth century. He writes, "In the eighteenth-century English arts, it is possible to see Swift and Hogarth especially, but even Gay and Fielding, as 'iconoclasts' ranged against Dryden, Pope, Reynolds, and Johnson in a latter-day reenactment of the image debate" (182–83).

12. See John Doebler, *Shakespeare's Speaking Pictures: Studies in Iconic Imagery* (Albuquerque: University of New Mexico Press, 1974), for a fairly comprehensive study of the issue; Dieter Mehl, "Emblems in English Renaissance Drama," *Renaissance Drama,* n.s., 2 (1969): 39–57, and "Visual and Rhetorical Imagery in Shakespeare's Plays," *Essays and Studies,* n.s., 25 (1972): 83–100; Martha Hester Fleischer, *The Iconography of the English History Play* (Salzburg: Institut für englische Sprache und Literatur, 1974); Rosalind King, "Black Vesper's Pageants: Emblems of Tragic Stagecraft in Shakespeare," in Palmer and Bradbury, *Shakespearean Tragedy,* 76–96; and Doebler's "Bibliography for the Study of Iconography in Renaissance English Literature," *Research Opportunities in Renaissance Drama* 22 (1979): 45–55. See also Alan Dessen, *Elizabethan Drama and the Viewer's Eye* (Chapel Hill: University of North Carolina Press, 1977); *Elizabethan Stage Conventions and Modern Interpreters* (Cambridge: Cambridge University Press, 1984), 130–79; "Shakespeare's Patterns for the Viewer's Eye: Dramaturgy for the Open Stage," in Homan, *Shakespeare's More Than Words Can Witness;* and Clifford Lyons, "Stage Imagery in Shakespeare's Plays," in *Essays on Shakespeare and Elizabethan Drama in Honor of Hardin Craig,* ed. Richard Hosley (Columbia: University of Missouri Press, 1962), 261–74. Lyons follows R. A. Foakes, "Suggestions for a New Approach to Shakespeare's Imagery," *Shakespeare Survey* 5 (1952): 81–92, in the latter's attempt to enlarge the category of "poetic imagery" to "dramatic imagery," which would include references to "visual and auditory effects," "historical placing," and "the subject-matter and object-matter of poetic imagery." On the vogue for collections of emblems in the Renaissance, see Mario Praz, *Studies in Seventeenth-Century Imagery,* vol. 1 (London: Warburg Institute, 1939), 9–45; and Rosemary Freeman, *English Emblem Books* (London: Chatto and Windus, 1948).

13. Two critics who anticipate much of what Foucault has to say about the Renaissance, but with more of an emphasis on English texts and contexts, are Marshall McLuhan, *The Gutenberg Galaxy: The Making of Typographic Man* (1962; rpt., New York: New American Library, 1969); and the largely parallel work of Walter J. Ong, whose relevant texts include *The Presence of the Word: Some Prolegomena for Cultural and Religious History* (New Haven: Yale University Press, 1967); *Rhetoric, Romance, and Technology: Studies in the Interaction of Expression and Culture* (Ithaca: Cornell University Press, 1971); *Interfaces of the Word: Studies in the Evolution of Consciousness and Culture* (Ithaca: Cornell University Press, 1977); and *Orality and Literacy: The Technologizing of the Word* (London: Methuen, 1982). As Foucault's takes a reading of *Don Quixote* as its point of departure, so does McLuhan's take off from a reading of *King Lear,* taking as symptomatic of the Renaissance "the separation of sight from the other senses" and "the isolation of the visual sense as a kind of blindness" in that play (19, 21).

14. Foucault, *The Order of Things,* 43.

15. Ibid., 133, 137.

16. Orgel, *Illusion of Power,* 24. The notion that images concealed a readable language

found expression not only in emblems and theatrical practices but also in the art of the frontispiece and in the Renaissance fascination with Egyptian hieroglyphs. See the discussion by Gilman, *Iconoclasm and Poetry,* 17f.

17. Orgel, *Illusion of Power,* 26.

18. Sherry, *A Treatise of Schemes & Tropes* (London, 1550), 50.

19. John Hoskins, *Directions for Speech and Style,* ed. Hoyt H. Hudson (Princeton: Princeton University Press, 1935).

20. Greenblatt, *Shakespearean Negotiations,* 64.

21. *Basilikon Doron,* in *Political Works of James I,* 39.

22. Ibid., 5.

23. On *Coriolanus* as a text marking the difference between Shakespeare's Elizabethan and Jacobean political orders, by opposing an order of the spectacular body (associated with the patrician class) with an order of the word (associated with the tribunes and plebeians), see Tennenhouse, "*Coriolanus:* History and the Crisis of Semantic Order." See also his more recent study, *Power on Display.* A very valuable essay on James's rejection of Elizabethan theatricalism and search for a stable self and political authority through the medium of print is Richard Helgerson, "Milton Reads the King's Book: Print, Performance, and the Making of a Bourgeois Idol," *Criticism* 29 (1987): 1–25. For an extended treatment of the relation of spectacle and politics in Shakespeare, see Pye, *Regal Phantasm.*

24. Phineas Fletcher, *The Purple Island* (1633), Canto 5.25, 5.38, in Giles and Phineas Fletcher, *Poetical Works,* vol. 2, ed. Frederick S. Boas (Cambridge: Cambridge University Press, 1909), 58, 61.

25. In *The Illusion of Power,* Orgel makes the argument (counter to the critical tradition) that courtly theaters were by our standards as auditory in their appeal as public theaters and that theater historians, ignoring the Renaissance standpoint, have falsely distinguished between visual and verbal Renaissance theaters in order to make court theaters, with their love of spectacle, the culprit that put an end to "the era of poetic drama" (16–19).

26. The explanation, it seems to me, lies not simply in the judgment that Shakespeare has become a better playwright, learning to spare the audience a potentially tedious recapitulation of events à la Friar Lawrence (5.3.229–69), by making that recitation (promised by Horatio) take place offstage. In fact, one reason that *Hamlet* strikes so many readers and viewers as a tragedy without a catharsis is that it denies us the cathartic effect of hearing the events of the play summarized and thereby subdued: denies us the translation from the visual to the verbal that among other things reaffirms the old bonds between eye and ear, words and things.

27. There was a well-established association in poetic texts of the Renaissance of rays presumed to be emitted by the eyes with Cupid's arrows. Such associations usually emphasized reciprocity, the possibility of a return dart from the other eye that was not possible with an object. Juliet herself relies on this association when she promises her mother to no further "endart mine eye / Than your consent gives strength to make it fly" (1.3.98–99). Macrobius states that eyes alone among the senses send or emit rays, while the other senses are purely receptive (*Saturnalia,* VII,xiv.5–7). Ficino discusses the rays of the eyes in detail in his commentary on Plato's *Symposium, Commentarium in Convivium,* VII.iv. And Aquinas ranked sight the highest or noblest sense because it was the most active in seeking impressions, the ear more passive, as Mercutio's lines also suggest.

28. I take the phrase from the title of an interview of Foucault, reprinted in *Power/Knowledge.*

29. The pervasive imagery of sight in *King Lear* has been variously explored by Paul J. Alpers, "*King Lear* and the Theory of the 'Sight Pattern,'" in *In Defense of Reading: A Reader's Approach to Literary Criticism,* ed. Reuben Brower and Richard Poirier (New York: E. P. Dutton, 1962), 133–52; and Stanley Cavell, "The Avoidance of Love," reprinted in Cavell, *Disowning Knowledge in Six Plays of Shakespeare* (Cambridge: Cambridge University Press, 1987), among many others. Marshall McLuhan, in *The Gutenberg Galaxy,* takes *King Lear* as a seminal and

exemplary text in his discussion of the isolation of the sense of sight from other senses in the Renaissance.

30. Phineas Fletcher in *The Purple Island* characterizes the ear as "Master of request," V.49, and also describes the labyrinth of the ear as "eye-deceiving," V.45. Here we have the two sides of the ear in *Othello,* Desdemona and Iago, compassion and craft.

31. See Martin Jay, "Scopic Regimes of Modernity," in Foster, *Vision and Visuality,* 3–23.

32. Cited in Janet Arnold, *Queen Elizabeth's Wardrobe Unlock'd* (Leeds: Maney, 1988), 81. For other accounts of the Rainbow Portrait, see Roy Strong, *The Cult of Elizabeth: Elizabethan Portraiture and Pageantry* (London: Thames and Hudson, 1977); and Frances Yates, *Astraea: The Imperial Theme in the Sixteenth Century* (London: Routledge and K. Paul, 1975).

33. See Michael O'Connell, "The Idolatrous Eye: Iconoclasm, Anti-Theatricalism, and the Image of the Elizabethan Theater," *ELH* 52 (1985): 279–310; and Siemon, *Shakespearean Iconoclasm.*

34. See Gilman, *Iconoclasm and Poetry,* esp. 61–83.

35. *The Poems of Sir John Davies,* ed. Robert Krueger (Oxford: Oxford University Press, 1975), 9.

36. Foucault, *Madness and Civilization,* 70.

37. See Foucault, *Discipline and Punish;* and the interview "The Eye of Power" in Foucault, *Power/Knowledge,* 145–65.

38. Ernest Tuveson has written, "From the nature of the mind as described by Locke, we could expect a new poetry to be highly visual in nature, for the faculty of sight came to monopolize the analysis of intellectual activity. Since ideas are images, since even complex ideas are multiple pictures, and since understanding itself is a form of perception, the visual and the intellectual would tend to become amalgamated." *The Imagination as a Means of Grace: Locke and the Aesthetics of Romanticism* (Berkeley and Los Angeles: University of California Press, 1960). See also Kenneth MacLean, *John Locke and English Literature of the Eighteenth Century* (New Haven: Yale University Press, 1936). Marjorie Hope Nicolson has analyzed the effect of Newton's theories of vision on poetic practice, in *Newton Demands the Muse* (Princeton: Princeton University Press, 1946).

39. See Jean Starobonski's classic study, *Jean-Jacques Rousseau: La transparence et l'obstacle* (Paris: Gallimard, 1971).

40. Foucault states that in the Panopticon "the principle of the dungeon is reversed; daylight and the overseer's gaze capture the inmates more effectively than darkness, which afforded after all a sort of protection" (*Power/Knowledge,* 147).

41. John Barrell, *English Literature in History, 1730–80: An Equal, Wide Survey* (London: Hutchinson, 1983), 51.

42. For a discussion of this tradition, see William K. Wimsatt, *The Verbal Icon: Studies in the Meaning of Poetry* (Lexington: University of Kentucky Press, 1954); Jean H. Hagstrum, *The Sister Arts: The Tradition of Literary Pictorialism and English Poetry from Dryden to Gray* (Chicago: The University of Chicago Press, 1958); Patricia Meyer Spacks, *The Poetry of Vision: Five Eighteenth-Century Poets* (Cambridge, Mass.: Harvard University Press, 1967); and M. H. Abrams, *The Mirror and the Lamp: Romantic Theory and the Critical Tradition* (New York: Norton, 1958). On the shifting nature and status of the visual in metaphysical poetry, especially the break between visual imagery and the correspondences or universal system of analogies inherited from the Middle Ages, see Mary Cole Sloane, *The Visual in Metaphysical Poetry* (Atlantic Highlands, N. J.: Humanities Press, 1981).

43. *The Spectator,* Thursday, March 1, 1711; George Aitken, ed. (New York: Longmans, 1898), vol. 1, p. 3.

44. Ibid., 5.

45. Neil Carson, "Shakespeare and the Dramatic Image," in *Mirror up to Shakespeare: Essays in Honour of G. R. Hibbard* (Toronto: University of Toronto Press, 1984), 41.

INDEX

Diehl, Huston, 195n.21, 205n.3
Doebler, John, 206n.12
Don Quixote, 67, 115–17
Dryden, John, 12, 184n.26
DuBois, Page, 185n.30
Durston, Christopher, 183n.8

Elam, Keir, 204n.13
Eliot, T. S., 84
Elizabeth I, 12, 47, 51, 73, 90, 106,
    179; "Golden Speech" (1601), 89;
    parliaments of, 20; Rainbow Portrait,
    176; relation to spectacle, 30, 130, 144,
    153–54, 175
Elton, G. R., 19
Elyot, Sir Thomas, 15, 110–15, 117, 127,
    201n.16
emblems, 161, 206n.12
Emden, Cecil S., 205n.6
Empson, William, 12, 99
enclosure, 34, 118
Engels, Frederick, 199n.1
English Civil Wars, 12, 109
epigrammatic style, 125
Essex, Earl of, 90
Ewbank, Inga-Stina, 198n.63, 204n.1

Felperin, Howard, 181n.6
Feltham, Owen, 118
Ficino, Marsilio, 207n.27
Fineman, Joel, 85, 205nn.4, 6
Flaubert, Gustave, 114
Fleischer, Martha Hester, 206n.12
Fletcher, Phineas, 44, 163–64, 208n.30
Fly, Richard, 198n.69, 203n.40
Foakes, R. A., 206n.12
Forset, Edward, 141
Foucault, Michel, 15, 135, 153, 157–58,
    169, 176, 192n.61, 206n.13; as
    antigeneralizing thinker, 78–79;
    antivisual bias of, 205n.9; difficulty
    applying to English contexts, 160–61;
    on "eye of power," 173–74, 203n.41,
    208n.40; on madness, 67, 149–51
Fowler, Thomas, 48
Freedman, Barbara, 205n.6
Freeman, Rosemary, 206n.12
Freud, Sigmund, 177, 191n.33
Fried, Michael, 205n.6
Frye, Northrop, 203n.3
Frye, Susan, 181n.2

Garber, Marjorie, 205n.3
generality: of scientific discourses, 75–76;
    of Shakespeare's characters, 35–36, 41,
    128–31
generalizing: by Shakespeare's characters,
    13; aspects of drama, 13, 14, 75,
    80–109, 111, 131; censoriousness
    of, 102–5; embarrassment to modern
    criticism, 74; endings of Shakespeare's
    tragedies, 93–97; links to authority
    and sovereignty, 87, 97–100, 111; and
    melancholy, 105–7; self-cancelling
    aspects of, 100–102
Gilman, Ernest B., 206n.11, 208n.34
Godwin, William, 53–54, 153–54
Goethe, Johann Wolfgang von, 63
Goldberg, Jonathan, 181n.2, 185n.37,
    205n.6
Goodman, Paul, 59–60, 191n.31
Gorboduc (Norton and Sackville), 14, 83
Gordon, D. J., 186n.43, 188n.56
Greenberg, Janelle Renfrow, 190n.28
Greenblatt, Stephen, 15, 163, 194n.15,
    205n.6
Greville, Fulke, 186n.46, 196n.28
Grontowski, Christine, 205n.6
Group μ, 193n.65
Gurr, Andrew, 185n.36, 187n.47, 189n.65
Gutenberg revolution, 177
Guy, John, 22, 194n.9

Hagstrum, Jean H., 208n.42
Hakewill, George, 151
Hale, David G., 185n.35, 189n.65,
    193n.67
Hall, Joseph, 197n.36
Hankins, John Erskine, 63
Harris, Tim, 188n.53
Hartley, T. E., 183n.8
Haydn, Hiram, 82, 131
Hazlitt, William, 97–98, 108
Helgerson, Richard, 207n.23
Hibbard, G. R., 199n.72
Hill, Christoper, 200n.6, 201n.12, 202n.37
Hirst, Derek, 182n.6
Hobbes, Thomas, 21, 22, 24, 45, 122,
    183n.20, 189n.12, 190n.29
Hodges, Devon, 189n.1
Holstun, James, 188n.58, 189n.64
Honigmann, E. A. J., 202n.29
Hoskyns, John, 162
Howard, Jean, 78